Date Due

INC. YOURSELF

INC.
YOURSELF

HOW TO PROFIT BY SETTING UP YOUR OWN CORPORATION

Judith H. McQuown

Revised and Updated

MACMILLAN PUBLISHING CO., INC.
NEW YORK

COLLIER MACMILLAN PUBLISHERS
LONDON

Macmillan Publishing Co., Inc.
866 Third Avenue, New York, N.Y. 10022
Collier Macmillan Canada, Ltd.

Library of Congress Cataloging in Publication Data
McQuown, Judith H
  Inc. yourself.
    1. Corporations—Handbooks, manuals, etc.
  2. One-man companies—Handbooks, manuals, etc.
  I. Title.
  HD2741.M22   1979   658'.1'145   79-18781
  ISBN 0-02-583720-6

First Revised Edition 1979

Printed in the United States of America

For
Alfred Bester

Contents

Acknowledgments

I am grateful to many people who gave so generously of their time—especially during income-tax season.

In particular, I would like to thank: Bernard Resh, lawyer, accountant, and professional corporation; Dean Ridlon, of the State Street Bank; Mary Ellen O'Brien and Jaye Fallar of The Bank of New York; Thomas F. McDermott and John J. Ryan of the Metropolitan Life Insurance Company; Richard E. Daniels, of the Vanguard Group of mutual funds; Stanley Sanders, of Haas Securities Corporation; and many people at the Internal Revenue Service in New York City.

Special thanks must go to Robert Willens, of Peat, Marwick, Mitchell & Co., who sat patiently for many hours of interviews and helped me with some of the charts and sample tax returns.

At Macmillan I am grateful for the help of Toni Lopopolo, my editor, and Carol Robinson, my copy editor.

And, most of all, my heartfelt thanks to Alfred Bester, for all his patience and advice.

Introduction

This book is not designed to substitute for your lawyer or accountant, but rather to serve as a guide and enable you to make the most of their professional help. While you *can* incorporate and set up tax shelters yourself, without legal advice, it is far more desirable not to go it alone. Tax laws are complicated and often change from year to year; it takes a skilled professional to stay on top of them.

You don't have to be a professional to incorporate—if you're a self-employed salesman, plumber, real-estate agent, antique dealer, hairdresser, this book can save you money. If you can show a net profit, this book can save you money. All you have to do is form a corporation, and this book will show you how it can be done, step by step.

While we'll discuss corporations completely in Chapter 1, "So You Want to Be a Corporation," for now let's define a corporation simply as a body of persons granted a charter which legally recognizes them as a separate entity with its own rights, privileges, and liabilities. But don't let the "body of persons" wording scare you;

most states permit one person to incorporate (see chart, Appendix A).

Depending on the state you live in, your business or profession may require you to incorporate as a *professional corporation* (see Appendix A), but this means only that your professional practice is now able to enjoy all the benefits and privileges of corporations that had earlier been prohibited. There is no difference in the *tax* treatment of professional vs. business corporations; the only difference is a legal and supervisory one: if you form a professional corporation, all the shareholders and officers of the corporation must be licensed as professional practitioners in the state of incorporation. Your husband or wife and children cannot own stock in the corporation—even as minority stockholders—unless they, too, are licensed as professionals.

Thus, in terms of the law, a professional corporation is more limited in structure than a general business corporation; if your state permits you to choose, it is better to incorporate as a general business corporation. But whatever you do, if you are earning enough money and want to shelter substantial portions of it from taxes, you should consider incorporation.

Now sit back, read carefully, and you, too, can *Inc. Yourself* and *Profit by Setting Up Your Own Corporation.*

1

So You Want to Be a Corporation

Now that your appetite has been sufficiently whetted by visions of tax-free sugarplums, let's get down to basics:

Until now, most self-employed people have been operating as sole (or individual) proprietorships, a form of business organization in which the individual provides the capital, starts and runs the business, and keeps all the net profits and is taxed on them. As a sole proprietorship, the individual assumes total liability.

One step up from the sole proprietorship in complexity is the partnership, in which two or more people act as joint proprietors: they provide joint funding, joint management, and joint financial responsibility. Unfortunately, like the sole proprietorship, the partners are personally liable for all the debts of the business: each partner is personally liable to an unlimited degree for all the other partners.

A corporation is the most sophisticated—and protective—form of business organization. It is a "legal person," completely separate from the individuals who own and control it. A corporation has the power to do anything any person may do: carry on business, own property, lend and borrow money, sue and be sued. Most impor-

1

tant, it offers its shareholders limited liability: its stockholders can lose no more than their original investment; they are not liable for the debts of the corporation.

In terms of limited exposure to liability alone, it pays to incorporate to protect your assets; if you incorporate, no one can attach your house, car, or Ming vases if your business fails or if you lose a lawsuit. While this point is particularly important in such obvious professions as medicine, dentistry, law, architecture, and the construction industry, there are lesser-known areas on which limited liability plays an important role:

One of my friends incorporated himself to produce illustrated science fiction and children's books. For him, too, the primary benefit of incorporation has been limited liability: "I publish authors whose work some people might find offensive, and they might sue me, as the publisher. Rather than reject authors whose work I respected, but who might be dangerous, it seemed safer to incorporate. If I were sued, I wouldn't be personally liable."

Although limited liability may be the most attractive feature of incorporating, there are many others. For many people, there is greater ease in doing business. Some stores favor corporate accounts and offer discounts. Yes, even Tiffany's.

Incorporating can make job possibilities more attractive to new or future employees. There's a feeling of working for a profitable enterprise associated with incorporation, you can offer them greater benefits out of pretax dollars, and, of course, you can always offer them a promotion in title instead of a raise.

Then, too, there are medical, life, and disability insurance benefits. There is even one kind of insurance you can't get as a self-employed person, but can get as the employee of your corporation, even if you are the *only* employee—workmen's compensation.

Although the maximum annual Keogh Plan (retirement fund) contributions for self-employed people have been raised recently from $2,500 to $7,500, your benefits will still be greater if you incorporate. As the "key employee" of your own corporation, you can set aside upwards of $25,000 a year, or more than three times as much. This fund will be taxed only when you retire, and then only at capital-gains rates, which are usually only half the ordinary income-tax rates. Is your business so profitable that you've been investing in stocks? Good. Whereas before, as a sole proprietor, you had to pay income tax on all your dividends over $100, now, if your corporation invests in those stocks, 85 percent of those dividends are completely excluded from income tax, and the remaining 15 percent are taxed at only 17 percent (if your corporate net taxable income was $25,000 or less) and at only 20 percent (if your corporate net taxable income was between $25,000 and $50,000). The maximum rate is 46 percent for corporate net income over $100,000.

That's the good news. There are a few drawbacks, but they're mostly minor ones. There will be more paper work, and you will have to set yourself a salary and live within it. There will be a greater number of taxes to pay, but your total tax bill will be much lower than it was as an individual proprietorship. It's pretty clear that the advantages far outweigh the disadvantages, and that's why more and more people are following their lawyers' and accountants' advice and incorporating!

Are You Ever Too Young to Incorporate?

Although the voting age has been lowered to 18, in many states you still must be 21 to incorporate. From a practical point of view, most experts recommend incorporating as soon as possible. Incorporation has many intangible benefits for young people. The young publisher I mentioned earlier says, "I find it easier to deal as a corporation. I have less trouble in getting good people to work for me; they feel that a corporation is more responsible financially. It seems to increase my financial stature, even in my personal life. I had fewer credit-investigation problems when I wanted to rent an expensive apartment."

Are You Ever Too Old?

Of course, the older you are, the fewer years you have in which to accumulate tax-sheltered retirement funds. Still, according to

Dean Ridlon of the State Street Bank and Trust Company of Boston, "People in their fifties can still incorporate profitably; it all depends on how much money they're earning every year. A successful professional can certainly make use of incorporation in order to provide substantial retirement funds even if retirement is ten, five, or even only three years away."

Are You Ever Too Rich to Incorporate?

Yes, Virginia, there is such a thing as making too much money to incorporate. Your corporation is allowed to accumulate $150,000—no questions asked. Above that figure, you must prove that your corporation needs the money for business purposes. Otherwise, the IRS will take the position that your company has liquid assets that are "greatly in excess of its reasonable business needs" (IRS regulations quoted) and will impose additional punitive taxes on the corporation.

The corporation then comes to the crossroads, where it must either declare a dividend, on which the stockholders would be taxed; or justify the accumulation by showing "specific, definite, and feasible plans" (IRS regulations quoted) for the use of that accumulation. (Office or inventory expansion would be considered such a reasonable use.) If the accumulation cannot be justified, the IRS sets a penalty tax on the "accumulated taxable income": the retained earnings in excess of $150,000. The tax is 27½ percent of the first $100,000 of this accumulated taxable income and 38½ percent of everything in excess of $100,000. This corporate tax is an *additional* tax on top of the normal corporate income tax, so the *total* tax can go as high as 75 percent.

Thus, if your corporation's retained earnings are approaching the $150,000 limit, it should pay a dividend to its stockholders in order to avoid this tax.

However, only a corporation which has been grossing about $200,000 or $250,000 a year, or a corporation which has been in existence a number of years (long enough to have accumulated a substantial surplus) and is considered "mature," is faced with these problems. For most people who are thinking of incorporating, the accumulated earnings tax on surplus is premature and should not be a factor in their decisions.

There's another point, too. Until 1976, the amount a corporation could set aside as surplus without penalty was only $100,000; the Tax Reduction Act of 1975 increased that allowance to $150,000. With inflationary pressures influencing legislation, it is likely that in another 5 or 10 years, that allowance will be increased again, just because money today isn't worth what it used to be. If your corporation's net after taxes is $15,000, it would take 10 years to reach the IRS limit, and many tax changes are likely between now and then.

Are You Ever Too Poor?

Yes, again. It really doesn't pay for someone who is earning $10,000 or $12,000 a year to incorporate. The real benefits start between $20,000 and $25,000 a year. At $25,000 net taxable income, a single person is in the 39-percent bracket. A married person is in the 32-percent bracket. However, if either draws a salary of $15,000 instead and retains $10,000 in the corporation, he or she is taxed at approximately 20 percent on the $15,000, and the corporation is taxed at 17 percent on the $10,000.

But You Can Be Too Undisciplined

For some people, the joys of corporate tax savings just don't outweigh the extra paper work and planning that are involved. In contrast to the "good old days" of sole proprietorship, when you could write yourself a check or raid petty cash whenever you ran short, now you must clearly differentiate between the corporation and yourself and act in accordance with the fact that you are now an employee of the corporation—even if at the same time you are its president and only employee. The corporation is a *separate legal entity*, and, as such, there are certain formalities and restrictions. One of the tests the IRS uses to disqualify a corporation is "the corporate pocketbook"—the mixing together of personal and corporate funds: are you recognizing that you and the corporation are two separate, distinct legal entities, and does your bookkeeping reflect that fact, or are you still commingling corporate and personal income and expenditures? Of course, I know one man who does this and even pays the milkman with a corporate check—he leaves the mess to his accountant, who straightens it out every year. But this procedure is—to say the least—highly inadvisable.

In order to avoid having your corporation disqualified on these grounds, it is necessary that you set yourself a liberal salary—and to live within it, since you can no longer tap the bank account whenever you run short.

More Talk About Salaries

But deciding on a salary is not as simple as it seems at first glance. If you operate a business as a sole proprietor, you pick up all the income of your business. But if you incorporate and pay yourself a high salary, the IRS may attack your salary as unreasonably high and disallow it. Or the IRS may hold that your salary is reasonable, but that if you don't have a history of paying dividends and your income has been accumulating, part of your salary may be deemed by the IRS to be a dividend and will be taxed to you accordingly.

Part of the question of reasonable vs. unreasonable salary depends upon what other people in the same business or profession or a comparable one are earning. However, even this point can be gotten around, to a certain extent. For example, if you are in a creative profession, the IRS really cannot find an equivalent: there's just no way of comparing two artists or two writers—or their income.

But what about too low a salary? If you pay yourself a very low salary, your personal income taxes will be minimal, and your retained corporate earnings, which will be proportionately greater, will also be taxed at minimal corporate rates—17 percent under $25,000 and 20 percent between $25,000 and $50,000, under the Revenue Act of 1978.

This sounds like a wonderful solution, but there are some drawbacks. First, you may not be able to live on a very low salary—and remember, you must avoid the corporate pocketbook at all costs. Second, the more rapidly money accumulates as corporate surplus, the more quickly you may reach the limit of $150,000 and be forced to declare a dividend or be liable for the punitive tax on accumulated taxable income over $150,000, as explained earlier.

There may also be other considerations involved in how much or how little you pay yourself. If your corporation earns $40,000 a year, the IRS may look askance at your paying yourself $5,000—even if you can live on it—and retaining $35,000 in the corporation at minimum tax rates of 17 percent on the first $25,000 and 20 percent on the remaining $10,000. If you drew $10,000 in salary and retained $30,000 in the corporation, there would be less question of the IRS's involvement in the issue of your salary.

Third—and possibly most important—both your Social Security and pension contributions (and eventually payments) are based on your salary; the lower your salary is, the lower these contributions and payments to you will be.

Let's look at that $40,000 to see how this might work with respective salaries of $15,000 and $25,000:

	$15,000 Salary	$25,000 Salary
Net pretax earnings before salary	$40,000	$40,000
Salary	15,000	25,000
	25,000	15,000
Pension contribution (25% of salary)	3,750	6,250
Net corporate earnings	$21,250	$ 8,750
Corporate income tax (17%)	3,613	1,488
Retained earnings—available for investment	$17,637	$ 7,262
Income if invested in common and preferred stocks yielding 8%	$ 1,410	$ 580

Tax-free dividends (85% dividend exclusion)	$ 1,199	$ 493
Salary (single)	$15,000	$25,000
Less standard deduction	2,300	2,300
	12,700	22,700
Less exemption	1,000	1,000
Net taxable income	$11,700	$21,700
Personal income tax	$ 1,771	$ 4,755
Corporate tax	3,613	1,488
Total taxes	$ 5,384	$ 6,243
Salary (married)	$15,000	$25,000
Less standard deduction	3,400	3,400
	11,600	21,600
Less exemptions	2,000	2,000
Net taxable income	$ 9,600	$ 19,600
Personal income tax	$ 990	$ 3,129
Corporate tax	$ 3,613	1,488
Total taxes	$ 4,603	$ 4,617

There is no hard-and-fast formula to follow in this area; there are too many individual considerations. Are you single? Are you married? Does your spouse work? How many exemptions do you have? Do you itemize or take the standard deduction? Discuss these trade-offs with your lawyer and accountant and get their advice. Whatever you decide, recognize that no salary decision must be permanent and inflexible. Your salary can be raised or lowered as long as such provisions are spelled out neatly in the bylaws of your corporation, which will be dealt with at length in Chapter 2, "Getting Ready."

Should Your Spouse Incorporate?

Most certainly, if your spouse is self-employed, and for the same reasons that you should incorporate. Furthermore, if at all possible, your spouse should form his or her own corporation, rather than incorporating with you. Yes, once more it's more paper work keeping two separate sets of corporate records, but there's a most compelling reason to do it this way. Since a corporation can accumulate $150,000 at minimum tax rates whether the corporation has one shareholder or 100, incorporating as two separate corporations permits the two of you to accumulate double that amount, or $300,000.

The Taxman Cometh

If you are a one-person corporation, as I am, the IRS may scrutinize your return very carefully, with an eye toward ruling that your corporation was created to avoid taxes and is therefore illegal. Here are some important arguments you can use to disprove the IRS's claim:

(1) Incorporation gives you greater ease in doing business and frequently offers special corporate accounts and discounts.

(2) Incorporation increases the attractiveness of your business to new or future employees.

(3) Incorporation provides insurance benefits (e.g., workmen's compensation) that may not be available to self-employed persons.

(4) Incorporation offers greater retirement benefits.

(5) Incorporation permits limited—rather than unlimited—liability.

But the most important test of whether a corporation is valid depends on how much business activity is being conducted by the corporation. Normally, if the corporation is clearly operating a business and earning income, there would be no reason for the IRS not to accept it as a valid corporation; it would be very difficult for the IRS to attack the corporation as a sham.

The Personal Holding Corporation Trap

However, even if your corporation is deemed valid by the IRS, there is still another pitfall to avoid: you do not want to be considered a personal holding corporation. A personal holding corporation is a corporation in which 60 percent or more of corporate income is derived from investments and less than 40 percent comes from actual operation of the business. This situation is to be avoided because personal holding corporations are subject to special heavy taxes and do not enjoy the preferential tax treatment of general business corporations and professional corporations.

In the past, some people who had a great deal of money incorporated and took their investments into the corporation since, by incorporating, 85 percent of their preferred and common stock dividend income would not be taxed. These people weren't really conducting a business, they were just managing their investments and collecting dividends. It was a tax loophole.

The personal holding corporation regulations, which were designed by the IRS to close this tax loophole and prevent further tax inequities, provide that if a corporation is held to be a personal holding corporation—and obviously this can vary from year to year depending on annual earned income vs. annual dividend income—the personal holding company income must be distributed to its shareholders. If it was a one-man corporation, without other shareholders, then he would be taxed on the dividend income as though he himself owned the stocks and not the corporation. If there are several shareholders, they will be taxed on the income as though they themselves owned the stocks, and not the corporation.

But there are ways around even this problem. Let's assume that your corporation has a portfolio of $100,000, which yields 7½ percent, or $7,500 in dividend income, and that for some reason your corporation earned only $5,000. Because the dividend income represents 60 percent—the crucial figure—of total income, your corporation is regarded as a personal holding corporation for that year.

To avoid this problem, you could sell one of the stocks before the final quarterly dividend is paid, to avoid reaching the $7,500 figure. Since many corporations pay dividends in December, all you have to do is to make certain that your corporation sells the stock before the record date for payment of the dividend.

Then, depending on your financial situation, you might either invest the proceeds of the sale of the stock in a lower-yielding "growth" stock to reduce your dividend income below the 60 percent figure, or buy municipal bonds, whose income is not counted by the IRS in making personal holding company determinations.

The Myth of Double Taxation

A little knowledge is a dangerous thing. Here's proof: If you tell friends and colleagues that you're thinking of incorporating, sooner or later one of them will say to you, "But you don't want to do that— you'll be subject to double taxation."

True—and false. You *will* have to pay two taxes—but you won't be taxed twice on the same money. What's more important, *your total taxes will be less*—often by 30 to 50 percent, as compared with an individual proprietorship.

Let's look at some examples. In the first set of figures, our subject hasn't incorporated. Using current tax rates, he would have to pay $11,040 if he were single and $7,940 if he were married, assuming no children and filing a joint return with no other income:

	Single	Married
Net income	$40,000	$40,000
Less standard deduction	2,300	3,400
	37,700	36,600
Less exemption(s)	1,000	2,000
Net taxable income	$36,700	$34,600
Income tax	$11,040*	$ 7,940*

*Less possible tax credit

However, if our subject incorporates, pays himself $20,000 a year, and retains $20,000 in the corporation, the numbers change dramatically:

	Single	Married
Retained corporate earnings	$20,000	$20,000
Taxed at corporate rate	× 17%	× 17%
Corporate tax	$ 3,400	$ 3,400

Salary	$20,000	$20,000
Less standard deduction	2,300	3,400
	17,700	16,600
Less exemption(s)	1,000	2,000
Net taxable income	$16,700	$14,600
Income tax	$ 3,115*	$ 1,971*
Corporate tax	3,400	3,400
Total taxes	$ 6,515	$ 5,371
Income tax on $40,000	11,040	7,940
Amount saved	$ 4,525	$ 2,569
Percentage saved	41%	32%

*Less possible tax credit

The more money you earn, the more you can save by incorporating. The table below shows how favorable corporate tax rates are compared to personal income-tax rates:

Corporate Tax Rates	Personal Income-Tax Rates*	
	Single	Married
$0-$ 25,000 17%	$25,000 39%	32%
$25,000-$ 50,000 20%	$40,000 49%	43%
$50,000-$ 75,000 30%	$50,000 55%	54%
$75,000-$100,000 40%	$75,000 63%	54%
$100,000 + 46%		

*Net income, after deductions and exemptions

Thus, for the first $50,000 in income each year, the personal income-tax rates are approximately *double* the corporate-tax rates. At that point the gap narrows, but it widens again, since the maximum corporate-tax rate is only 46 percent, compared to the maximum personal income-tax rate of 70 percent.

But the most important point, of course, is that by incorporating you can divide your income into two portions, as shown earlier, *each of which is taxed at a lower rate.*

Getting Ready

Both incorporating and dissolving your corporation later, when you are ready to retire, or earlier, are especially easy if you are the only stockholder and officer. This is legal in every state.

Once you decide to incorporate, the first, crucial step is applying to the IRS for an Employer Identification Number: you will not be able to open corporate savings or checking accounts without it.

If you already have an Employer Identification Number (e.g., for your Keogh Plan account), it's no good—you'll need to apply for another one in the corporate name—even if you're just adding "Inc." to your own name. In the eyes of the IRS, the corporation is a separate "person" and must have a separate number.

The form to file is SS-4, Application for Employer Identification Number. Think of this number as your corporation's Social Security number. The length of time before your number is issued will depend on where you live and on the closeness to April 15—the IRS's busy season. At any rate, it should not take more than 6 weeks.

Therefore, if you're planning to start your corporate business on January 1, apply for your Employer Identification Number on October 15, to give yourself plenty of leeway.

You don't have to have corporate stationery and business cards, but if you want them, order them now so that you will have them on hand before January 1. You may wish to have cards printed and sent to your clients and customers, announcing that on January 1 your business or profession will be conducted under your new corporate name:

As of January 1, 1980

J. ENTREPRENEUR

Will Be Doing Business As

J. ENTREPRENEUR & CO., INC.

123 EASY STREET

NEW YORK, NEW YORK 10021

Now you're ready for the big step: applying for your Certificate of Incorporation. This is a procedure that varies from state to state; the different state requirements, forms, and fees are shown in Appendix A. In any case, your first step would be writing to the secretary of state or appropriate department or agency for your state, as shown on the chart.

For purposes of illustration, in this chapter I will walk you through the procedure of incorporation, using New York State laws, procedures, and forms. (Many of the states will differ in detail, but New York State is fairly representative.)

In New York State, the Certificate of Incorporation forms can be bought for approximately 25 cents each at most commercial stationers. Ask for Form A 234—Certificate of Incorporation, Business Corporation Law § (Section) 402, and get several blanks. You'll be sending one copy to Albany, you'll want a duplicate for your files, and you may want one or two forms to practice on.

Following is a sample Certificate of Incorporation. Of course, the

Certificate of Incorporation

of

JUDITH H. McQUOWN & CO., INC.

under Section 402 of the Business Corporation Law

Filed By: Judith H. McQuown

Office and Post Office Address
134 Franklin Avenue
Staten Island, NY 10301

15

A 234—Certificate of Incorporation
Business Corporation Law §402 ; 9-75

COPYRIGHT 1975 BY JULIUS BLUMBERG, INC., LAW BLANK PUBLISHERS
80 EXCHANGE PL. AT BROADWAY, N. Y. C. 10004

Certificate of Incorporation of

JUDITH H. McQUOWN & CO., INC.

under Section 402 of the Business Corporation Law

IT IS HEREBY CERTIFIED THAT:

(1) The name of the proposed corporation is JUDITH H. McQUOWN & CO., INC.

(2) The purpose or purposes for which this corporation is formed, are as follows, to wit:

To carry on all or any of the business of an editorial consulting firm and to do all other things necessary and relating thereto;

To carry on all or any of the business of a public relations, literary, and publicity agency and to do all other things necessary and relating thereto:

To purchase, acquire, hold and dispose of the stocks, bonds, and other evidences of indebtedness of any corporation, domestic or foreign, and to issue in exchange therefor its stocks, bonds, or other obligations, and to exercise in respect thereof all the rights, powers and privileges of individual owners, including the right to vote thereon; and to aid in any manner permitted by law any corporation of which any bonds or other securities or evudences of indebtedness or stocks are held by this corporation, and to do any acts or things designed to protect, preserve, improve or enhance the value of any such bonds or other securities or evidence of indebtedness or stock.

The corporation, in furtherance of its corporate purposes above set forth, shall have all of the powers enumerated in Section 202 of the Business Corporation Law, subject to any limitations provided in the Business Corporation Law or any other statute of the State of New York.

16

(3) *The office of the corporation is to be located in the* city
(city) (town) (incorporated village)

of New York. *County of* Richmond *State of New York.*

(4) *The aggregate number of shares which the corporation shall have the authority to issue is*

One Hundred (100) no par

17

(5) *The Secretary of State is designated as agent of the corporation upon whom process against it may be served. The post office address to which the Secretary of State shall mail a copy of any process against the corporation served upon him is*

134 Franklin Avenue, Staten Island, New York   10301

(6) *The accounting period which the corporation intends to establish as its first calendar or fiscal year for reporting the franchise tax shall end on* December 31   *19*77

The undersigned incorporator, or each of them if there are more than one, is of the age of eighteen years or over.

IN WITNESS WHEREOF, *this certificate has been subscribed this* 20th *day of* December   *19*76 *by the undersigned who affirm(s) that the statements made herein are true under the penalties of perjury.*

Judith H. McQuown
....
Type name of Incorporator

134 Franklin Avenue, Staten Island, NY   10301
....
Address

....
Type name of Incorporator

....
Address

....
Type name of Incorporator

....
Address

....
Signature

....
Signature

....
Signature

18

purpose of your corporation may be different from the one shown; for the wording you need, consult §§ (Sections) 202 and 402 of the Business Corporation Law.

In New York State, this form is sent to New York State Division of Corporations, 162 Washington Avenue, Albany, New York 12231, along with a money order or bank cashier's check for $60. Unless you are a lawyer, New York State will not accept your personal check.

Choosing a Fiscal Year

You will note that the IRS Request for Employer Identification Number and the New York State Certificate of Incorporation both ask for your fiscal year. Of course, it is much easier and more desirable to choose the calendar year as your corporation's fiscal year. You will have fewer tax forms to file that way. However, if that is impossible, a second choice would be July 1 to June 30. In that case, for your first year of incorporation, you would have to file two sets of income-tax forms. For the first half of the year, you would file as a sole proprietor (individual return), using Schedule C and any other appropriate schedules. For the second half of the year, you would file a corporate return (Form 1120 or Form 1120S if you make the Subchapter S election, as explained later in this chapter) and an individual return—because you are now an employee of your corporation.

Similarly, if you choose April 1 or October 1 as the beginning of your fiscal year, you will have to file the same two sets of tax returns. If you choose April 1, you would file as a sole proprietor for the first quarter (January 1 to March 31), and you would file corporate and individual returns for the last three quarters (April 1 to December 31). If you choose October 1, you would file as a sole proprietor for the first three quarters (January 1 to September 30), and you would file corporate and individual returns for the last quarter (October 1 to December 31).

As you can see, this situation is so complicated that it would be desirable to shift your corporate fiscal year to the calendar year as soon as possible, by using a corporate resolution, as shown later in this chapter.

Par-Value vs. No-Par-Value Stock

Most states' Certificate of Incorporation forms ask whether the corporation plans to issue par-value stock or no-par-value stock, as in the preceding illustration. Par value (sometimes called "face value") means the value or price at which the corporation's stock is issued; if a share of stock has a par value of $10, there must be $10 in the treasury to back it when the stock is initially sold or transferred. An entering stockholder would have to pay $1,000 for 100 shares, and the $1,000 would go into the corporate treasury to back the shares of stock ($10 per share).

No-par-value stock has no money behind the shares; no stockholder investment is necessary. Usually, in an ongoing sole proprietorship, the assets and liabilities of the proprietorship are transferred to the corporation in exchange for the corporation's stock.

Generally, if you are offered the option, issue no-par-value stock, rather than par-value stock. No par-value stock is easier to set up, cheaper, and requires less paper work. Some states assess taxes based on the par value of the issued and outstanding stock; if you have 100 shares of $100 par-value stock issued and outstanding, your total par value is $10,000; if those 100 shares have no par value, your total par value is $0.

In most states, corporations which deal in services can choose either par-value or no-par-value stock; it is just those businesses which use a great deal of capital (e.g., manufacturing) which may not be given the choice and would have to issue par-value stock so that the corporation would start with substantial cash assets.

Your Corporate Records

If you incorporate in New York State, shortly after you submit your Certificate of Incorporation and cashier's check or money order for $60 to the Division of Corporations, you will receive a filing receipt. Now you are able to proceed to the next step: ordering a set of corporate records and a corporation seal at a commercial stationer; both of these are required by law. Depending on where you live, it may take one to three weeks for you to receive your order. You must present your filing receipt to the stationer, or your order will not be accepted.

The simplest and cheapest corporate record set is a looseleaf binder (approximately $30, including corporation seal) which contains stock certificates, a stock transfer ledger in which the shareholders' names and addresses are recorded, pages to which you attach the filing receipt and a copy of the Certificate of Incorporation, and sample minutes of meetings and bylaws that are set up so that you can just fill in the blanks. (A sample set of corporate minutes and bylaws is shown in Appendix B.) Even if you are the sole stockholder, officer, and employee of your corporation, alas, it is necessary to go through this paper work. Or, if you put a higher value on your time than on your money, you can have your lawyer set up your corporation.

Your Corporate Bank Accounts

After you receive your new Employer Identification Number and your corporate seal, you will be able to open your new corporate bank accounts; I find it best to keep both a savings account and a checking account. Both these types of accounts require the impression of your corporate seal.

Following is a typical commercial bank checking-account corporate resolution, which you would sign and affix the corporate seal to; since a savings bank corporate resolution is much less detailed, a sample is not given.

RESOLUTIONS

I, the undersigned, hereby certify to _____ Bank, New York, N. Y., that at a meeting of the Board

of Directors of _____

_____

a Corporation organized and existing under the laws of _____

duly called and duly held on the _____ day of _____, 19____, the
following resolutions were duly adopted, and that the said resolutions have been entered upon the regular
minute book of the said Corporation, are in accordance with the By-Laws and are now in full force and effect.

RESOLVED: 1. That the officers of this Corporation, or any one or more of them, are hereby
authorized to open a bank account or accounts from time to time with the _____ Bank (hereinafter
referred to as the "Bank"), for and in the name of this Corporation with such title or titles as he or they may
designate.

2. That the _____

_____ of this Corporation,

(Indicate by Title persons authorised to sign, viz.: President, Vice-President, Treasurer, etc.)

signing _____

(Indicate how checks etc. are to be signed, viz.: singly, jointly, any two, etc.)

and their successors in office, and any other person hereafter authorized to sign on behalf of this Corporation,
are hereby authorized to sign checks, drafts, notes, acceptances, and other instruments, and orders for the
payment or withdrawal of moneys, credits, items and property at any time held by the Bank for account of
this Corporation, and the Bank is hereby authorized to honor any or all thereof and other instruments and
orders authorized to be paid by the Bank, including such as may bring about an overdraft and such as may
be payable to or for the benefit of any signer thereof or other officer or employee individually without in-
quiry as to the circumstances of the issue or the disposition of the proceeds thereof and without limit as to
amount.

3. That the bank is hereby authorized to accept for deposit for the account of this Corporation for
credit, or for collection, or otherwise, any or all checks, drafts, notes and other instruments of every kind
indorsed by any person or by hand stamp impression in the name of this Corporation or without indorsement.

4. That the _____

_____ of this Corporation,

(Indicate by Title person authorised to effect Loans, Advances, etc., viz.: President, Vice-President, Treasurer, etc.)

signing _____

(Indicate how Notes etc. are to be signed, viz.: singly, jointly, any two, etc.)

and their successors in office are hereby authorized to effect loans and advances at any time for this Corporation from the Bank, and for such loans and advances to make, execute and deliver promissory notes and
other written obligations or evidences of indebtedness of this Corporation, applications for letters of credit,
and any agreements or undertakings, general or specific, giving liens on, and rights and powers with respect
to, any property of this Corporation, and other agreements and undertakings, and as security for the payment
of loans, advances, indebtedness and liabilities of this Corporation to pledge, hypothecate, mortgage, assign,
transfer, indorse and deliver property of any description, real or personal, and any interest in and evidences
of any thereof at any time held by this Corporation, and to execute instruments of transfer, powers of attorney
and other instruments which may be necessary or desirable in connection therewith; and also to sell to, or discount with, the Bank commercial paper, bills receivable, accounts receivable and other instruments and
evidences of debt at any time held by this Corporation, and to that end to indorse, assign, transfer and deliver
the same, and also to give any orders or consents for the delivery, sale, exchange or other disposition of
any property or interest therein or evidences thereof belonging to this Corporation and at any time in the
hands of the Bank, whether as collateral or otherwise.

5. That all loans, discounts and advances heretofore obtained on behalf of this Corporation and all
notes and other obligations or evidences thereof of this Corporation held by the Bank are hereby approved,
ratified, and confirmed.

6. That the officers of this Corporation or any one or more of them are hereby authorized to act for
this Corporation in all other matters and transactions relating to any of its business with the Bank.

7. That each of the foregoing resolutions and the authority thereby conferred shall remain in full
force and effect until written notice of revocation or modification shall be received by the Bank; that the Secretary or any Assistant Secretary or any other officer of this Corporation is hereby authorized and directed
to certify, under the seal of this Corporation or not, but with like effect in the latter case, to the Bank the
foregoing resolutions, the names of the officers and other representatives of this Corporation, any changes
from time to time in the said officers and representatives and specimens of their respective signatures; and
that the Bank may conclusively assume that persons at any time certified to it to be officers or other representatives of this Corporation continue as such until receipt by the Bank of written notice to the contrary.

In Witness Whereof, I have hereunto set my hand as Secretary and affixed the seal of

the said Corporation this _____ day of _____, 19____

*ATTEST: _____

_____   Secretary

Official Designation

SEAL

*NOTE:— In case the Secretary is authorized to sign by the above resolutions, this certificate should be
attested by a second officer or director of the Corporation.

Transferring Assets to Your New Corporation

On the date on which you begin corporate life, you can either cut off your sole proprietorship and start afresh, or transfer the proprietorship's assets and liabilities to the new corporation. Note that these are assets and liabilities, such as office equipment and accounts receivable and payable, not earnings and profits from the proprietorship. In general, a corporation's assumption of the proprietorship's liabilities is beneficial; a dentist who had ordered silver would rather have the corporation pay the bill than pay it out of his own pocket.

The only danger—in terms of federal tax—is transferring more liabilities than assets, which can lead to punitive taxes. This situation can be avoided fairly easily; you can always throw in a personal asset to equalize the balance, even if it's only another chair for your office or a few more reams of paper.

The asset/liability balance is probably a question of magnitude. If the liabilities exceed the assets by $50, it is unlikely that the IRS would bother with your case; if they exceed the assets by $5,000, that's another story. Just to be on the safe side, though, get your accountant's advice; theoretically, even a difference of $50 or $100 could get you in trouble with the IRS.

Seed Money

Whether you transfer your sole proprietorship's assets and liabilities to your new corporation or close down everything and start from scratch, there will probably be a period of a month or two in which the corporation will need some kind of seed money until funds start coming into the corporation. This would usually be money for new stationery, petty cash, one months's operating capital, and similar expenses.

Of course, the simplest—but also most expensive—route would be taking out a 30-, 60-, or 90-day bank loan. But it is possible for you to lend the corporation money with an interest-free loan as long as the amount of money you are lending the corporation is not too great and as long as the corporation repays you within a short period of time. The IRS suggests that if you choose to lend money to the corporation for start-up expenses, you should limit the loan to no more than about $2,500 and the corporation should repay you within three months. There really isn't any point in your charging the corporation interest on your loan: although it is an expense to the corporation, the interest is income to you, and, in most cases, during the first year of corporate operation, you will be in a higher tax bracket than your corporation will, so, in effect, you will be penalized by accepting interest on the loan.

However, the IRS points out some possible pitfalls in your lending money to the corporation. If the loan is on the corporation's books for an extended period of time, and if there is no provision for interest, the IRS could maintain that this money is not really a loan, that instead it is equity capital (money that the corporation must have to stay alive). If the IRS can prove that you need all that money for a fairly long time to keep your business afloat, then, whether or not you call it a loan, the IRS will hold that the money is equity capital.

If the IRS does establish that the loan is really equity capital, then, when the loan is repaid, it may be deemed to be a dividend (and therefore taxable to you), rather than a repayment of the loan: you would be distributing part of that equity capital to yourself, and such a distribution is considered a dividend.

However, this is generally only a problem that affects companies which need a great deal of capital; small business and professional corporations can usually stay within the loan-size and repayment-time limitations that satisfy the IRS.

The worksheets that follow show how I handled the problem of seed money for my corporation. In this case, because I had to wait for my Employer Identification Number, I paid some corporate expenses with personal checks and then reimbursed myself when the corporate checking account was activated. I delayed paying myself salary until corporate income could be transferred to the checking

			Receipts	Expenses / Notes	
Jan 5	Client A		3750 —	The following expenses were incurred	
				at various times and were repaid (or	
Jan 7	Client B		455 —	paid) on or after February 15, 1977	
	Client C		11580	when employer id number was issued by IRS.	
Jan 13	Client D		35 —	Dec 20 New York State —	
				Corporation Fee	60 —
Jan 17	Client B		17750		
				Jan 3 Chemical Bank —	
Jan 19	Client E		30560	Cash Advance to open	
	Client F		125 —	checking a/c	100 —
Jan 25	Client C		9075	Jan 6 M.T. P/T Sec'y	50 —
	Client B		75 —	(personal ck #512)	
Jan 28	Client B		80 —	Feb 10 Paragon Ans. Svce	52 —
	Client D		444 —	(personal ck #826)	
				Gump's - Desk Acc.	14 —
Jan 31	Client G		246 —	(personal ck #817)	
			589935	Mfrs. Hanover (#522)	2604
				business portion	
				Chemical Bank (#501)	7554
	(of this:	3,000 checking		business portion	
		500 special savings		Con Ed (#525) bus. portion	1220
		balance - temp svgs			
				Feb 13 Print Craft (Xeroxing) #527	5882
				Misc. Cash Expenses -	
				Xeroxing, Cab Fares,	
				Supplies, etc.	
				Jan 1 - Feb 15	100 —
				Jan & Feb Rent @ 100	200 —
				ck #1003	79860

25

FEBRUARY 1977

Date	Description	Amount		Date	Description	Amount	
Feb 1	Client B	1 50 —		Feb 18	Me - Back Salary (#1001)	1 4 29 40	1
					IRS - Back Withholding (#1002)	5 25 35	2
Feb 7	Client B	1 62 50			Me - Reimbursement (#1003)	7 48 60	3
					NY Telephone - Jan (#1004)	75 90	4
Feb 10	Client A	6 21 —			QED Transcription (#1005)	1 76 40	5
							6
Feb 18	Client B	5 95 —		Feb 25	Me - Salary (#1007)	20 4 20	7
							8
Feb 25	Client B	1 45 —		Feb 26	Mrs Hanover (#1018)	1 4 04	9
		1 6 73 50			(Editor's Xmas Present)		10
							11
				Feb 28	Sec'y of State - ND (#1008)	2 —	12
					Sec'y of State - CT (#1009)	2 —	13
						3 1 77 89	14
							15
							16

account, and then paid myself back salary and reimbursed expenses in two large lump-sum checks: one for salary, and one for expenses. This procedure might well work for you and your new corporation.

Shortly after you incorporate, you will have to decide whether you want a Subchapter S corporation and/or whether you want to issue §1244 stock. These are independent choices; you may choose either, both, or neither. *Do not make either decision without consulting a lawyer and/or an accountant.*

Subchapter S Corporations

Subchapter S corporations are "small business corporations" (no more than 15 shareholders, only one class of stock) which are permitted to be taxed as partnerships for income-tax purposes. Corporate income or losses are credited or debited to the shareholders in proportion to their holdings. If you choose Subchapter S status, you must file Form 2553 with the District Director of the IRS within the first calendar month of the taxable year or the calendar month preceding the first calendar month.

There are two main advantages to Subchapter S election. If a corporation has losses in its early years, these losses can be passed through to the stockholders and can be used to offset their income from other sources, thus lowering their individual income taxes. When the corporation becomes profitable, the stockholders can either continue it as a Subchapter S corporation, now picking up the profits and paying taxes on them, or can vote to terminate the Subchapter S corporate status; the corporation would then no longer be taxed as a partnership, but would be taxed as an ordinary corporation. Once a corporation terminates its Subchapter S election, normally it has to wait 5 years before it can choose Subchapter S status again. Only the Commissioner of Internal Revenue can waive the 5-year waiting period.

There is a second advantage to Subchapter S status. If the IRS examines the corporation and disallows certain expenses, deeming them to be distributions of the corporation's earnings to the stockholders, in a general business or professional corporation, the disallowances are taxed twice: first the corporation must pay taxes on the distribution, and then the individual who received it must pay taxes on it since it is held to be a dividend. This is especially painful if the shareholder is in a 50-percent or higher tax bracket.

On the other hand, if the expenses were disallowed in a Subchapter S corporation, there would be only one tax. Only the shareholders would be taxed on the dividend because all the profits and losses (including dividends and disallowances) are picked up by the shareholders; the corporation itself pays no taxes.

There are many pitfalls in electing Subchapter S status, and most of them involve punitive tax penalties. Generally, most accountants and lawyers feel that Subchapter S election is more trouble and paper work than it's worth.

There is one major disadvantage, too. In pension planning, a Subchapter S corporation is treated like a sole proprietorship or partnership; its annual payments to defined-contribution plans which are not taxed to the employee are limited to the Keogh Plan maximum of 15 percent of salary or $7,500, whichever is smaller. (Above this limit, excess contributions are treated as additional income to the shareholder-employee.) This allowable contribution is much lower than the permitted corporate contribution of 25 percent or $25,000, whichever is smaller.

§1244 Stock

If the officers of a corporation decide to issue §1244 stock—a decision which must be made and recorded before the stock is issued—any shareholder who subsequently sells or exchanges that stock at a loss can take the loss as an ordinary loss—as opposed to the less favorable capital loss—on his or her personal income-tax return. The rules governing this tax shelter are too technical to describe in detail in a general book like this one; if you feel that issuing §1244 stock might benefit your stockholders and your corporation (usually only if you think that at some point outsiders may buy your stock), you should consult your lawyer and/or your accountant.

Appendix B consists of a sample set of minutes and bylaws for a corporation registered in New York State. They include minutes of the organizational meeting, the bylaws, minutes of a board of directors' meeting, minutes of a shareholders' meeting, and minutes of a special meeting of the board of directors to approve a change in the fiscal year so that it becomes identical to the calendar year. Minutes of a special meeting of the board of directors to approve a medical care reimbursement plan and the plan itself are found in Chapter 8, "Medical Benefits."

3

And Now the
Paper Work

Once you've come this far, the rest is easy. Changing from sole proprietor to corporate status doesn't require vastly more complicated bookkeeping; I find that my routine bookkeeping takes me only ten or fifteen minutes a day, or perhaps an hour or so on Saturday morning.

Your corporate bookkeeping can be very simple; any bookkeeping method that you can walk the IRS through is acceptable. For many people, single-entry bookkeeping is much simpler than double-entry. Your ledger can show what funds came in, what was paid out, what money was left, and how it was allocated.

No matter how accurate your records are, the IRS may be somewhat reluctant to accept records written on index cards or stray pieces of paper. From the standpoint of creating a good corporate impression, it may be wise to invest in a ledger and to learn to use it. It increases your credibility and, as always, neatness counts.

The worksheets that follow compare several months' books of an individual proprietorship and a corporation. As you can see, the individual proprietorship is taxed far more than the corporation, and

29

J. ENTREPRENUR

October 1977

		Income				Expenses		
Oct	3	Client A	300 —	Oct	3	Rent	200 —	1
		Client B	475 —					2
				Oct	14	Phone	100 —	3
Oct	7	Client C	250 —			Electric	20 —	4
		Client A	125 —					5
				Oct	31	Entertainment	100 —	6
Oct	12	Client B	850 —			(Receipts in File)		7
						Misc. Expenses	100 —	8
Oct	21	Client B	500 —			(Receipts in File)		9
							520 —	10
Oct	31	Client A	150 —					11
		Client D	350 —			Retirement Plan	872 —	12
			3000 —					13
						Federal Income		14
						Tax (40%)	843 20	15
								16
						Social Security	108 62	17
							1843 82	18
								19
								20
								21
								22
								23
								24
								25
								26
								27
								28
								29
								30
								31
								32
								33
								34
								35
								36

J. Entrepreneur & Co., Inc.

October 1977

Date	Income	Amount	Date	Expense	Amount	#
Oct 3	Client A	300 —	Oct 3	Rent	200 —	1
	Client B	475 —				2
			Oct 7	Salary		3
Oct 7	Client C	250 —		($300 gross, $224.95 Net)	224 95	4
	Client A	125 —				5
			Oct 14	Salary	224 95	6
Oct 12	Client B	850 —		Phone	100 —	7
				Electric	26 —	8
Oct 21	Client B	500 —				9
			Oct 21	Salary	224 95	10
Oct 31	Client A	150 —				11
	Client D	350 —	Oct 28	Salary	224 95	12
		3000 —				13
			Oct 31	Entertainment	100 —	14
				(Receipts in File)		15
				Misc. Expenses	100 —	16
				(Receipts in File)		17
					1419 80	18
						19
				Federal Income +	300 20	20
				S.S. Taxes		21
						22
				Retirement Plan	300 —	23
					2020 —	24
						25
						26
						27
						28
						29
						30
						31
						32
						33
						34
						35
						36

J. ENTREPRENGUR

NOVEMBER 1977

Nov 1	CLIENT D	575 —	Nov 4	RENT	200 —	1
						2
Nov 4	CLIENT C	825 —	Nov 18	PHONE	100 —	3
				ELECTRIC	20 —	4
Nov 10	CLIENT A	500 —				5
	CLIENT B	600 —	Nov 30	ENTERTAINMENT	100 —	6
				(RECEIPTS IN FILE)		7
Nov 25	CLIENT C	500 —		MISC. EXPENSES	100 —	8
				(RECEIPTS IN FILE)		9
Nov 30	CLIENT A	500 —			520 —	10
		3000 —				11
				RETIREMENT PLAN	372 —	12
						13
				FEDERAL INCOME	843 20	14
				TAX (40%)		15
						16
				SOCIAL SECURITY	108 62	17
					1843 82	18
						19

32

J. Entrepreneur & Co., Inc.
November 1977

Date	Description	Amount	Date	Description	Amount	Line
Nov 1	Client D	575 —	Nov 4	Salary	224 95	1
				Rent	200 —	2
Nov 4	Client C	825 —				3
			Nov 11	Salary	224 95	4
Nov 10	Client A	500 —				5
	Client B	600 —	Nov 18	Salary	224 95	6
				Phone	100 —	7
Nov 25	Client C	500 —		Electric	20 —	8
						9
Nov 30	Client A	500 —	Nov 25	Salary	224 95	10
		3000 —				11
			Nov 30	Entertainment	100 —	12
				(Receipts in file)		13
				Misc. Expenses	100 —	14
				(Receipts in file)		15
					1419 80	16
						17
						18
				Federal Income & SS Taxes	300 20	19
						20
				Retirement Plan	300 —	21
					2020 —	22
						23
						24
						25
						26
						27
						28
						29
						30
						31
						32
						33
						34
						35
						36

Dec 2	CLIENT E	1000 —	Dec 2	RENT	200 —	1
						2
Dec 8	CLIENT A	675 —	Dec 15	EMERGENCY	250 —	3
	CLIENT C	800 —		DENTAL WORK		4
				(TAX-DOLLAR		5
Dec 15	DIVIDENDS	500 —		VALUE OF $1000 —)		6
						7
Dec 21	CLIENT B	750 —	Dec 16	PHONE	100 —	8
				ELECTRIC	20 —	9
Dec 23	CLIENT A	225 —				10
			Dec 30	ENTERTAINMENT	100 —	11
Dec 30	CLIENT B	550 —		(RECEIPTS IN FILE)		12
		4500 —		MISC. EXPENSES	100 —	13
				(RECEIPTS IN FILE)		14
					770 —	15
						16
				RETIREMENT PLAN	522 —	17
						18
	SUMMARY			FEDERAL INCOME		19
	GROSS INCOME	10500 —		TAX (40% OF		20
				$2,188 + 40%		21
	EXPENSE	1,810 —		OF $475 DIVIDEND =		22
	RETIREMENT	1,266 —		$500 — $25 EXEMPTION)	1065.20	23
	FEDERAL					24
	INCOME + S.S.			SOCIAL SECURITY	1086.3	25
	TAXES	3,077.17			2465.83	26
			6153.47			27
	NET FOR QUARTER		4346.53			28
						29
	TOTAL TAXES FOR QUARTER		3077.47			30
						31
						32
						33
						34
						35
						36

34

J. Entrepreneur & Co., Inc.

December 1977

		Income			Expenses	
Dec 2	Client E	1000 —	Dec 2	Salary	224 95	1
				Rent	200 —	2
						3
Dec 8	Client A	675 —				4
	Client C	800 —	Dec 9	Salary	224 95	5
						6
Dec 15	Dividends	500 —	Dec 15	Emergency		7
				Dental Work		8
Dec 21	Client B	750 —		(Totally Deductible)	1000 —	9
						10
Dec 23	Client A	225 —	Dec 16	Salary	224 95	11
				Phone	100 —	12
Dec 30	Client B	550 —		Electric	20 —	13
		4500 —				14
			Dec 23	Salary	224 95	15
						16
	Summary		Dec 30	Salary	224 95	17
	Gross Income	10500 —		Entertainment	100 —	18
				(Receipts in File)		19
	Expense* 2,560 —			Misc. Expenses	100 —	20
	Retirement 975 —			(Receipts in File)		21
	Federal Income &				2644 75	22
	SS Taxes-Employee 975.65					23
	Federal Income &			Federal Income &		24
	SS Taxes - Corp. 911 —			SS Taxes	3752 5	25
		5421 65				26
	Net for Quarter	5078 35		Retirement Plan	375 —	27
					3395 —	28
	Total Taxes for Quarter	1886 65				29
				Tax on 15% of		30
				Dividends	15 —	31
					3410 —	32
				Quarterly Fed. Tax	1106 0	33
				Corp. Tax @ 20%		34
	*$5,845.35 - $2,924.35 Taken			of Net Income	786 —	35
	As Salary				4306 60	36

35

much less of its profits can be sheltered from taxes in a pension plan.

Getting down to specifics, always remember that you and your corporation are two separate, distinct legal entities. The corporation is now your employer and should pay your salary regularly, just as any other employer would. It will also withhold taxes from your salary and send them to the appropriate government agencies.

Your corporation will send out all the bills, and all income must now go into corporate bank accounts. I prefer using both a savings account and a checking account: all income goes directly into a corporate savings account which earns interest; when money is needed to pay salary and bills, it is transferred from the savings account to the checking account.

Paying bills is a little more complicated now than it used to be. As an individual proprietor, your personal check paid for all expenses—personal and business; it was only at the end of the year that you had to figure out what part of a check to a credit-card company covered business expenses and what part represented personal items. Now you will have to make these calculations in advance and pay many bills with two checks: corporate and personal. There is a bonus, though: when you come to the end of the year, your business and personal expenses will already have been segregated, and tax preparation of these items will take no time at all.

You may find it simpler to use one credit card for business only; many people use their American Express or Diner's Club cards for corporate expenditures and their Master Charge or BankAmericards for personal ones.

Paying office bills isn't difficult, but it deserves a chapter all its own; mortgages, rent, phone, and utilities are covered in the next chapter, "Your Office: Home or Away?"

Your Office: Home or Away?

If you have been renting an office as an individual proprietor, corporate status doesn't mean much of a change: from the date of incorporation, you'll be paying your rent and office expenses with company checks instead of personal checks, as you had when you were an individual proprietor.

If your office is at home—one or more rooms of an apartment or house that you rent—you would now use a corporate check to pay for the rent on that portion of the apartment or the house that you use as an office. If your rent was $400 a month for a four-room apartment and you used one room of the apartment exclusively as an office, you would now pay the rent with two checks: a corporate check for $100 for the office portion of your apartment, and a personal check for the personal living portion of your apartment. Using these proportions, you would send the electric utility company a corporate check for 25 percent of your electric bill and a personal check for 75 percent of it. Or you might be able to make a convincing case for a larger share to be allocated to your office—an electric typewriter and lights in constant use, perhaps—and write off 33 or 40 percent as a corporate office expense and 67 or 60 percent for personal use.

Your telephone bill is a bit more complicated. If you have a separate business phone, the bill gets paid with a corporate check, of course, and your private phone bill gets paid with a personal check. If your home office has only one phone, you will have to pro-rate business and personal use and pay the appropriate shares with corporate and personal checks. Be especially careful to allocate long-distance calls properly; you should be able to document business long-distance calls if the IRS audits your tax return.

Still more complicated is the situation where your office is part of a house, cooperative apartment, or condominium you own and live in. In this case, in order to preserve the separation between your corporation and you, one accountant suggests that the corporation rent its office space from you, the shareholder, in an arm's-length transaction. In this kind of transaction, it is clear that there are two separate entities, and that there is no favoritism shown; e.g., if you would not rent anyone else office space at $10 per month, you must not rent space to the corporation at this price.

You can even profit from this transaction: as the stockholder, you could take the position that the fair rental value of the corporate offices is higher than the proportionate share of the mortgage and the real estate tax payments you have to make. For example, if your mortgage and tax payments total $200 a month and your corporation uses two rooms of your eight-room house, you could conceivably and reasonably argue that $100 a month (rather than the $50 that would be the proportionate share) is a reasonable rent for a two-room office in your neighborhood. Then, as the homeowner (or cooperative or condominium owner), you would be able to take 100 percent of all the deductions on your individual tax return: interest amortization, real estate taxes, etc. You would have to report the rent your corporation pays you as income, but this way you are withdrawing funds from your corporation that will be deductible by the corporation: sales, rentals, anything but dividends, since dividends would be taxed twice.

As you can see, the corporation is defraying a larger part of your home's expenses than the proportion of the actual physical space it is using, and yet the $100 a month rent, in this example, is quite reasonable and not likely to be questioned by the IRS.

Especially for Women

Self-employed women, like self-employed men, can enjoy such benefits of incorporation as limited liability, increased pension benefits, minimally taxed dividend income, and medical and insurance programs.

But there are special benefits for women, too. One talented young *Vogue* photographer puts it this way: "Incorporating sets me apart from a hundred other free-lance photographers. It shows clients and prospective clients that I'm successful and financially sophisticated. It's that extra bit—that extra little touch—that helps them remember *me*, not just my work."

Nowadays, more and more women are self-employed, and with increasing financial sophistication, more women are incorporating. But very often women suffer from the legacy of the past: they are not as knowledgeable about banking and establishing credit as men are, and all too often, wives, widows, and divorcées suddenly find that they have no financial history. Quite simply, this means that lenders don't know whether or not to lend them money.

Whether you'll ever use it or not, establish a credit record immediately; you never know when you'll need it. The best way to do this is to open a checking account—*in your own name alone*—and to become known to your bank manager.

Next, ask for a line of credit: overdraft privileges for your checking account. Most banks give this a fancy name—Privilege Checking, Executive Credit, The No-Bounce Check. All it means is that if you overdraw your account, your checks will be honored—but at the same time you will have automatically borrowed money to cover them, at a hefty 12 to 18 percent. Formerly, the traditional advice on establishing credit was: "Take out a loan, make the payments promptly, and pay the final installment a little early." However, if you can show your bank manager that you have assets, you should be granted a line of credit without having to go through the rigmarole of a bank loan that you don't need.

What assets will impress a bank manager? A savings account in your name and property in your name. A savings account is particularly good because it shows that you are not a spendthrift, and also that there is money at your disposal even if your income should fluctuate.

A good credit-card or charge-account history will also show that you are fiscally responsible. Like your checking and savings accounts, your credit card and charge plates should also be in your name alone.

Whatever method you use—checking account, line of credit, credit cards—always use your own name alone, even if it involves what seems like duplication and extra service charges. One of my friends who'd worked for 20 years finally decided to go into business for herself and applied for a bank loan to furnish her home office. Alas, the bank manager required her husband to cosign the loan because my friend had never built up an independent credit record—all her accounts were in joint name, and thus all the credit records were in her husband's name.

Now, if you incorporate, there's an additional reason to keep separate accounts: to prove to the IRS that there's no "corporate pocketbook" at work, that you are not lumping together your corporate and personal expenditures.

In most corporate situations, women experience the same problems as men: setting up a corporation, making it successful, investing corporate surplus profitably, etc. But there is one area in which women (and, incidentally, artists and writers who may produce only one major money-making work every two, three, or more years) are particularly vulnerable.

Women as Personal Holding Corporations

Because women will often curtail their workload during pregnancy and for a time after their children are born, women who incorporate may frequently have years in which their corporation receives much more dividend income from the stocks the corporation has bought than earned income from the work the corporation has performed for customers and clients, and thus be in danger of being held by the IRS to be a personal holding corporation. This situation would be especially likely if a woman had accumulated around $100,000 in a corporate portfolio which was invested in high-yield stocks paying $7,000 or $8,000 a year at the time of her maternity leave.

As explained earlier, a woman in this position could easily avoid having her corporation deemed a personal holding corporation simply by selling one or more of the corporation's stocks to bring the dividend income down to 59 percent or less of the total corporate income, and then reinvesting the proceeds of the stock sales in either low-yielding growth stocks (but making sure to keep the dividend income down to 59 percent), or municipal bonds (whose income is not counted by the IRS in making these calculations), depending on how aggressive or conservative an investor she is.

When she returns to work full time and her corporation is earning enough so that it is no longer in danger of being classified as a personal holding corporation, she can—and should—reverse the procedure so that her corporation can benefit from the 85-percent tax-free dividend exclusion. She should sell the corporation's municipal bonds or growth stocks and reinvest the proceeds of the sales in high-yielding common or preferred stocks.

Now that women are finally achieving their own in the business world and are earning enough money to make it worthwhile, doesn't it make sense for a woman to incorporate?

Your Employees

Up until now, we've been discussing the sometimes-idyllic situation where you are truly a one-man band: in your one-person corporation, you are everything from president down to file clerk.

But what if you have employees? Then it gets more complicated, though not necessarily more expensive.

If your corporation is able to hire what the IRS calls "independent contractors," you will not have to withhold taxes on their pay or cover them for Social Security. At the end of the year, the corporation just sends them an IRS Form 1099, which shows how much you paid them. Obviously, then, your corporation does not have to include independent contractors in its pension or profit-sharing plans because they are not considered to be the corporation's employees. (These independent contractors can set up their own Keogh Plans, of course, but that's another subject for another book.)

If your corporation hires part-timers who are held by the IRS to be your employees, you will have to withhold income taxes on their salaries and furnish them with W–2 forms showing the amounts withheld. Depending upon how much they earn each quarter, the corporation may or may not have to contribute to their Social Security accounts. State regulations on contributions to workmen's compensation and unemployment insurance funds vary too widely to be discussed here. The important point: unless your corporation's part-time employee completes 1,000 hours a year (an average of 20 hours a week), you do not have to include him or her in the corporation's pension or profit-sharing plans.

This means, of course, that your corporation could hire two or three part-timers instead of one full-time employee and save thousands of dollars every year by not having to contribute to employees' plans.

Hiring part-timers has social as well as financial benefits. Very often you can hire more intelligent and qualified people—college students, mothers, retirees—who are unable to work a full week, but who perform splendidly on a part-time basis and are often delighted to work flexible hours. (I know from personal experience: I worked my way through college assisting the president of a small legal-services corporation.)

Even if you have full-time employees, though, you may not have to include them in your pension and profit-sharing plans immediately—and there are even ways to exclude them permanently.

First, there is a minimum-age requirement: an employer does not have to include anyone under the age of 24½ in its pension and profit-sharing plans.

Second, if an employer is willing to vest 100 percent of its contributions to an employee pension plan immediately, it can legally delay including that employee in the plan for 3 years. Then, of course, all employer contributions are 100 percent vested, and if the employee leaves after 5 years of employment, he or she could take 100 percent of 2 years' worth of your contributions. Compare this with the figures shown in Section 6.4 of Appendix C, where, if the employee is included after completion of 1,000 hours, after 5 years of employment, the employer's contribution is only 45 percent vested. This means that if your employee leaves after 5 years, he or she can take only 45 percent of your corporation's contribution to the pension and profit-sharing plans; the remaining 55 percent reverts to the corporation. If he or she leaves before working 4 years, no funds are vested and all the corporation's contributions revert to the corporation.

These two options present an obvious trade-off. If your corporation is in an industry where people move around frequently (advertising, Wall Street, and publishing are typical examples), it might be wise to wait the 3 years and then vest 100 percent of the contributions, because the odds are that none of your employees will stay the 3 years, and you won't have to make any contributions at all. On the other hand, if your corporation is in an industry where employee turnover is low, it might be best to include an employee in the plan immediately, so that if he or she leaves after 4 or 5 years, only 40 or 45 percent of your corporation's contributions will be vested. What it boils down to in the case where an employee leaves after 5 years is your risking 100 percent of 2 years' contributions vs. 45 percent of 4½ years' contributions. Check with your lawyer and accountant before you decide.

But don't think that you can hire employees and then fire them just before their 3 years' waiting time is up and they become eligible to join your corporation's pension and profit-sharing plans. You may get away with it for the first two 3-year periods. But when the IRS audits your corporation's plan and discovers that your corporation terminates its employees as soon as they become eligible, the IRS will disqualify the plan. The plan then becomes a taxable trust, and the employer really has problems. Besides, this kind of behavior just isn't ethical.

There's still another gimmick, though, for eliminating low-paid employees from pension and profit-sharing plans. Here's how it works: the plan—called an integrated plan because it is integrated with Social Security—is constructed to cover employees earning amounts over the Social Security maximum, which is $22,900 in 1979. Under those amounts, the employer pays the Social Security tax, and above the cut-off point, the employer contributes to the pension and profit-sharing plans. Thus, if a secretary earned $12,000 in 1979, the corporation would pay only the Social Security tax on the $12,000. If the president of the corporation earned $42,900 in 1979, the corporation would pay the Social Security tax on the first $22,900 of salary and would contribute to the pension and profit-sharing plans on a base of $20,000 ($42,900 minus $22,900).

Of course, the base doesn't have to be the maximum Social Security salary. In the preceding illustration, the cut-off point could have been $12,000; then the secretary would still be excluded from the pension and profit-sharing plans and would be covered only by the Social Security tax, but the base on which the corporation would contribute to its president's pension and profit-sharing plans would rise to $30,900 ($42,900 minus $12,000). If the corporation were being generous, it might make the cut-off point $10,000. Then the corporation would pay the Social Security tax on $12,000 and make a contribution based on $2,000 for the secretary, and would pay the Social Security tax on $22,900 and make a contribution based on $32,900 for the president. *Notice that because the cut-off point is less than the maximum Social Security, the secretary is getting retirement coverage on $14,000, and the president is getting retirement coverage on $55,800 ($22,900 + $32,900).*

The important thing to note is that the Social Security level is a maximum; our corporation could not make the cut-off point $30,000—unless the Social Security maximum had risen to $30,000 by that time.

Again, the constant refrain: consult a lawyer or accountant before you decide how to cover (or not to cover) your employees. Good employees should be rewarded somehow; you *do* want them to stay, don't you?

"Free" Insurance

As a key employee of your corporation, you can get "free" life insurance and disability insurance. Workmen's compensation, a third form of insurance, is available *only* to employees; sole proprietors are ineligible. By "free" insurance, I mean that the insurance premiums are fully deductible by the corporation and reduce its pretax income, while at the same time they are not treated by the IRS as income to the insured.

The "free" life insurance—sometimes called §79 insurance—is limited to one-year renewable term policies of up to $50,000 face value as group insurance in groups of 10 people or more. However, smaller groups—including a "group" of one—can qualify for similar renewable term policies which get similar tax treatment from the IRS. It is possible to discriminate on an employee's class basis in choosing the face value for these policies; a common choice would be for officer/employees to have $50,000 policies, and for other employees to have $10,000 policies.

If additional life-insurance coverage above $50,000 is desired, the IRS insists that the employee pay taxes on what is called "imputed income." This is a figure per $1,000 of coverage that is based solely on the age of the employee; it is not a percentage of the monthly premium. The following table shows monthly premiums and im- puted income:

Age	Approximate Monthly Premium Per $10,000	Monthly Imputed Income Per $10,000
30–34	$ 2.00	$ 1.00
35–39	2.30	1.40
40–44	3.00	2.30
45–49	4.40	4.00
50–54	7.10	6.80
55–59	11.10	11.10
60–64	18.80	16.30

Since, at all ages, the imputed income is less than the premium for the additional insurance, it pays for the corporation to pay for the additional insurance and for the shareholder/employee to accept the imputed income.

But as important as life insurance is, many people worry far more about disability. There are many people who don't need life insurance; they have no family to protect. However, they all need disability insurance: some form of income protection to provide for them if they are unable to work because of illness or injury. Disability insurance premiums, too, are fully deductible by the corporation and are not considered by the IRS to be income to the insured.

It is difficult to set up hard-and-fast guidelines about insurance coverage—especially disability insurance coverage. There are too many variables: riskiness of work, riskiness of life-style, extent of medical insurance coverage, living expenses, escalating medical costs, etc. This is an area which really needs individual treatment and frequent examination and revision. However, as a general rule, it may make sense to arrange for generous—if not maximum— coverage. What little extra the corporation may pay for your being overinsured against possible disability is certainly worth the price in terms of peace of mind. Besides, the premiums are paid out of pre-tax dollars, so they're less expensive than they may seem, and may even pull your corporation down from the 30-percent bracket into the 20-percent bracket.

Medical Benefits

First, the bad news. Prior to the Tax Reform Act of 1976, employees of corporations (but not individual proprietors) were able to take a sick-pay exclusion (and, in effect, receive tax-free income) when they were absent from work due to illness or injury. The Tax Reform Act has virtually put an end to these benefits for corporate employees, except in the case of permanent and total disability.

Now, the good news. Corporate employees can still enjoy "free" medical insurance and payment of medical expenses and drugs for themselves and their families. They are "free" in that the corporation can write off the payments as a business expense, but they are not held by the IRS to be income to the individuals receiving them.

Although the IRS calls them "medical reimbursement plans," your corporation can actually pay your medical bills for you and your family directly, rather than reimbursing you for your medical expenses. While legally this plan can be informal and unwritten (especially if you are the sole employee and stockholder) and can consist of the understanding that the corporation will pay all medical bills, in actual practice, where the IRS is concerned, a formal written corporate resolution of the type shown later in this chapter carries much more weight.

In a one-person corporation, that one officer/stockholder/employee unquestionably provides significant services as an employee and can be covered, along with his or her family. In larger corporations, it has been held that medical reimbursement plans must benefit employees, rather than stockholders as such. The basis of the plan must be the employer-employee relationship, and not the stockholder relationship. Of course, covered employees can also be stockholders, and, in fact, many closely held corporations limit participation in their medical reimbursement plans to officers who are also stockholders. If these officers contribute substantial services as employees, the medical reimbursement plan will resist challenge.

In a one-person reimbursement plan, the corporation can—and should—arrange to reimburse 100 percent of medical expenses. In a larger corporation, thought must be given to the total medical expenses among the plan's participants; it may be wise to set a limit on the amount of reimbursement per eligible employee. It may also be advisable to set up a medical care reimbursement plan for stockholder/employees and to provide a more limited plan—or just Blue Cross/Blue Shield for ordinary employees.

Following is a sample medical care reimbursement plan and minutes of a meeting of the board of directors approving the plan. As in other areas of corporate life, remember that your plan can be amended as situations change: as the corporation covers an increasing number of employees, it may be wise to lower the reimbursement limit per employee.

(NAME OF YOUR CORPORATION)
MEDICAL REIMBURSEMENT PLAN

ARTICLE I — Benefits

The Corporation shall reimburse all eligible employees for expenses incurred by themselves and their dependents, as defined in

IRC S152, as amended, for medical care, as defined in IRC S213(e), as amended, subject to the conditions and limitations as hereinafter set forth. It is the intention of the Corporation that the benefits payable to eligible employees hereunder shall be excluded from their gross income pursuant to IRC S105, as amended.

ARTICLE II — Eligibility

All corporate officers employed on a full-time basis at the date of inception of this Plan, including those who may be absent due to illness or injury on said date, are eligible employees under the Plan. A corporate officer shall be considered employed on a full-time basis if said officer customarily works at least seven months in each year and twenty hours in each week. Any person hereafter becoming an officer of the Corporation, employed on a full-time basis shall be eligible under this Plan.

ARTICLE III — Limitations

(a) The Corporation shall reimburse any eligible employee (without limitation) (no more than $_____) in any fiscal year for medical care expenses.

(b) Reimbursement or payment provided under this Plan shall be made by the Corporation only in the event and to the extent that such reimbursement or payment is not provided under any insurance policy(ies), whether owned by the Corporation or the employee, or under any other health and accident or wage-continuation plan. In the event that there is such an insurance policy or plan in effect, providing for reimbursement in whole or in part, then to the extent of the coverage under such policy or plan, the Corporation shall be relieved of any and all liability hereunder.

ARTICLE IV — Submission of Proof

Any eligible employee applying for reimbursement under this Plan shall submit to the Corporation, at least quarterly, all bills for medical care, including premium notices for accident or health insurance, for verification by the Corporation prior to payment. Failure to comply herewith may, at the discretion of the Corporation, terminate such eligible employee's right to said reimbursement.

ARTICLE V — Discontinuation

This Plan shall be subject to termination at any time by vote of the board of directors of the Corporation; provided, however, that medical care expenses incurred prior to such termination shall be reimbursed or paid in accordance with the terms of this Plan.

ARTICLE VI — Determination

The president shall determine all questions arising from the administration and interpretation of the Plan except where reimbursement is claimed by the president. In such case, determination shall be made by the board of directors.

MINUTES OF SPECIAL MEETING OF DIRECTORS
OF
(NAME OF YOUR CORPORATION)

A special meeting of the board of directors of (name of your corporation) was held on (date) at (time) at (address where meeting was held).

All of the directors being present, the meeting was called to order by the chairman. The chairman advised that the meeting was called to approve and adopt a medical care expense reimbursement plan. A copy of the plan was presented to those present and upon motion duly made, seconded, and unanimously carried, it was

RESOLVED, that the "Medical Care Reimbursement Plan" presented to the meeting is hereby approved and adopted, that a copy of the Plan shall be appended to these minutes, and that the proper officers of the corporation are hereby authorized to take whatever action is necessary to implement the Plan, and it is further

RESOLVED, that the signing of these minutes by the directors shall constitute full ratification thereof and waiver of notice of the meeting by the signatories.

There being no further business to come before the meeting, upon motion duly made, seconded, and unanimously carried, the meeting was adjourned.

_____
SECRETARY

_____   _____
CHAIRMAN   DIRECTOR

_____   _____
DIRECTOR   DIRECTOR

The advantages of your corporation's paying all your medical bills are enormous. If you were to pay your medical bills yourself, as a sole proprietor (or if your corporation hadn't adopted the medical reimbursement plan), the totals would be reduced first by 1 percent and then by 3 percent of your adjusted gross income, as shown below. The dollar amount of these reductions can be quite sizable, and in some cases can completely wipe out your medical deductions.

However, a corporation is not subject to the 1 percent and 3 percent reductions; every penny of medical expense counts.

Let's look at some simple Schedule A returns. We'll assume that Entrepreneur's adjusted gross income is $20,000 and Worldly Wise's adjusted gross income is $40,000. We'll give them identical medical expenses:

Medical insurance	800.00
Medicine and drugs	250.00
Doctors, dentists, etc.	300.00
Other (eyeglasses)	200.00
	$1,550.00

ENTREPRENEUR

Schedule A—Itemized Deductions

Medical and Dental Expenses (not paid by insurance or otherwise) (See page 15 of Instructions.)		
1 One-half (but not more than $150) of insurance premiums you paid for medical care. (Be sure to include in line 10 below.) . ▶	150	—
2 Medicine and drugs	250	—
3 Enter 1% of Form 1040, line 31 . . .	200	—
4 Subtract line 3 from line 2. If line 3 is more than line 2, enter zero	50	—
5 Balance of insurance premiums for medical care not entered on line 1	650	—
6 Other medical and dental expenses:		
a Doctors, dentists, nurses, etc. . . .	300	—
b Hospitals		
c Other (itemize—include hearing aids, dentures, eyeglasses, transportation, etc.) ▶ EYEGLASSES	200	—
7 Total (add lines 4 through 6c)	1200	—
8 Enter 3% of Form 1040, line 31 . . .	600	—
9 Subtract line 8 from line 7. If line 8 is more than line 7, enter zero	600	—
10 Total medical and dental expenses (add lines 1 and 9). Enter here and on line 33 . ▶	750	—

WORLDLY WISE

Schedule A—Itemized Deductions

Medical and Dental Expenses (not paid by insurance or otherwise) (See page 15 of Instructions.)		
1 One-half (but not more than $150) of insurance premiums you paid for medical care. (Be sure to include in line 10 below.) . ▶	150	—
2 Medicine and drugs	250	—
3 Enter 1% of Form 1040, line 31 . . .	400	—
4 Subtract line 3 from line 2. If line 3 is more than line 2, enter zero	0	
5 Balance of insurance premiums for medical care not entered on line 1	650	—
6 Other medical and dental expenses:		
a Doctors, dentists, nurses, etc. . . .	300	—
b Hospitals		
c Other (itemize—include hearing aids, dentures, eyeglasses, transportation, etc.) ▶ EYEGLASSES	200	—
7 Total (add lines 4 through 6c)	1150	—
8 Enter 3% of Form 1040, line 31 . . .	1200	—
9 Subtract line 8 from line 7. If line 8 is more than line 7, enter zero	0	
10 Total medical and dental expenses (add lines 1 and 9). Enter here and on line 33 . ▶	150	—

Entrepreneur's medical deductions have been sliced in half: from $1,550 to $750. If he is in the 25-percent tax bracket, his medical deductions are now worth only $187.50 in tax dollars.

Poor Worldly Wise has fared even worse. His medical deductions have dwindled to less than 10 percent of his cost—from $1,550 to $150—and that only because of line 1's $150 tax exclusion for medical insurance. Even if he is in the 50-percent tax bracket, his medical deductions are worth only $75 in tax dollars.

But your corporation is not subject to those 1 percent and 3 percent reductions. The total medical expenditures remain at $1,550, and consequently their value in tax dollars is much greater:

Corporate Income	Tax Bracket as Percentage	Dollar Value of $1,550 Deduction
$ 0–$ 25,000	17%	$263.50
$25,000–$ 50,000	20	310.00
$50,000–$ 75,000	30	465.00
$75,000–$100,000	40	620.00
$100,000 +	46	713.00

Amazing, isn't it!

All About ERISA:
Tax-Sheltered Pension and
Profit-Sharing Plans

ERISA—the Employees' Retirement Income Security Act—is one of the most complicated and confusing pieces of legislation ever to be enacted. Even lawyers and accountants have trouble interpreting it, so if you find this chapter difficult to understand, you're not alone. There is a lot of paper work to file with the IRS and the Labor Department (in some cases, the Labor Department will be satisfied with the IRS form), but the results are worth it. Your corporation will be able to put away for you, its (sole) employee, up to 25 percent of your annual compensation, even including bonuses, if you like—up to $25,000. Furthermore, *you* can add up to 6 percent of your annual compensation to this retirement fund as what is called a Voluntary Contribution.

The simplest, cheapest, and easiest-to-adopt plans are the money-purchase and profit-sharing plans, both of which are classified as defined-contribution plans.

Defined-Contribution Plans

Defined-contribution plans are just what they sound like: a set contribution which is made every year. The contribution is defined as a percentage of the employee's annual compensation.

Money-Purchase Plan

A money-purchase plan is a defined-contribution plan with a specific contribution formula. Unlike a profit-sharing plan, which is also a defined-contribution plan, contributions to a money-purchase plan must be made *each year, whether or not the employer has a profit.* The annual contribution is based on a stated percentage of the employee's compensation. The contribution can range from less than 1 percent to 25 percent of compensation if the money-purchase plan is used alone. The money-purchase plan can also be combined with a profit-sharing plan or a defined-benefit plan, as explained later in this chapter.

Example: The employer agrees to contribute 10 percent of each employee's compensation each year. The contributions and earnings thereon are accumulated until the employee retires or leaves the employer. The benefit that the employee will receive depends on the amount to his or her credit and whether or not the terminated participant has a vested interest. An employee is always fully vested at normal retirement age, and usually at death or retirement because of disability. The rate of vesting depends on provisions in the plan. (A more thorough discussion of vesting is found in Chapter 6, "Your Employees," and in Appendix C, the "Model Profit-Sharing Plan.")

Profit-Sharing Plan

As its name implies, a profit-sharing plan is a defined-contribution plan in which contributions are made only in years in which the employer shows a profit. Contributions can range from less than 1 percent to 15 percent of compensation. Furthermore, there are unwritten IRS assumptions (which come to light if the employer's tax return is audited) that contributions not only be a percentage of the employee's compensation, but also not exceed a certain percentage of the employer's profit. Thus, even though the employer has a profit for the year, contributions to an employee profit-sharing plan probably should not exceed 60 percent of the employer's profits. After all, the IRS doesn't want 80 or 90 percent of the employer's profits being eaten up by retirement-plan contributions; it wants some profits left over so the employer can pay income tax on them. Thus, in wording the "Trust Agreement" (sample shown in Appendix D) and the "Adoption Agreement" (sample shown in Appendix E), to be discussed later in this chapter, the employer should construct limits on profit-sharing contributions first on the basis of the corporation's profits, and second on the basis of the desired contribution as a percentage of compensation.

Example: The employer's Adoption Agreement could say: "So long as retirement-plan contributions are less than 60 percent of net profits, contributions to employee profit-sharing plans shall be made on the basis of 15 percent of compensation. If retirement-plan contributions are in excess of 60 percent of net profits, contributions to employee profit-sharing plans shall be reduced to 10 percent of compensation," or words to that effect. The simplest wording, with the greatest flexibility, is: "The employer shall contribute such amount to the profit-sharing plan as annually determined by its board of directors."

If the employer provides both a money-purchase plan and a profit-sharing plan, the maximum annual additions to an individual account cannot exceed the lesser of 25 percent of compensation or $25,000. Since the profit-sharing contribution maximum is 15 percent, most employers choose a combination of a 15 percent (remember: this is a flexible maximum, meaning 0 to 15 percent) profit-sharing plan and a 10 percent money-purchase plan.

If you are thinking of choosing defined-contribution plans, it pays to investigate the pros and cons of money-purchase and profit-sharing plans. If you choose the money-purchase plan for a maximum contribution of 25 percent, your corporation doesn't have to show a profit in order to be entitled to make that 25 percent contribution. In the first few years of a new corporation's existence, this may be an important advantage, since under a money-purchase plan it could make contributions which it could not make if it were bound by profit-sharing-plan regulations. The corporation would have to borrow the money to make the initial contributions, but both it and the employee would have the benefit of those contributions.

On the other hand, the set-percentage contribution (not a set amount, because raises in employee salaries automatically increase the contributions) feature of the money-purchase plan is also a liability: as long as it remains in effect, the corporation is locked into a fixed liability. It must make contributions every year. There are no options under the money-purchase plan, and this plan's lack of flexibility can be quite detrimental to many corporations, when management realizes that a fixed liability of what may run into thousands of dollars a year for many years has been created.

Profit-sharing plans offer the flexibility of determining contributions that money-purchase plans lack, but are limited to a maximum of 15 percent, compared to the money-purchase plan's maximum of 25 percent. Many corporate employers try to optimize the benefits of both plans by adopting profit-sharing plans that permit them to contribute 15 percent and 10 percent money-purchase plans for the total of 25 percent. In this way they can effectively choose contributions from a mandatory 10 percent to the full permitted 25 percent each year. And, of course, many corporations choose only the 15 percent profit-sharing plan option, rather than the combined 25 percent.

Generally speaking, the 25 percent money-purchase plan can be compared to the forced-saving element of Christmas Club bank accounts; the combined 10 percent money-purchase plan and 15 percent profit-sharing plan can be compared to an ordinary savings account, where the amount of money saved depends entirely upon the saver, with no element of coercion or penalty for not saving. If you feel that you are psychologically oriented to saving by yourself, the combined 10 percent money-purchase plan and 15 percent profit-sharing plan will offer you greater flexibility. If, however, you need a spur to put away retirement funds every year, the 25 percent money-purchase plan is probably better for you; otherwise, you might find that your corporation is putting away only the mandatory 10 percent in the money-purchase plan.

Setting up the profit-sharing plan is fairly easy. If the "Model Profit-Sharing Plan" shown in Appendix C suits your purposes, all you need do is file IRS Form 5613, which states that your corporation has adopted this plan, already approved by the IRS. Otherwise, your lawyer will have to draw up a profit-sharing plan and submit it to the IRS for approval. It's a good idea to draw up the plan and submit it shortly after you incorporate; the IRS has a very large backlog of plans to approve, stemming from corporations' necessity to rewrite plans to conform to ERISA, and you want IRS approval before your corporation files its taxes and makes its retirement-plan contribution the following April. You will need to have your lawyer draw up a money-purchase plan, which is somewhat more complicated.

Both Appendix D, the "Trust Agreement," and, in some cases, Appendix E, the "Adoption Agreement," are integral parts of Appendix C, the "Model Profit-Sharing Plan." The "Model Profit-Sharing Plan" sets the rules and regulations that bind your corporation; the "Trust Agreement" goes further in discussing the areas your corporation is empowered to invest in, and the means by which investments will be made and the funds administered; the "Adoption Agreement," while usually used by mutual funds, can be used effectively by your corporation to nail down exactly which employees are covered, how contributions are calculated, how vesting is accomplished, and many other important details.

There is one refinement on the defined-contribution plan which was discussed in Chapter 6, "Your Employees": the defined-contribution plan which is integrated with Social Security contributions and which is thus called the integrated defined-contribution plan.

Integrated Defined-Contribution Plan

Under this type of defined-contribution plan, the employer can choose to cover employees earning amounts above the Social Security maximum ($22,900 in 1979). If this option is chosen, the employer pays only the Social Security tax for employees who are earning $22,900 or less, and contributes 7 percent of salaries over $22,900 to the defined-contribution plan. The 7 percent figure is set by regulations issued by the Secretary of the Treasury. It is an actuarial value of the 6.13 percent the employer contributes for Social Security. As explained earlier, a base lower than the Social Security maximum (presently $22,900) may be chosen, but not a base higher than that figure.

The 7 percent contribution can be increased only if a percentage is contributed for the excluded taxable wage base.

Example: If a corporation's president earns $42,900 and employees who earn $22,900 or less are covered only by Social Security, the corporation can contribute $1,400 to the president's retirement account (7 percent × $20,000). If, however, the corporation contributes 3 percent to the retirement fund of employees earning $22,900 or less, then it can contribute $2,890 to the president's account (3 percent × $20,000 plus 10 percent × $22,900).

Thus, for each percent contributed for the amount below the taxable wage base, or any base below that which is chosen by the employer, the employer can add 1 percent to the 7 percent above the taxable wage base or the base that is chosen by the employer.

Now we get to the hard part: the defined-benefit plans.

Defined-Benefit Plans

The benefits in these plans are usually stated as an annual amount. The amount could be (a) a percentage of compensation; (b) a fixed dollar amount; (c) a dollar amount per month times the number of years of service; or (d) an annual percentage of compensation multiplied by years of service.

When the benefit is a percentage of compensation, compensation is usually defined as the average of the highest 3 or 5 *consecutive* years of compensation multiplied by years of service.

Examples of types of defined-benefit plans:

(a) percentage of compensation—if the highest average compensation during years of participation is $50,000, the annual benefit at normal retirement age (normally age 65) would be $15,000 per year if the percentage were 30 percent.

(b) fixed dollar amount—$1,000 per month.

(c) dollar amount per month times number of years of service—If the monthly figure is $10 per year of service, someone with 20 years of service would receive $200 per month; someone with 10 years of service would receive $100 per month.

(d) annual percentage of compensation times years of service—If the plan provides 1 percent of compensation each year times years of service, a participant worked for 25 years, and his average compensation was $50,000, his benefit would be 25 percent (1 percent ×25) of $50,000, for an annual benefit of $12,500.

The benefit in a defined-benefit plan is limited to the lesser of $75,000 or 100 percent of compensation based on a straight-life annuity. The $75,000 limit is decreased for a benefit that is payable to an individual with less than 10 years of service at normal retirement age. A minimum benefit of $10,000 can be provided; it, too, is reduced for less than 10 years of service.

An employer can provide both a defined-benefit plan and a defined-contribution plan covering the same employees. In addition to the statutory limits of each plan, the combined limit is 1.4, which is computed as follows:

If the defined-benefit plan provides a benefit of $75,000 to an individual, this is equal to 1.0. In this case, the annual addition to the defined-contribution plan cannot exceed 40 percent of the lesser of 25 percent of compensation, or $25,000. If the defined-benefit plan provides a benefit of $37,500, which is equal to 0.5 (50 percent of $75,000), then the defined-contribution plan contribution can equal 0.9, or 90 percent of the lesser of 25 percent of compensation or $25,000 (0.5+ 0.9 = 1.4).

Unlike the defined-contribution plans, where determining the contribution is as simple as calculating a percentage, the defined-benefit plans require the work of an actuary, since they are based on such individual factors as the participants' ages, the number of years to work before normal retirement age, and the retirement benefits desired. If your corporation chooses a defined-benefits plan through a bank or insurance company—usually in the form of an annuity—these institutions will prepare all the actuarial work and all the filing with the IRS. They usually have a master plan which has already been approved by the IRS and which your corporation can adopt simply by your signing your name as president of the corporation.

(Incidentally, in all these plans, if you are a one-person corporation, you can be plan administrator, trustee, and fiduciary. You needn't have any other person acting in any capacity in supervising the plan.)

How and What to Invest In

While most corporations wait until the end of the year or the following April to make contributions to their retirement funds, it's often better to make periodic contributions during the year, to take advantage of more months of tax-preferred accumulation.

If you are a one-person or husband-and-wife corporation, your universe of investment choices is nearly boundless. Not only can your corporation invest in stocks, bonds, and mutual funds, but also in real estate, antiques, works of art, gemstones, jewelry, rare books, stamps, coins—in fact, any investment that "a prudent man might reasonably make." Legally, this concept, which is called "the prudent-man rule," governs most investments that are made on behalf of other people or institutions.

If your corporation includes outsiders, it would be wisest to stick to securities—stocks, bonds, and mutual funds. When retirement or other benefits have to be paid, it's much easier to sell shares of stock, bonds, or mutual funds than it is to figure out who owns what part of the antiques collection and to sell it quickly but profitably; or to try to divide a rare stamp or coin—or to sell it, pay out the benefits, and reinvest the remainder in another rare stamp or coin.

Regardless of what investment vehicles are purchased, make sure that they are registered in the name of the corporation's retirement funds, as follows:

John Smith & Co., Inc. Retirement Fund—Profit-Sharing Plan
Jane Smith & Co., Inc. Retirement Fund—Money-Purchase Plan
Smith & Associates, Inc. Retirement Fund—Defined-Benefits Plan

If stocks and bonds are purchased, your corporation will probably have to furnish the brokerage house where it has an account with corporate resolutions appointing the brokerage house as its broker and with copies of whichever retirement plans are being used.

If a mutual fund is chosen, your corporation will have to furnish it with whatever documents it requires: usually copies of the retirement plans being used, a Trust Agreement, and an Adoption Agreement, samples of which are shown in Appendix D and Appendix E.

Do not feel that your corporation must stick to only one type of investment. If the Trust Agreement permits, your corporation can invest in a combination of stocks, bonds, antiques, and art, choosing according to market conditions—or according to whim, for that matter.

What If the Retirement Plans Have Profits or Losses?

In a defined-contribution plan, the gains and losses are divided among all the participants, based on the account balance of each participant as a ratio to the total of all participants' balances. Simply put, profits and losses are pro-rated according to the size of each participant's account.

In a defined-benefit plan, once again, the situation is a little more complicated. As explained earlier, the employer's contribution each year is based on actuarial calculations and includes an assumption that the fund will earn a stated percentage each year. If the fund does not earn the stated percentage, the employer's contribution will be greater the following year, to bring it up to the required balance. Conversely, if the fund earns more than the stated percentage, the next annual employer contribution will be lower. This will assure that when an employee is ready to retire, there is enough in the fund to provide his or her benefits. To ensure that the employer will make his annual contribution, ERISA provides an excise tax penalty of 5 percent each year if the minimum funding standard is not met.

Before choosing any ERISA plan, discuss all the options with your lawyer and your accountant. These plans are very tricky, and an entire book could easily be written about any of the plans. This chapter is merely an overview. Get more information before you decide. But remember: if you decide to change your plan, you can. You don't have to be saddled with a bad choice. All it will take is the money to have another retirement plan drawn up and the time to have the IRS approve it.

10

But I Already Have a Keogh Plan!

If you have a Keogh Plan at the time that you incorporate, you have three major choices: you can switch it to an ERISA account at the same institution (bank, insurance company, mutual fund) and take advantage of larger contributions and their concomitant tax savings; you can discontinue it and invest your ERISA funds elsewhere, in which case the Keogh Plan is frozen until you retire, when you will collect from both the Keogh Plan and your corporate retirement fund; or, under certain circumstances, you can transfer it.

If you choose the first option—a transfer to an ERISA account at the same institution—your paper work will be minimal. Just write to the bank, insurance company, or mutual fund, notifying them of your incorporation and your desire to continue the investment program, but using the more generous contribution allowances permitted to corporations. Give the institution your new Employer Identification Number. You will be sent some forms to fill out to effect the transfer, and you will be told what to do.

If you choose the second option—discontinuing the Keogh and

investing your ERISA funds elsewhere—just keep on collecting and filing the material you are sent by the Keogh Plan institution every year. You will need it to calculate your tax liability on your pension when you retire. You would set up your corporate pension and profit-sharing plans as shown in Chapter 9, "All About ERISA," just as though you had never had a Keogh Plan.

The last option—transferring your Keogh Plan—is the most complicated, but by no means impossible. Under proposed regulation 1.402(a)–3(c)(2) of the Internal Revenue Code, it will be possible to roll over an existing Keogh Plan to a corporate pension and profit-sharing plan.

If you are transferring from one mutual fund to another, there are a number of steps to take involving the old Keogh Plan mutual fund and the new ERISA mutual fund. First, you will want to get credit for your final contribution to the Keogh Plan in your last year as sole proprietor. Accordingly, when you file your income-tax return, you would send your Keogh contribution to the custodian bank and deduct the contribution on IRS Form 5500–K.

Then, at some point during your first corporate year, but as soon as possible, you would apply to the new mutual fund you had chosen, either directly or through its custodian bank, and file the necessary forms to set up an ERISA plan with the fund. You would probably send a token check of $100 or $500 just to start the plan; the balance, of course, would be contributed in April of the following year, or whenever the corporation's tax returns were filed. Having established an ERISA plan with a new mutual fund, you could then write to the Keogh custodian bank and the ERISA custodian bank to effect the transfer, using the following letters or similar wording:

ABC Bank as Custodian for
   DEF Mutual Fund
Address

To whom it may concern:
   Please transfer the funds in my DEF mutual fund Keogh Plan account *directly* to GHI Bank as custodian for my ERISA

account with the JKL mutual fund. My ERISA account number
is _____.

Very truly yours,

cc: GHI Bank as Custodian
    for JKL Mutual Fund

GHI Bank as Custodian for
    JKL Mutual Fund
Address

To whom it may concern:

Please accept, as custodian of the JKL mutual fund, the
funds being transferred from ABC Bank as custodian of my
Keogh Plan account with the DEF mutual fund, and use the
funds to immediately purchase shares of the JKL mutual fund
for my ERISA account number _____.

Very truly yours,

cc: ABC Bank as Custodian
    for DEF Mutual Fund

In this way, when your Keogh custodian bank liquidates your mutual fund, rather than sending you a check for the proceeds which
you would then send to the ERISA custodian bank to purchase new
shares for your ERISA account, it sends a check directly to your new
custodian bank.

These details may sound very picky, but they're extremely important. At all costs, you must avoid what the IRS calls "constructive
use" of the funds, which would invalidate your Keogh Plan and subject you to taxes and penalties. In fact, if you should receive the
liquidating check from the Keogh custodian bank by mistake, *do not
endorse it.* This would be constructive use. Don't even think of en-
dorsing it and sending the new ERISA custodian bank your own corporate check. The safest procedure is to return the check to the
Keogh custodian bank with another letter explaining what happened
and what you want the bank to do.

Let's take a slightly more complicated case: transferring your

Keogh Plan funds to a brokerage house so that you can buy your own securities for your corporate retirement fund. First, of course, you would need a trust agreement that had been approved by the IRS; the one shown in Appendix D, designed to permit all prudent-man investments (stocks, bonds, mutual funds, antiques, works of art, etc.), might be suitable.

With the IRS approval, you would open a brokerage account for your corporate retirement fund; this would be a completely separate account from your corporate account, if any. Then you would write to the Keogh custodian bank and to your brokerage house to effect the transfer of your Keogh funds, using the following letters or similar wording:

ABC Bank as Custodian for
   DEF Mutual Fund
Address

To whom it may concern:
   Please transfer the funds in my DEF mutual fund Keogh Plan account *directly* to GHI brokerage house to be deposited to the (name of your corporation) Retirement Fund. The account number is _____.

Very truly yours,

cc: GHI Brokerage House

GHI Brokerage House
Address

To whom it may concern:
   Please accept the funds being transferred from ABC Bank as custodian of my Keogh Plan account and deposit them in the (name of your corporation) Retirement Fund. The account number is _____.

Very truly yours,

cc: ABC Bank as Custodian
   for DEF Mutual Fund

Again, as in the previous case, under no circumstances should the liquidating check from the Keogh custodian bank come to you; if it should, return it. It's easier than trying to explain to the IRS that even though the check was sent to you, you didn't really have constructive use of the funds.

11

Fabulous ESOP

For many corporations, an ESOP (Employees' Stock Ownership Plan) is an even better choice than the other ERISA profit-sharing plans discussed in Chapter 9, "All About ERISA." As a profit-sharing plan, of course, it can be combined with either a money-purchase plan or a defined-benefits plan, if desired. Although this plan, created by Louis Kelso, a California lawyer, is used most frequently by large corporations whose stock is traded publicly and has actual value, an ESOP can benefit a one-person corporation. Its use has been approved by the Los Angeles division of the IRS, and many major accounting firms are recommending ESOPs for their one-person general business and professional corporations.

The beauty of an ESOP is that your corporation generates tax deductions at the corporate level *without its having to contribute any actual money to the plan*. It's all playing games with paper, in a sense—a one-person-corporation ESOP is designed for people who really aren't concerned with retirement benefits . . . because there are no *direct* benefits under the plan.

An ESOP is just a way of generating legitimate "cashless" deductions at the corporate level, not of really providing retirement benefits. Hopefully your retirement benefits will be funded by your 10 percent money-purchase contribution or your defined-benefit contribution, by the corporation's accumulated profits, and by all the cumulative tax savings of having a cashless deduction. Your corporation might have accumulated a write-off of $100,000 over a period of 20 years. In a sense, the tax savings that your corporation is realizing fund your retirement benefit because you would be entitled to all the assets of your corporation at liquidation, and the assets would be increased by all of your tax savings on money you never even had to contribute.

How an ESOP Works

That's the philosophy behind ESOP. Now let's see how an ESOP actually works in a one-person corporation.

With an ESOP, your corporation would continually contribute its own stock to the ESOP and receive tax deductions for the value of the stock without making any cash expenditure for it. The stock would be beneficially owned by the sole stockholder, so both before and after the contributions began, the stockholder would own 100 percent of the stock. The net effect would be that the corporation would be getting tax deductions without really dispersing the ownership of its stock at all or spending any money.

Let's say that our stockholder has 100 shares—all the issued and outstanding shares of the corporation. The first step would be a corporate resolution authorizing the corporation to issue 400 additional shares, for a total of 500 shares (authorized but unissued). In conjunction with this, let's say that our stockholder is earning a salary of $20,000. Since the ESOP belongs to the broad category of profit-sharing plans, the corporation can deduct up to 15 percent of his compensation ($3,000). The corporation can then contribute stock equal to $3,000.

But how does this stock acquire value? *This has nothing to do with either par value, discussed in Chapter 2, or basis value, discussed in Chapter 14.* In effect, the corporation can assign the ESOP stock nearly any value it likes and then give the stock to the sole stockholder. In the case of donating $3,000 of stock, the stockholder could assign each share of stock a value of $100. Then he would donate 30 shares to the ESOP, but of course he would still be the beneficial owner and control 100 percent of the stock. If, after a number of years, he had issued all the authorized stock (all the 400 shares), he would simply make another corporate resolution (amending the Certificate of Incorporation, if necessary in his state), authorizing and issuing more stock.

This is how the arithmetic looks:

If the corporate gross income is $40,000
   − 20,000 salary
   $20,000
   − 3,000 ESOP contribution
   $17,000
   − 2,000 money-purchase contr.
   $15,000 corporate net
   − 2,550 federal taxes
   $12,450 net corporate profit

And so it would go each year, the ESOP contribution and the money-purchase or defined-benefit contribution increasing only when the stockholder's salary was increased.

What Happens at Retirement?

At retirement, the value of the stock that is distributed to the stockholder as beneficiary of the ESOP will be taxable at that point. If you choose an ESOP, you will have to get a lump-sum distribution for more favorable tax treatment (discussed thoroughly in Chapter 14, "Retire with the Biggest Tax Break Possible"). But for all this time, your corporation has not paid tax on the "paper" contributions to

ESOP, so you have had use of these funds at the corporate level for all these years.

ESOP is often preferable to other profit-sharing plans because the corporation can take a deduction without spending any of its money. In other profit-sharing plans, the corporation actually would have to pay the $3,000 in cash to a trustee, who would then invest it. With ESOP the $3,000 is just written off on the books, and in this case, the $510 saved in taxes (17 percent × $3,000) remains in the corporation.

The advantages of ESOP are even greater as your corporation becomes more profitable and its tax bracket increases. If you're entitled to contribute $15,000 worth of stock and your corporation is in the 46-percent bracket, the corporation is saving $6,900 in taxes each year without having to make any $15,000 contribution. The $6,900 saved in taxes each year would compound to over $250,000 in corporate assets at the end of 20 years and would be an asset of the corporation, translating into a higher liquidating value when you liquidated the corporation. And remember that all this time, the corporation hasn't spent a penny—it's just issued paper to a trust, of which you are the trustee.

Present Tax Status of ESOP

As mentioned earlier, ESOP has been approved by the Los Angeles division of the IRS. There hasn't been any litigation on ESOP yet, but the intent of Congress is to encourage ESOP, so the legislative climate is favorable. You may be gambling on future legislation's closing up ESOPs for one-person corporations, but so far the Senate Finance Committee is behind the ESOP program and doesn't seem likely to move to close up the loopholes.

To set up an ESOP, you or your accountant must apply to the IRS for an Application for a Determination Letter; this is a standard form which is self-explanatory. In a one-person corporation, the form is really a formality.

If you think the ESOP is the profit-sharing plan for you, consult your lawyer or accountant and get an opinion. As with so many other one-person corporations, ESOP may be fabulous for you, too.

Investing Your Corporate Surplus

Let's hope you're running a successful business or you're a successful professional. After contributing to corporate pension and profit-sharing plans and paying taxes, your corporation still has a surplus which you'd like to invest profitably. For the most part, investing your corporate surplus (after-tax profits) depends on the following variables:

(1) how aggressive an investor you are;
(2) the length of time before your retirement;
(3) how much money you can invest each year.

The first two factors are closely interrelated; if you are 30 years old and plan to retire in 35 years, you can afford to assume more risks than if you are 50 and plan to retire in 10 years.

But this is the classic textbook approach to investment planning. In real life there are supercautious 23-year-olds and crapshooting 53-year-olds. While bearing the classic investment strategies in mind, always take only the amount of risk you feel comfortable with.

Perhaps the most important variable—in terms of its limiting your choices—is the last one: how much money you can invest every year. This amount will determine what kind of professional investment management help you can expect. After all, if you can invest $10,000 a year, your choices are much wider than if you can invest $1,000 a year.

Up until the time that your corporate portfolio reaches $25,000 to $50,000, it's virtually impossible to get any kind of professional management for your investments. About the best you can do is buy a mutual fund (preferably a no-load fund with a good track record); choose a good broker with excellent research capabilities; or subscribe to one or more investment services, do your own research, and have your orders executed by a discount broker, so that you save on commissions.

At $25,000 to $50,000, some banks will manage your portfolio on a pooled-trust basis, combining your portfolio with those of other investors with the same investment goals and creating, in effect, a mini-mutual fund. The fees for this service vary, but generally run about 1 to 2 percent per year—tax deductible, of course. When your portfolio reaches anywhere from $100,000 to $200,000, nearly all banks will manage your portfolio as a separate portfolio.

When your corporation does get big enough for a bank to handle its investment, there is one major advantage—apart from professional investment advice—that a bank can offer. As an institution (as banks are known in the investment community), a bank has access to the negotiated commission market because its trading volume is so much greater than any individual's. These commissions can range from about 20 percent to about 50 percent of individual commissions, or a discount of from 50 percent to 80 percent. If your corporation invests or trades heavily, this may be an important consideration for you.

In order to get the best executions of orders for its clients, a bank will often use different brokers for different orders or will use what is called the "third market" (trading between the institutions themselves, as opposed to on the stock exchanges). This "shopping around" is aimed at getting both the best prices and the smallest commissions.

Banks do offer economies of size. The question you must answer for yourself is: are the bank's fees worth the savings in executions and commissions?

Without exception, all the professional investment analysts and money managers I interviewed emphasized the necessity of common stocks in a corporate portfolio. Not only are their dividends 85 percent tax-free at the corporate level, but also they are one of the most powerful hedges against long-term inflationary pressures. Even at the present low inflationary levels of economic recovery, the rate of inflation is still higher than the interest rate of AA-rated bonds, after taxes; and no one can predict long-term trends, except that inflation at one level or another is certain to be with us. Common stocks can help protect the investor against that inflation and erosion of his purchasing power. Over a period of years, common stocks have outperformed bonds and other money-market instruments (e.g., commercial paper) and preferred stocks.

Another advantage of common stocks over bonds is less obvious, but by no means less real. The stock market is far more liquid than the bond market: stocks are traded more frequently and in smaller quantities than bonds, so a buy order for 100 shares—or even less—is less likely to raise the price you pay, and a sell order for 100 shares or less is less likely to lower the price you receive. In contrast, the bond market deals with much greater numbers and dollar amounts: an "average" order is usually for 25 or 50 bonds ($25,000 or $50,000 face value). Orders from smaller investors for 1, 5, or 10 bonds are penalized at both ends: they pay more for the bonds when they buy them and receive less for the bonds when they sell them. Small orders tend to have a disproportionately large effect on bond prices, both up and down, but always to the disadvantage of the small investor.

Preferred stocks are a hybrid, but in this respect they seem more like bonds: their liquidity is very limited, and they offer no protection against inflation. All they do offer, like common stocks, is the 85 percent dividend exclusion.

The stocks shown in the portfolio that follows are not to be construed as being recommendations; they are merely high-quality, high-yielding stocks suitable for corporate investment. The preferred stocks are all AAA-rated by Standard & Poor's Corporation; the common stocks are characterized by low P/E (price/earnings) ratio and high yield, combined with moderate growth.

REPRESENTATIVE CORPORATE PORTFOLIO

Standard & Poor's Rating	Preferred Stocks	Price 5/18/79	Dividend	Yield	Income from 100 Shares
AAA	duPont pfd 4.50	55¾	$4.50	8.07%	$ 450
AAA	General Motors pfd 3.75	45¼	3.75	8.29	375
AAA	General Motors pfd 5.00	60¾	5.00	8.23	500
					$1,325
	Common Stocks				
B	Alexander & Baldwin	18¾ *	1.20	6.40	120
	Continental Corp.	25⅞	2.00	7.73	200
A	Gulf Oil	25⅝	2.05	8.00	205
A	Houston Industries	29¼	2.36	8.07	236
	Johns-Manville	23⅞	1.92	8.04	192
	Northwest Energy	37¼	2.60	6.98	260
	Tampax	29¾ *	2.35**	7.90	235
A	Texaco	25⅝	2.16	8.43	216
A−	Wrigley	65⅞	3.90**	5.92	390
					2,054
					$3,379

*OTC—asked price
**Paid in 1978

The purpose of such a high-yield portfolio is the compounding of dividends, 85 percent of which are totally excluded from taxes, and

15 percent of which are taxed at 17 percent if net corporate income is less than $25,000 and 20 percent if net corporate income is between $25,000 and $50,000.

To illustrate this point, let's assume a portfolio consisting of 100 shares of each security. The annual income from the portfolio would be $3,379.

If the owner of the portfolio was a sole proprietor in the 40-percent bracket, he would have to pay $1,311.60 in taxes on his dividend income, and could keep only $2,067.40:

Dividend income	$3,379.00
Less $100 exclusion	100.00
	$3,279.00
Tax rate	×.40
Tax	$1,311.60
Net dividend income	$2,067.40

However, if his corporation owned the portfolio, the taxes are *more than ten times lower:*

	Assuming 17-Percent Bracket Net Corp. Taxable Income Under $25M	Assuming 20-Percent Bracket Net Corp. Taxable Income $25–$50M
Dividend income	$3,379.00	$3,379.00
Less 85 percent exclusion	2,872.15	2,872.15
	$ 506.85	$ 506.85
Tax rate	×.17	×.20
Tax	$ 86.16	$ 101.37
Net dividend income	$3,292.84	$3,277.63
Amount saved from individual tax	$1,225.44	$1,210.23
Percent saved from individual tax	93%	92%

Furthermore, if we project this unchanged portfolio for 5 or 10 years, it is easy to see how the more than $1,000 saved each year on the corporate stock portfolio alone can compound itself to more than $5,000 or $10,000. And if we go further and conceive of this portfolio as a unit, with an additional unit purchased each year, so that at the end of 5 years there are 500 shares each and at the end of 10 years there are 1,000 shares each, the savings are truly staggering.

The only thing we would have to worry about is that the portfolio income would not exceed 60 percent of total corporate income in any year, so that the corporation would not be construed by the IRS as a personal holding corporation, as discussed more fully in Chapter 1 and Chapter 5.

How and When Your Corporation Declares Dividends

So far we've talked about your corporation's *receiving* dividends from other corporations: dividends that are 85 percent tax-free. But what about your corporation's *paying* dividends to its stockholder(s)? In general, of course, you want to keep dividend income from common and preferred stocks in the corporation; if you draw the dividends out for your own use, you will be taxed on them. Furthermore, they won't be able to accumulate at minimal tax rates.

However, there are always times or special occasions that may warrant taking money out of the corporation, and this necessitates the corporation's declaring a dividend to the stockholders. A meeting of the board of directors of the corporation is called, and someone proposes that a dividend of X dollars per share be paid on a certain date to all stockholders who owned stock on a certain earlier date. The proposal is turned into a motion and voted on. When it is approved, as it is certain to be, it is recorded as Minutes of a Special Meeting of the Board of Directors and entered into the corporation's minute book. Then, on the payment date, the corporation gives or sends the dividend checks to its stockholders. Dividends do not have to be paid on a regular basis; it is thus wiser to declare each dividend as a special dividend.

When you declare these dividends, you can income-average, a procedure which gives you much more leeway and flexibility in tax planning. You can say, in effect, "The market looks pretty good this year, but I don't know about next year. I think I'll pull $10,000 out of the corporate portfolio and declare a special dividend." You can then spread the dividend over 5 years by using Schedule G, the income-averaging schedule, to minimize your taxes. In this way, your net effect is to have received $2,000 in each of the past 5 years, rather than to have received the $10,000 in one lump sum.

Treatment of Capital Gains

Up to now, I've stressed dividends because dividend payments to corporations are 85 percent tax-free. Bond interest is taxed as though it were ordinary income: at 17 percent, 20 percent, 30 percent, or up to 46 percent, depending upon the corporation's tax bracket. Ordinarily, short-term capital gains (securities held 12 months or less) are also taxed as though they are ordinary income: at 17 percent, 20 percent, 30 percent, or up to 46 percent. Long-term capital gains are taxed at 28 percent.

Recently, however, two new mutual funds have been set up to take advantage of federal tax laws which permit regulated investment companies (the legal term for mutual funds) to treat short-term capital-gains distributions and earned interest—provided the latter does not exceed 25 percent of gross investment income—as "dividend income," so that it, too, qualifies for the 85 percent dividend exclusion. This means, in effect, that everything except long-term gains is now taxed at only 15 percent of the corporation's tax rate: 2.6 percent (instead of 17 percent), 3 percent (instead of 20 percent), and a maximum of 6.9 percent (instead of 46 percent). These funds—QDP, which invests primarily in high-yielding common stocks with growth of capital and income potential, convertible securities, preferred stocks, and bonds; and QDP II, which invests primarily in high-yielding preferred stocks and bonds, and does not invest in common stocks—are no-load funds which are structured so that no long-term gains will be taken. All securities will be sold before they become long-term holdings, and the attractive ones will be repurchased to qualify for a new short-term holding period. So far, QDP and QDP II are the only mutual funds which offer corporations the advantage of an effective 85 percent dividend exclusion on bond interest and short-term gains as well as dividend income and which are structured so that there will be no long-term gains. For additional information, write to:

> QDP/QDP II
> P.O. Box 1100
> Valley Forge, PA 19482

Other Corporate Investments

Your corporation can make other investments besides stocks, bonds, mutual funds, and other securities. It can invest in real estate, antiques, art, gemstones or jewelry, or, in fact, anything of value that is tangible and not likely to depreciate in value. Your investment universe consists of anything and everything that would be selected by "a prudent man." (A company car would be a corporate possession, but would not be considered a prudent corporate investment because of its depreciability. A 1936 Rolls-Royce, however, would certainly qualify as an investment.)

If you are more comfortable with English furniture or Ming porcelain, nineteenth-century photographs or Old Master drawings, Lalique or Fabergé jewelry or just plain old diamonds or emeralds, set or unset, feel free to invest in them. Just make sure that you are paying for them with a corporate check and that they are insured in the name of the corporation. Antiques and art that are owned by the corporation must stay clearly on corporate territory: they may be displayed in your office, but not in your home. However, if your office is in your home, you do have more leeway about where to place them.

Summing Up

This chapter, like the rest of this book, has been written primarily for the one-person or husband-and-wife corporation. If you are part of a larger, nonfamily corporation, think more carefully about investing in the more unusual corporate investments. They will be more difficult to liquidate, and this may generate problems. They will certainly be less divisible than stocks, bonds, or mutual fund shares, and surely be more difficult to value.

13

Putting It All Together

It's often said that one picture is worth 10,000 words. Let's look, then, at three pictures. Following are tax returns for three businesses at three different income levels, both as corporations and as sole proprietorships. To simplify matters, the individuals are assumed to be single and will take the standard deduction. Tax forms for 1978 have been used. For 1979, both corporate and personal tax brackets have been lowered.

First, there is George Gordon, a real estate broker whose earnings are $45,000 a year, with dividend income of $1,275. George prefers to retain as much corporate income as possible, so his corporation pays him a salary of $15,000 a year. His corporate return and his employee tax return, followed by his tax return as a sole proprietor, as shown on pages 88–98.

Because George chose a low salary, his retirement-plan contribution as a sole proprietor is higher than his corporation's contribution: $6,000 vs. $3,750. However, by accepting the low salary, he saves over 43 percent in taxes: $11,810.70 as a sole proprietor vs. a total of $6,707; $4,250 in corporate taxes and $2,457 in employee income taxes.

Geoffrey Fourmyle, an engineer, has chosen a higher salary of $25,000, although his gross income is also $45,000. This option gives him a slightly higher corporate pension contribution: $6,250 vs. $6,000. By taking the higher salary, however, he cuts his tax saving to slightly over 33 percent: $11,334.90 as a sole proprietor vs. a total of

$7,580; $1,750 in corporate taxes and $5,830 in employee income taxes. He is sheltering less of his income at the preferential corporate rate; thus, his tax savings are smaller. See pages 99–109 for his tax returns.

Last, there is Tiffany Field, a successful designer who earned $70,000 last year and had dividend income of $2,000. By taking a salary of $30,000, she cuts her total tax bill from a maximum tax of $17,612.16 as a sole proprietor (note Form 4726, Maximum Tax on Earned Income) to $10,842.50, for a saving of $6,769.66 in just one year. At these levels, the corporate retirement-plan contribution and the sole-proprietor Keogh Plan contribution are identical: $7,500. If Tiffany took a higher salary, her corporate contribution would continue to rise; at $50,000, her corporation could contribute $12,500, compared to the Keogh Plan maximum of $7,500. However, she would be sheltering less income at low corporate rates. In this return, take special notice of the $2,000 dividend income. Tiffany's corporation is able to shelter $1,700 of it (see line 29(b) page 110), and is taxed on $300, for a tax liability of only $60. If Tiffany owned the stock herself, she would be taxed on the full $1,900 ($2,000 less $100 dividend exclusion), for a tax liability of approximately $740, more than twelve times greater than the corporate tax. For her tax returns, see pages 110–121.

Let's summarize the tax savings of incorporation shown on the sample returns this way:

Name	Corporate Taxes	Employee Income Taxes	Total	Sole Proprietor	Amount Saved	Percent Saved
Gordon	$4,250.00	$2,457.00	$ 6,707.00	$11,810.70	$5,103.70	43.21%*
Fourmyle	1,750.00	5,830.00	7,580.00	11,334.90	3,754.90	33.13
Field	2,960.00	7,882.50	10,842.50	17,612.16	6,769.66	38.44

*The percentages saved in the 1977 edition of *Inc. Yourself* (1976 tax returns) were 40.33%, 32.90%, and 38.44% respectively. Thus, now more than ever, it pays to incorporate.

Just for fun, why don't you pull out last year's tax return and pencil your numbers in on one of the sample returns. If your figures show savings of several thousand dollars a year, it might be a good idea for you to incorporate.

Form 1120

Department of the Treasury
Internal Revenue Service

U.S. Corporation Income Tax Return

For calendar year 1978 or other taxable year beginning
.... 1978, ending .... 19......

1978

Check If a—			
A Consolidated return ☐	Use IRS label. Otherwise please print or type.	Name GEORGE GORDON + CO., INC.	D Employer identification number (see instruction W) 00-0000000
B Personal Holding Co. ☐		Number and street 350 FIFTH AVENUE	E Date incorporated 1/1/78
C Business Code No. (See Page 8 of instructions) 8599		City or town, State, and ZIP code NEW YORK, NY 10001	F Enter total assets (see instruction X) $50,000.00

Gross Income

1 Gross receipts or gross sales......................Less: Returns and allowances..........	1	
2 Less: Cost of goods sold (Schedule A) and/or operations (attach schedule)	2	
3 Gross profit	3	
4 Dividends (Schedule C)	4	1,275.00
5 Interest on obligations of the United States and U.S. instrumentalities	5	
6 Other interest	6	
7 Gross rents	7	
8 Gross royalties	8	
9 (a) Capital gain net income (attach separate Schedule D)	9(a)	
(b) Net gain or (loss) from Form 4797, line 11, Part II (attach Form 4797)	9(b)	
10 Other income (see instructions—attach schedule)	10	45,000.00
11 TOTAL income—Add lines 3 through 10	11	46,275.00

Deductions

12 Compensation of officers (Schedule E)	12	15,000.00
13 (a) Salaries and wages................... 13(b) Less new jobs credit.................... Balance ▶	13(c)	
14 Repairs (see instructions)	14	
15 Bad debts (Schedule F if reserve method is used)	15	
16 Rents	16	
17 Taxes	17	
18 Interest	18	
19 Contributions (not over 5% of line 30 adjusted per instructions—attach schedule)	19	
20 Amortization (attach schedule)	20	500.00
21 Depreciation from Form 4562 (attach Form 4562) ...., less depreciation claimed in Schedule A and elsewhere on return ...... 500.00 ...., Balance ▶	21	500.00
22 Depletion	22	
23 Advertising	23	
24 Pension, profit-sharing, etc. plans (see instructions) (enter number of plans ▶ .....|.......) .	24	3,750.00
25 Employee benefit programs (see instructions)	25	
26 Other deductions (attach schedule)	26	4,191.00
27 TOTAL deductions—Add lines 12 through 26	27	23,941.00
28 Taxable income before net operating loss deduction and special deductions (subtract line 27 from line 11) . .	28	22,334.00
29 Less: (a) Net operating loss deduction (see instructions—attach schedule) . . 29(a)		
(b) Special deductions (Schedule I) . . . . 29(b) 1,084.00	29	1,084.00
30 Taxable income (subtract line 29 from line 28)	30	21,250.00

Tax

31 TOTAL TAX (Schedule J)	31	4,250.00
32 Credits: (a) Overpayment from 1977 allowed as a credit . . .		
(b) 1978 estimated tax payments 3,000.00		
(c) Less refund of 1978 estimated tax applied for on Form 4466 . ( )		
(d) Tax deposited: Form 7004................... Form 7005 (attach)................... Total ▶		
(e) Credit from regulated investment companies (attach Form 2439) . .		
(f) U.S. tax on special fuels, nonhighway gas and lubricating oil (attach Form 4136) . .	32	3,000.00
33 TAX DUE (subtract line 32 from line 31). See instruction G for depositary method of payment .	33	1,250.00
(Check ▶ ☐ if Form 2220 is attached. See page 3 of instructions.) ▶ $...............		
34 OVERPAYMENT (subtract line 31 from line 32).	34	
35 Enter amount of line 34 you want: Credited to 1979 estimated tax .... Refunded ▶	35	

Under penalties of perjury, I declare that I have examined this return, including accompanying schedules and statements, and to the best of my knowledge and belief, it is true, correct, and complete. Declaration of preparer (other than taxpayer) is based on all information of which preparer has any knowledge.

Please Sign Here

▶		
Signature of officer	Date	Title

Paid Preparer's Information

Preparer's signature ▶		Preparer's social security no.	Check if self-employed ▶ ☐
Firm's name (or yours, if self-employed), address and ZIP code ▶		E.I. No. ▶	
		Date ▶	

263-104-1

88

Schedule A Cost of Goods Sold (See instruction 2)

1 Inventory at beginning of year . . . .
2 Merchandise bought for manufacture or sale . . . .
3 Salaries and wages . . . .
4 Other costs (attach schedule) . . . .
5 Total . . . .
6 Less: Inventory at end of year . . . .
7 Cost of goods sold—Enter here and on line 2, page 1 . . . .
8 (a) Check valuation method(s) used for total closing inventory:
    ☐ Cost ☐ Lower of cost or market ☐ Other (if "other," attach explanation)
 (b) Check if this is the first year LIFO inventory method was adopted and used. (If checked, attach Form 970.) . . . . . . ☐
 (c) If the LIFO inventory method was used for this taxable year, enter percentage (or amounts) of closing inventory computed under LIFO . . . .
 (d) Is the corporation engaged in manufacturing activities? . . . . ☐ Yes ☐ No
    If "Yes," are inventories valued under Regulations section 1.471–11 (full absorption accounting method)? . ☐ Yes ☐ No
 (e) Was there any substantial change in determining quantities, cost, or valuations between opening and closing inventory? . . . ☐ Yes ☐ No
    If "Yes," attach explanation.

Schedule C Dividends (See instruction 4)

1 Domestic corporations subject to 85% deduction 1,275.00
2 Certain preferred stock of public utilities . . . .
3 Foreign corporations subject to 85% deduction . . . .
4 Dividends from wholly-owned foreign subsidiaries subject to 100% deduction (section 245(b)) . . . . .
5 Other dividends from foreign corporations . . . .
6 Includable income from controlled foreign corporations under subpart F (attach Forms 3646) . . . . . .
7 Foreign dividend gross-up (section 78) . . . .
8 Qualifying dividends received from affiliated groups and subject to the 100% deduction (section 243(a)(3)) . .
9 Taxable dividends from a DISC or former DISC not included in line 1 (section 246(d)) . . . .
10 Other dividends . . . .
11 Total—Enter here and on line 4, page 1 . . . . 1,275.00

Schedule E Compensation of Officers (See instruction 12)

1. Name of officer	2. Social security number	3. Time devoted to business	Percent of corporation stock owned		6. Amount of compensation	7. Expense account allowances
			4. Common	5. Preferred		
GEORGE GORDON	000-00-0000	ALL	100		15,000.00	

Total compensation of officers—Enter here and on line 12, page 1 . . . . . . 15,000.00

Schedule F Bad Debts—Reserve Method (See instruction 4)

1. Year	2. Trade notes and accounts receivable outstanding at end of year	3. Sales on account	Amount added to reserve		6. Amount charged against reserve	7. Reserve for bad debts at end of year
			4. Current year's provision	5. Recoveries		
1973						
1974						
1975						
1976						
1977						
1978						

Schedule I Special Deductions

1 (a) 85% of Schedule C, line 1 . . . . 1,084.00
 (b) 60.208% of Schedule C, line 2 . . . .
 (c) 85% of Schedule C, line 3 . . . .
 (d) 100% of Schedule C, line 4 . . . .
2 Total—See instructions for limitation 1,084.00
3 100% of Schedule C, line 8 . . . .
4 Dividends paid on certain preferred stock of public utilities (see instructions) . . . .
5 Western Hemisphere trade corporations (see instructions) . . . .
6 Total special deductions—Add lines 2 through 5. Enter here and on line 29(b), page 1 . . . . 1,084.00

263-104-2

89

(Fiscal year corporations, omit lines 1 through 8 and enter on line 9, the amount from Form 1120-FY (1978-79), line 5, Part III)

1	Taxable income (line 30, page 1)	21,250.00
2	Enter line 1 or $25,000, whichever is less. (Members of a controlled group enter one-half of surtax allocation, see instructions) .	21,250.00
3	Subtract line 2 from line 1	0
4	Enter line 3 or $25,000, whichever is less. (Members of a controlled group enter one-half of surtax allocation, see instructions) .	O
5	Subtract line 4 from line 3	O
6	20% of line 2	4,250.00
7	22% of line 4	O
8	48% of line 5	O
9	Income tax (Sum of lines 6, 7 and 8 or alternative tax from separate Schedule D, whichever is less)	4,250.00
10 (a)	Foreign tax credit (attach Form 1118)	
(b)	Investment credit (attach Form 3468)	
(c)	Work incentive (WIN) credit (attach Form 4874)	
(d)	New jobs credit (attach Form 5884)	
11	Total of lines 10(a), (b), (c), and (d)	
12	Subtract line 11 from line 9	
13	Personal holding company tax (attach Schedule PH (Form 1120))	
14	Tax from recomputing a prior year investment credit (attach Form 4255)	
15	Tax from recomputing a prior year WIN credit (see instructions—attach computation)	
16	Minimum tax on tax preference items (see instructions—attach Form 4626)	
17	Total tax—Add lines 12 through 16. Enter here and on line 31, page 1	4,250.00

Schedule K Record of Federal Tax Deposits Tax Class Number 503
(List deposits in order of date made—See instruction G)

Date of deposit	Amount	Date of deposit	Amount	Date of deposit	Amount
				12/15/78	1,000.00
6/15/78	1,000.00	9/15/78	1,000.00		

	Yes	No
G (1) Did you claim a deduction for expenses connected with:		
(a) Entertainment facility (boat, resort, ranch, etc.)? . . .		✓
(b) Living accommodations (except for employees on business)?		✓
(c) Employee's families at conventions or meetings? . . .		✓
If "Yes," were any of these conventions or meetings outside the United States or its possessions?	✓	
(d) Employee or family vacations not reported on Form W-2? .		✓
(2) Enter total amount claimed on Form 1120 for entertainment, entertainment facilities, gifts, travel, and conventions of the type for which substantiation is required under section 274(d). (See instruction Y.) ▶		

H (1) Did you at the end of the taxable year own, directly or indirectly, 50% or more of the voting stock of a domestic corporation? (For rules of attribution, see section 267(c).) . . . [No ✓]

If "Yes," attach a schedule showing: (a) name, address, and identifying number; (b) percentage owned; (c) taxable income or (loss) (e.g., if a Form 1120: from Form 1120, line 28, page 1) of such corporation for the taxable year ending with or within your taxable year; (d) highest amount owed by you to such corporation during the year; and (e) highest amount owed to you by such corporation during the year.

(2) Did any individual, partnership, corporation, estate or trust at the end of the taxable year own, directly or indirectly, 50% or more of your voting stock? (For rules of attribution, see section 267(c).) If "Yes," complete (a) through (e) . . . [Yes ✓]

(a) Attach a schedule showing name, address, and identifying number; (b) Enter percentage owned ▶ 100

(c) Was the owner of such voting stock a person other than a U.S. person? (See instruction S.) . . . . . . [No ✓]

If "Yes," enter owner's country ▶

(d) Enter highest amount owed by you to such owner during the year ▶

	Yes	No
(e) Enter highest amount owed to you by such owner during the year ▶		
(Note: For purposes of H(1) and H(2), "highest amount owed" includes loans and accounts receivable/payable.)		
I Did you ever declare a stock dividend?		✓
J Taxable income or (loss) from Form 1120, line 28, page 1, for your taxable year beginning in: 1975 ...., 1976 ...., 1977		
K Were you a member of a controlled group subject to the provisions of section 1561? If "Yes," check the type of relationship . .		✓

(1) ☐ parent-subsidiary   (2) ☐ brother-sister
(3) ☐ combination of (1) and (2) (See section 1563.)

L Refer to page 8 of instructions and state the principal:
Business activity
Product or service

	Yes	No
M Did you file all required Forms 1087, 1096 and 1099? . . .	N/A	
N Were you a U.S. shareholder of any controlled foreign corporation? (See sections 951 and 957.) If "Yes," attach Form 3646 for each such corporation		✓
O Did you, at any time during the taxable year, have an interest in or signature or other authority over a bank, securities or other financial account in a foreign country (see instruction V)? . .		✓
P Were you the grantor of, or transferor to, a foreign trust during any taxable year, which foreign trust was in being during the current taxable year, whether or not you have any beneficial interest in such trust? If "Yes," you may be required to file Forms 3520, 3520-A, or 926		✓
Q During this taxable year, did you pay dividends (other than stock dividends and distributions in exchange for stock) in excess of your current and accumulated earnings and profits? (See sections 301 and 316.)		✓

If "Yes," file Form 5452. If this is a consolidated return, answer here for parent corporation and on Form 851, Affiliation Schedule, for each subsidiary.

263-104-2

90

Schedule L — Balance Sheets

ASSETS	Beginning of taxable year		End of taxable year	
	(A) Amount	(B) Total	(C) Amount	(D) Total
1 Cash		7,000.00		12,500.00
2 Trade notes and accounts receivable				
(a) Less allowance for bad debts				
3 Inventories				
4 Gov't obligations: (a) U.S. and instrumentalities .				
(b) State, subdivisions thereof, etc.				
5 Other current assets (attach schedule)				
6 Loans to stockholders		4,000.00		10,000.00
7 Mortgage and real estate loans				
8 Other investments (attach schedule) (STOCK).		10,000.00		15,000.00
9 Buildings and other fixed depreciable assets . .	5,000.00		5,000.00	
(a) Less accumulated depreciation		5,000.00	500.00	4,500.00
10 Depletable assets				
(a) Less accumulated depletion				
11 Land (net of any amortization)				
12 Intangible assets (amortizable only)				
(a) Less accumulated amortization				
13 Other assets (attach schedule)		2,250.00		8,000.00
14 Total assets		28,250.00		50,000.00
LIABILITIES AND STOCKHOLDERS' EQUITY				
15 Accounts payable		8,250.00		5,000.00
16 Mtges., notes, bonds payable in less than 1 yr. .				
17 Other current liabilities (attach schedule) . . .				
18 Loans from stockholders				
19 Mtges., notes, bonds payable in 1 yr. or more . .				2,666.00
20 Other liabilities (attach schedule)				
21 Capital stock: (a) Preferred stock				
(b) Common stock	10,000.00	10,000.00	10,000.00	10,000.00
22 Paid-in or capital surplus		10,000.00		10,000.00
23 Retained earnings—Appropriated (attach sch.) . .				
24 Retained earnings—Unappropriated				22,334.00
25 Less cost of treasury stock		( )		( )
26 Total liabilities and stockholders' equity . . .				50,000.00

Schedule M-1 — Reconciliation of Income Per Books With Income Per Return

1 Net income per books	22,334.00		7 Income recorded on books this year not included in this return (itemize)		
2 Federal income tax			(a) Tax-exempt interest $_____		
3 Excess of capital losses over capital gains			_____		
4 Income subject to tax not recorded on books this year (itemize)_____			_____		
_____			8 Deductions in this tax return not charged against book income this year (itemize)		
5 Expenses recorded on books this year not deducted in this return (itemize)			(a) Depreciation . . $_____		
(a) Depreciation . . . $_____			(b) Depletion . . . $_____		
(b) Depletion . . . . $_____			_____		
_____			9 Total of lines 7 and 8		
6 Total of lines 1 through 5	22,334.00		10 Income (line 28, page 1)—line 6 less 9 .	22,334.00	

Schedule M-2 — Analysis of Unappropriated Retained Earnings Per Books (line 24 above)

1 Balance at beginning of year	—	5 Distributions: (a) Cash		
2 Net income per books	22,334.00	(b) Stock		
3 Other increases (itemize)_____		(c) Property		
_____		6 Other decreases (itemize)_____		
_____		_____		
_____		7 Total of lines 5 and 6 . . .		
4 Total of lines 1, 2, and 3	22,334.00	8 Balance at end of year (line 4 less 7) . . .		22,334.00

For Privacy Act Notice, see page 3 of Instructions | For the year January 1–December 31, 1978, or other tax year beginning _____ , 1978, ending _____ , 19

Use IRS label. Otherwise, please print or type.	Your first name and initial (if joint return, also give spouse's name and initial)	Last name	Your social security number
	GEORGE	GORDON	000 00 0000
	Present home address (Number and street, including apartment number, or rural route)		Spouse's social security no.
	350 FIFTH AVENUE		
	City, town or post office, State and ZIP code		Your occupation
	New York NY 10001		REAL ESTATE BROKER

Do you want $1 to go to the Presidential Election Campaign Fund? ✓ Yes ___ No
If joint return, does your spouse want $1 to go to this fund? . . ___ Yes ___ No

Note: Checking Yes will not increase your tax or reduce your refund.

Spouse's occupation

Filing Status
Check only one box.

1 ✓ Single
2 ___ Married filing joint return (even if only one had income)
3 ___ Married filing separate return. If spouse is also filing, give spouse's social security number in the space above and enter full name here ▶ ....
4 ___ Unmarried head of household. Enter qualifying name ▶ .... See page 6 of Instructions.
5 ___ Qualifying widow(er) with dependent child (Year spouse died ▶ 19___). See page 6 of Instructions.

Exemptions
Always check the box labeled Yourself. Check other boxes if they apply.

6a ✓ Yourself ___ 65 or over ___ Blind

Enter number of boxes checked on 6a and b ▶ | 1 |

b ___ Spouse ___ 65 or over ___ Blind

c First names of your dependent children who lived with you ▶ ....

Enter number of children listed ▶ | |

d Other dependents: (1) Name	(2) Relationship	(3) Number of months lived in your home	(4) Did dependent have income of $750 or more?	(5) Did you provide more than one-half of dependent's support?

Enter number of other dependents ▶ | |

Add numbers entered in boxes above ▶ | 1 |

7 Total number of exemptions claimed . . . .

Income
Please attach Copy B of your Forms W–2 here.

If you do not have a W–2, see page 5 of Instructions.

Please attach check or money order here.

8	Wages, salaries, tips, and other employee compensation	8	15,000 00
9	Interest income (If over $400, attach Schedule B)	9	
10a	Dividends (If over $400, attach Schedule B)............., 10b Exclusion...........		
10c	Subtract line 10b from line 10a	10c	
11	State and local income tax refunds (does not apply unless refund is for year you itemized deductions)	11	
12	Alimony received	12	
13	Business income or (loss) (attach Schedule C)	13	
14	Capital gain or (loss) (attach Schedule D)	14	
15	Taxable part of capital gain distributions not reported on Schedule D (see page 9 of Instructions) .	15	
16	Net gain or (loss) from Supplemental Schedule of Gains and Losses (attach Form 4797)	16	
17	Fully taxable pensions and annuities not reported on Schedule E	17	
18	Pensions, annuities, rents, royalties, partnerships, estates or trusts, etc. (attach Schedule E)	18	
19	Farm income or (loss) (attach Schedule F)	19	
20	Other income (state nature and source—see page 10 of Instructions) ▶	20	
21	Total income. Add lines 8, 9, and 10c through 20 . . . . ▶	21	15,000 00

Adjustments to Income

22	Moving expense (attach Form 3903)	22	
23	Employee business expenses (attach Form 2106) . .	23	
24	Payments to an IRA (see page 10 of Instructions) . .	24	
25	Payments to a Keogh (H.R. 10) retirement plan . . .	25	
26	Interest penalty due to early withdrawal of savings	26	
27	Alimony paid (see page 10 of Instructions)	27	
28	Total adjustments. Add lines 22 through 27 . . . . ▶	28	0

Adjusted Gross Income

29	Subtract line 28 from line 21	29	15,000 00
30	Disability income exclusion (attach Form 2440)	30	0
31	Adjusted gross income. Subtract line 30 from line 29. If this line is less than $8,000, see page 2 of Instructions. If you want IRS to figure your tax, see page 4 of Instructions . . . . ▶	31	15,000 00

263–053–2 ☆ U.S. GOVERNMENT PRINTING OFFICE : 1978—O–263-053

Form 1040 (1978)

Tax Compu-tation	32 Amount from line 31	32	15,000 00
	33 If you do not itemize deductions, enter zero . . . . } If you itemize, complete Schedule A (Form 1040) and enter the amount from Schedule A, line 41. . . . }	33	0
	Caution: If you have unearned income and can be claimed as a dependent on your parent's return, check here ▶ ☐ and see page 11 of the Instructions. Also see page 11 of the Instructions if:		
	• You are married filing a separate return and your spouse itemizes deductions, OR		
	• You file Form 4563, OR		
	• You are a dual-status alien.		
	34 Subtract line 33 from line 32. Use the amount on line 34 to find your tax from the Tax Tables, or to figure your tax on Schedule TC, Part I	34	15,000 00
	Use Schedule TC, Part I, and the Tax Rate Schedules ONLY if:		
	• The amount on line 34 is more than $20,000 ($40,000 if you checked Filing Status Box 2 or 5), OR		
	• You have more exemptions than those covered in the Tax Table for your filing status, OR		
	• You use any of these forms to figure your tax: Schedule D, Schedule G, or Form 4726.		
	Otherwise, you MUST use the Tax Tables to find your tax.		
	35 Tax. Enter tax here and check if from ☑ Tax Tables or ☐ Schedule TC	35	2,457 00
	36 Additional taxes. (See page 11 of Instructions.) Enter total and check if from ☐ Form 4970, } ☐ Form 4972, ☐ Form 5544, ☐ Form 5405, or ☐ Section 72(m)(5) penalty tax . . . }	36	0
	37 **Total.** Add lines 35 and 36 . . . . ▶	37	2,457 00
Credits	38 Credit for contributions to candidates for public office . .	38		
	39 Credit for the elderly (attach Schedules R&RP)	39		
	40 Credit for child and dependent care expenses (attach Form 2441) .	40		
	41 Investment credit (attach Form 3468)	41		
	42 Foreign tax credit (attach Form 1116)	42		
	43 Work Incentive (WIN) Credit (attach Form 4874)	43		
	44 New jobs credit (attach Form 5884)	44		
	45 Residential energy credits (see page 12 of Instructions, attach Form 5695) . . .	45		
	46 Total credits. Add lines 38 through 45	46		
	47 **Balance.** Subtract line 46 from line 37 and enter difference (but not less than zero) . ▶	47		
Other Taxes	48 Self-employment tax (attach Schedule SE)	48		
	49 Minimum tax. Check here ▶ ☐ and attach Form 4625	49		
	50 Tax from recomputing prior-year investment credit (attach Form 4255)	50		
	51 Social security (FICA) tax on tip income not reported to employer (attach Form 4137) . .	51		
	52 Uncollected employee FICA and RRTA tax on tips (from Form W-2)	52		
	53 Tax on an IRA (attach Form 5329)	53		
	54 **Total tax.** Add lines 47 through 53 . . . . ▶	54		
Payments Attach Forms W-2, W-2G, and W-2P to front.	55 Total Federal income tax withheld	55		
	56 1978 estimated tax payments and credit from 1977 return .	56		
	57 Earned income credit. If line 31 is under $8,000, see page 2 of Instructions. If eligible, enter child's name ▶	57		
	58 Amount paid with Form 4868	58		
	59 Excess FICA and RRTA tax withheld (two or more employers)	59		
	60 Credit for Federal tax on special fuels and oils (attach Form 4136) .	60		
	61 Regulated Investment Company credit (attach Form 2439)	61		
	62 **Total.** Add lines 55 through 61 . . . . ▶	62		
Refund or Due	63 If line 62 is larger than line 54, enter amount **OVERPAID** . . . . ▶	63		
	64 Amount of line 63 to be **REFUNDED TO YOU** . . . . ▶	64		
	65 Amount of line 63 to be credited on 1979 estimated tax . ▶	65		
	66 If line 54 is larger than line 62, enter **BALANCE DUE.** Attach check or money order for full amount payable to "Internal Revenue Service." Write your social security number on check or money order . . ▶ (Check ▶ ☐ if Form 2210 (2210F) is attached. See page 14 of instructions.) ▶ $	66		

Please Sign Here

Under penalties of perjury, I declare that I have examined this return, including accompanying schedules and statements, and to the best of my knowledge and belief, it is true, correct, and complete. Declaration of preparer (other than taxpayer) is based on all information of which preparer has any knowledge.

▶ Your signature   Date |▶ Spouse's signature (if filing jointly, BOTH must sign even if only one had income)

Paid Preparer's Information	Preparer's signature ▶		Preparer's social security no.	Check if self-employed ▶ ☐
	Firm's name (or yours, if self-employed), address and ZIP code ▶		E.I. No. ▶	
			Date ▶	

Form **1040** Department of the Treasury—Internal Revenue Service
U.S. Individual Income Tax Return 19**78**

For Privacy Act Notice, see page 3 of Instructions | For the year January 1–December 31, 1978, or other tax year beginning , 1978, ending , 19

Use IRS label. Otherwise, please print or type.	Your first name and initial (if joint return, also give spouse's name and initial) GEORGE	Last name GORDON	Your social security number 000 00 0000
	Present home address (Number and street, including apartment number, or rural route) 350 FIFTH AVENUE		Spouse's social security no.
	City, town or post office, State and ZIP code NEW YORK, NY 10001		Your occupation REAL ESTATE BROKER

Do you want $1 to go to the Presidential Election Campaign Fund? ✔ Yes ☐ No | Note: Checking Yes will not increase your tax or reduce your refund. | Spouse's occupation
If joint return, does your spouse want $1 to go to this fund? . . ☐ Yes ☐ No

Filing Status
Check only one box.

1 ✔ Single
2 ☐ Married filing joint return (even if only one had income)
3 ☐ Married filing separate return. If spouse is also filing, give spouse's social security number in the space above and enter full name here ▶
4 ☐ Unmarried head of household. Enter qualifying name ▶ .... See page 6 of Instructions.
5 ☐ Qualifying widow(er) with dependent child (Year spouse died ▶ 19). See page 6 of Instructions.

Exemptions
Always check the box labeled Yourself.
Check other boxes if they apply.

6a ✔ Yourself ☐ 65 or over ☐ Blind } Enter number of boxes checked on 6a and b ▶ **1**
b ☐ Spouse ☐ 65 or over ☐ Blind
c First names of your dependent children who lived with you ▶ .... Enter number of children listed ▶

d Other dependents: (1) Name	(2) Relationship	(3) Number of months lived in your home	(4) Did dependent have income of $750 or more?	(5) Did you provide more than one-half of dependent's support?	Enter number of other dependents ▶

Add numbers entered in boxes above ▶ **1**

7 Total number of exemptions claimed . . . .

Income
Please attach Copy B of your Forms W–2 here.
If you do not have a W–2, see page 5 of Instructions.

8	Wages, salaries, tips, and other employee compensation	8	
9	Interest income (If over $400, attach Schedule B)	9	
10a	Dividends (If over $400, attach Schedule B) 1,275 00, 10b Exclusion 100 00		
10c	Subtract line 10b from line 10a	10c	1,175 00
11	State and local income tax refunds (does not apply unless refund is for year you itemized deductions)	11	
12	Alimony received	12	
13	Business income or (loss) (attach Schedule C)	13	34,309 00
14	Capital gain or (loss) (attach Schedule D)	14	
15	Taxable part of capital gain distributions not reported on Schedule D (see page 9 of Instructions) .	15	
16	Net gain or (loss) from Supplemental Schedule of Gains and Losses (attach Form 4797)	16	
17	Fully taxable pensions and annuities not reported on Schedule E	17	
18	Pensions, annuities, rents, royalties, partnerships, estates or trusts, etc. (attach Schedule E)	18	
19	Farm income or (loss) (attach Schedule F)	19	
20	Other income (state nature and source—see page 10 of Instructions) ▶	20	
21	Total income. Add lines 8, 9, and 10c through 20 . . . . ▶	21	35,484 00

Please attach check or money order here.

Adjustments to Income

22	Moving expense (attach Form 3903)	22	
23	Employee business expenses (attach Form 2106) . .	23	
24	Payments to an IRA (see page 10 of Instructions)	24	
25	Payments to a Keogh (H.R. 10) retirement plan . . .	25	
26	Interest penalty due to early withdrawal of savings	26	
27	Alimony paid (see page 10 of Instructions)	27	
28	Total adjustments. Add lines 22 through 27 . . . . ▶	28	0

Adjusted Gross Income

29	Subtract line 28 from line 21	29	35,484 00
30	Disability income exclusion (attach Form 2440)	30	0
31	Adjusted gross income. Subtract line 30 from line 29. If this line is less than $8,000, see page 2 of Instructions. If you want IRS to figure your tax, see page 4 of Instructions . . . . ▶	31	35,484 00

263–053–2 ☆ U.S. GOVERNMENT PRINTING OFFICE : 1978—O-263-053 Form 1040 (1978)

Tax Compu- tation	32 Amount from line 31	32	35,484	00
	33 If you do not itemize deductions, enter zero . . . . }		
	If you itemize, complete Schedule A (Form 1040) and enter the amount from Schedule A, line 41 . . . . }	33	0
	Caution: If you have unearned income and can be claimed as a dependent on your parent's return, check here ▶ ☐ and see page 11 of the Instructions. Also see page 11 of the Instructions if:		
	• You are married filing a separate return and your spouse itemizes deductions, OR		
	• You file Form 4563, OR		
	• You are a dual-status alien.		
	34 Subtract line 33 from line 32. Use the amount on line 34 to find your tax from the Tax Tables, or to figure your tax on Schedule TC, Part I	34	35,484	00
	Use Schedule TC, Part I, and the Tax Rate Schedules ONLY if:		
	• The amount on line 34 is more than $20,000 ($40,000 if you checked Filing Status Box 2 or 5), OR		
	• You have more exemptions than those covered in the Tax Table for your filing status, OR		
	• You use any of these forms to figure your tax: Schedule D, Schedule G, or Form 4726.		
	Otherwise, you MUST use the Tax Tables to find your tax.		
	35 Tax. Enter tax here and check if from ☐ Tax Tables or ☑ Schedule TC	35	10,377	00
	36 Additional taxes. (See page 11 of Instructions.) Enter total and check if from ☐ Form 4970, }		
	☐ Form 4972, ☐ Form 5544, or ☐ Form 5405, or ☐ Section 72(m)(5) penalty tax . . . }	36	0
	37 Total. Add lines 35 and 36 . . . . ▶	37	10,377	00

Credits	38 Credit for contributions to candidates for public office . .	38	
	39 Credit for the elderly (attach Schedules R&RP)	39	
	40 Credit for child and dependent care expenses (attach Form 2441) .	40	
	41 Investment credit (attach Form 3468)	41	
	42 Foreign tax credit (attach Form 1116)	42	
	43 Work Incentive (WIN) Credit (attach Form 4874)	43	
	44 New jobs credit (attach Form 5884)	44	
	45 Residential energy credits (see page 12 of Instructions, attach Form 5695) . . .	45	
	46 Total credits. Add lines 38 through 45	46	0
	47 Balance. Subtract line 46 from line 37 and enter difference (but not less than zero) . ▶	47	10,377	00

Other Taxes	48 Self-employment tax (attach Schedule SE)	48	1,433	70
	49 Minimum tax. Check here ▶ ☐ and attach Form 4625	49	
	50 Tax from recomputing prior-year investment credit (attach Form 4255)	50	
	51 Social security (FICA) tax on tip income not reported to employer (attach Form 4137) . .	51	
	52 Uncollected employee FICA and RRTA tax on tips (from Form W–2)	52	
	53 Tax on an IRA (attach Form 5329)	53	
	54 Total tax. Add lines 47 through 53 . . . . ▶	54	11,810	70

Payments Attach Forms W–2, W–2G, and W–2P to front.	55 Total Federal income tax withheld	55	
	56 1978 estimated tax payments and credit from 1977 return .	56	
	57 Earned income credit. If line 31 is under $8,000, see page 2 of Instructions. If eligible, enter child's name ▶	57	
	58 Amount paid with Form 4868	58	
	59 Excess FICA and RRTA tax withheld (two or more employers)	59	
	60 Credit for Federal tax on special fuels and oils (attach Form 4136) .	60	
	61 Regulated Investment Company credit (attach Form 2439)	61	
	62 Total. Add lines 55 through 61 . . . . ▶	62	

Refund or Due	63 If line 62 is larger than line 54, enter amount OVERPAID . . . . ▶	63	
	64 Amount of line 63 to be REFUNDED TO YOU . . . . ▶	64	
	65 Amount of line 63 to be credited on 1979 estimated tax . ▶	65	
	66 If line 54 is larger than line 62, enter BALANCE DUE. Attach check or money order for full amount payable to "Internal Revenue Service." Write your social security number on check or money order . . ▶ (Check ▶ ☐ if Form 2210 (2210F) is attached. See page 14 of instructions.) ▶ $	66	

Please Sign Here

Under penalties of perjury, I declare that I have examined this return, including accompanying schedules and statements, and to the best of my knowledge and belief, it is true, correct, and complete. Declaration of preparer (other than taxpayer) is based on all information of which preparer has any knowledge.

▶ Your signature	Date	▶ Spouse's signature (if filing jointly, BOTH must sign even if only one had income)	

Paid Preparer's Information	Preparer's signature ▶		Preparer's social security no.	Check if self-employed ▶ ☐
	Firm's name (or yours, if self-employed), address and ZIP code ▶		E.I. No. ▶	
			Date ▶	

Profit or (Loss) From Business or Profession

(Sole Proprietorship)

Partnerships, Joint Ventures, etc., Must File Form 1065.

▶ Attach to Form 1040. ▶ See Instructions for Schedule C (Form 1040).

1978

Name of proprietor	Social security number of proprietor
GEORGE GORDON	000 : 00 : 0000

A Main business activity (see Instructions) ▶ REAL ESTATE BROKER ; product ▶ ....

B Business name ▶ GEORGE GORDON ....

C Employer identification number ▶ .....

D Business address (number and street) ▶ 350 FIFTH AVENUE ....

City, State and ZIP code ▶ NEW YORK, N Y 10001

C

E Accounting method: (1) ☑ Cash (2) ☐ Accrual (3) ☐ Other (specify) ▶ ....

F Method(s) used to value closing inventory:

(1) ☐ Cost (2) ☐ Lower of cost or market (3) ☐ Other (if other, attach explanation)

	Yes	No
G Was there any major change in determining quantities, costs, or valuations between opening and closing inventory? . . If "Yes," attach explanation.		✓
H Does this business activity involve oil or gas, movies or video tapes, or leasing personal (section 1245) property to others? (See page 25 of the Instructions.)		✓
I Did you deduct expenses for an office in your home?		✓

Part I Income

1 a Gross receipts or sales.	1a		
b Returns and allowances	1b		
c Balance (subtract line 1b from line 1a).		1c	
2 Cost of goods sold and/or operations (Schedule C–1, line 8)		2	
3 Gross profit (subtract line 2 from line 1c).		3	
4 Other income (attach schedule)		4	45,000 00
5 Total income (add lines 3 and 4) . . . . ▶		5	45,000 00

Part II Deductions

6 Advertising		28 Telephone		300 00
7 Amortization		29 Travel and entertainment . .		450 00
8 Bad debts from sales or services .		30 Utilities		191 00
9 Bank charges		31 a Wages . . .		
10 Car and truck expenses		b New Jobs Credit .		
11 Commissions		c Subtract line 31b from 31a .		
12 Depletion		32 Other expenses (specify):		
13 Depreciation (explain in Schedule C–2)	500 00	a Books + Subscriptions		50 00
		b		
14 Dues and publications . . .		c		
15 Employee benefit programs . . .		d		
16 Freight (not included on Schedule C–1)		e		
17 Insurance		f		
18 Interest on business indebtedness		g		
19 Laundry and cleaning		h		
20 Legal and professional services .		i		
21 Office supplies	100 00	j		
22 Pension and profit-sharing plans .	6,000 00	k		
23 Postage	100 00	l		
24 Rent on business property . . .	3,000 00	m		
25 Repairs		n		
26 Supplies (not included on Schedule C–1)		o		
27 Taxes		p		
		q		
		r		

33 Total deductions (add amounts in columns for lines 6 through 32r) . . . . ▶	33	10,691	00
34 Net profit or (loss) (subtract line 33 from line 5). Enter here and on Form 1040, line 13. ALSO enter on Schedule SE (Form 1040), line 5a. (For "at risk" provisions, see page 25 of Instructions.) . . . . ▶	34	34,309	00

263–056–2

SCHEDULE C–1.—Cost of Goods Sold and/or Operations (See Schedule C Instructions for Part I, Line 2)

1 Inventory at beginning of year (if different from last year's closing inventory, attach explanation) .	**1**	
2 a Purchases **2a**		
b Cost of items withdrawn for personal use **2b**		
c Balance (subtract line 2b from line 2a)	**2c**	
3 Cost of labor (do not include salary paid to yourself)	**3**	
4 Materials and supplies	**4**	
5 Other costs (attach schedule)	**5**	
6 Add lines 1, 2c, and 3 through 5	**6**	
7 Inventory at end of year	**7**	
8 Cost of goods sold and/or operations (subtract line 7 from line 6). Enter here and on Part I, line 2 . ▶	**8**	

SCHEDULE C–2.—Depreciation (See Schedule C Instructions for line 13)
If you need more space, please use Form 4562.

Description of property (a)	Date acquired (b)	Cost or other basis (c)	Depreciation allowed or allowable in prior years (d)	Method of computing depreciation (e)	Life or rate (f)	Depreciation for this year (g)
1 Total additional first-year depreciation (do not include in items below)——————▶						
2 Other depreciation:						
Buildings						
Furniture and fixtures	1,1,78	5,000.00		STRAIGHT LINE	10 Yrs,	500 00
Transportation equipment . .						
Machinery and other equipment .						
Other (Specify)						
3 Totals		5,000.00	. . . .		**3**	500 00
4 Depreciation claimed in Schedule C–1					**4**	0
5 Balance (subtract line 4 from line 3). Enter here and on Part II, line 13 . . . . ▶					**5**	500 00

SCHEDULE C–3.—Expense Account Information (See Schedule C Instructions for Schedule C–3)

Enter information for yourself and your five highest paid employees. In determining the five highest paid employees, add expense account allowances to the salaries and wages. However, you don't have to provide the information for any employee for whom the combined amount is less than $25,000, or for yourself if your expense account allowance plus line 34, page 1, is less than $25,000.

Name (a)	Expense account (b)	Salaries and Wages (c)
Owner		
1		
2		
3		
4		
5		

Did you claim a deduction for expenses connected with:	Yes	No
A Entertainment facility (boat, resort, ranch, etc.)?		
B Living accommodations (except employees on business)?		
C Employees' families at conventions or meetings?		
If "Yes," were any of these conventions or meetings outside the U.S. or its possessions? (See page 26 of Instructions.) .		
D Vacations for employees or their families not reported on Form W–2?		

Computation of Social Security Self-Employment Tax

► Each self-employed person must file a Schedule SE.   ► Attach to Form 1040.
► See Instructions for Schedule SE (Form 1040).

1978

● If you had wages, including tips, of $17,700 or more that were subject to social security or railroad retirement taxes, do not fill in this schedule (unless you are eligible for the Earned Income Credit). See Instructions.

● If you had more than one business, combine profits and losses from all your businesses and farms on this Schedule SE.

Important.—The self-employment income reported below will be credited to your social security record and used in figuring social security benefits.

NAME OF SELF-EMPLOYED PERSON (AS SHOWN ON SOCIAL SECURITY CARD)	Social security number of self-employed person ►
GEORGE GORDON	000 00 0000

● If you have only farm income complete Parts I and III.   ● If you have only nonfarm income complete Parts II and III.
● If you have both farm and nonfarm income complete Parts I, II, and III.

Part I   Computation of Net Earnings from FARM Self-Employment

You may elect to compute your net farm earnings using the OPTIONAL METHOD, line 3, instead of using the Regular Method, line 2, if your gross profits are: (1) $2,400 or less, or (2) more than $2,400 and net profits are less than $1,600. However, lines 1 and 2 must be completed even if you elect to use the FARM OPTIONAL METHOD.

REGULAR METHOD	a Schedule F, line 58 (cash method), or line 76 (accrual method) .	1a	
1 Net profit or (loss) from:	b Farm partnerships	1b	
2 Net earnings from farm self-employment (add lines 1a and b)		2	
FARM OPTIONAL METHOD 3 If gross profits from farming¹ are:	a Not more than $2,400, enter two-thirds of the gross profits . .		
	b More than $2,400 and the net farm profit is less than $1,600, enter $1,600	3	

¹ Gross profits from farming are the total gross profits from Schedule F, line 32 (cash method), or line 74 (accrual method), plus the distributive share of gross profits from farm partnerships (Schedule K–1 (Form 1065), line 3) as explained in instructions for Schedule SE.

4 Enter here and on line 12a, the amount on line 2, or line 3 if you elect the farm optional method .	4	

Part II   Computation of Net Earnings from NONFARM Self-Employment

	a Schedule C, line 34. (Enter combined amount if more than one business.) .	5a	34,309 00
	b Partnerships, joint ventures, etc. (other than farming)	5b	
REGULAR METHOD 5 Net profit or (loss) from:	c Service as a minister, member of a religious order, or a Christian Science practitioner. (Include rental value of parsonage or rental allowance furnished.) If you filed Form 4361 and have not revoked that exemption, check here ► ☐ and enter zero on this line	5c	
	d Service with a foreign government or international organization	5d	
	e Other—Specify ►	5e	
6 Total (add lines 5a through e)		6	34,309 00
7 Enter adjustments if any (attach statement, see page 27 of instructions)		7	
8 Adjusted net earnings or (loss) from nonfarm self-employment (line 6, as adjusted by line 7) . .		8	34,309 00

If line 8 is $1,600 or more OR if you do not elect to use the Nonfarm Optional Method, skip lines 9 through 11 and enter amount from line 8 on line 12b, Part III.

Note: You may use the nonfarm optional method (line 9 through line 11) only if line 8 is less than $1,600 and less than two-thirds of your gross nonfarm profits,² and you had actual net earnings from self-employment of $400 or more for at least 2 of the 3 following years: 1975, 1976, and 1977. The nonfarm optional method can only be used for 5 tax years.

SE

NONFARM OPTIONAL METHOD

9 a Maximum amount reportable, under both optional methods combined (farm and nonfarm) . .	9a	$1,600 00
b Enter amount from line 3. (If you did not elect to use the farm optional method, enter zero) .	9b	
c Balance (subtract line 9b from line 9a)	9c	
10 Enter two-thirds of gross nonfarm profits ² or $1,600, whichever is smaller	10	
11 Enter here and on line 12b, the amount on line 9c or line 10, whichever is smaller	11	

² Gross profits from nonfarm business are the total of the gross profits from Schedule C, line 3, plus the distributive share of gross profits from nonfarm partnerships (Schedule K–1 (Form 1065), line 15(a)) as explained in instructions for Schedule SE. Also, include gross profits from services reported on line 5c, d, and e, as adjusted by line 7.

Part III   Computation of Social Security Self-Employment Tax

12 Net earnings or (loss): a From farming (from line 4)	12a	
b From nonfarm (from line 8, or line 11 if you elect to use the Nonfarm Optional Method) . . .	12b	34,309 00
13 Total net earnings or (loss) from self-employment reported on lines 12a and 12b. (If line 13 is less than $400, you are not subject to self-employment tax. Do not fill in rest of schedule.)	13	34,309 00
14 The largest amount of combined wages and self-employment earnings subject to social security or railroad retirement taxes for 1978 is	14	$17,700 00
15 a Total "FICA" wages (from Forms W–2) and "RRTA" compensation . . .	15a	0	
b Unreported tips subject to FICA tax from Form 4137, line 9 or to RRTA . .	15b	0	
c Add lines 15a and b	15c	0
16 Balance (subtract line 15c from line 14)	16	34,309 00
17 Self-employment income—line 13 or 16, whichever is smaller	17	34,309 00
18 Self-employment tax. (If line 17 is $17,700, enter $1,433.70; if less, multiply the amount on line 17 by .081.) Enter here and on Form 1040, line 48	18	1,433 70

Form **1120** Department of the Treasury Internal Revenue Service	**U.S. Corporation Income Tax Return** For calendar year 1978 or other taxable year beginning ...., 1978, ending ...., 19......	**1978**

Check if a—
A Consolidated return ☐
B Personal Holding Co. ☐
C Business Code No. (See Page 8 of instructions)
8599

Use IRS label. Otherwise please print or type.	Name GEOFFREY FOURMYLE
	Number and street 5217 CERES BOULEVARD
	City or town, State, and ZIP code SAN FRANCISCO CA 94701

D Employer identification number (see instruction W) 000-00-0000
E Date incorporated 1 1 73
F Enter total assets (see instruction X) $ 50,000.00

Gross Income

1	Gross receipts or gross sales...............Less: Returns and allowances............	1	
2	Less: Cost of goods sold (Schedule A) and/or operations (attach schedule)	2	
3	Gross profit	3	
4	Dividends (Schedule C)	4	525.00
5	Interest on obligations of the United States and U.S. instrumentalities	5	
6	Other interest	6	
7	Gross rents	7	
8	Gross royalties	8	
9	(a) Capital gain net income (attach separate Schedule D)	9(a)	
	(b) Net gain or (loss) from Form 4797, line 11, Part II (attach Form 4797)	9(b)	
10	Other income (see instructions—attach schedule)	10	45,000.00
11	TOTAL income—Add lines 3 through 10	11	45,525.00

Deductions

12	Compensation of officers (Schedule E)	12	25,000.00
13	(a) Salaries and wages....................13(b) Less new jobs credit.................... Balance ▶	13(c)	
14	Repairs (see instructions)	14	
15	Bad debts (Schedule F if reserve method is used)	15	
16	Rents	16	
17	Taxes	17	
18	Interest	18	
19	Contributions (not over 5% of line 30 adjusted per instructions—attach schedule)	19	
20	Amortization (attach schedule)	20	500.00
21	Depreciation from Form 4562 (attach Form 4562) ...., less depreciation claimed in Schedule A and elsewhere on return ...., Balance ▶	21	500.00
22	Depletion	22	
23	Advertising	23	
24	Pension, profit-sharing, etc. plans (see instructions) (enter number of plans ▶ .....1........) . .	24	6,250.00
25	Employee benefit programs (see instructions)	25	
26	Other deductions (attach schedule)	26	4,079.00
27	TOTAL deductions—Add lines 12 through 26	27	36,329.00
28	Taxable income before net operating loss deduction and special deductions (subtract line 27 from line 11) .	28	9,196.00
29	Less: (a) Net operating loss deduction (see instructions—attach schedule) . . 29(a)		
	(b) Special deductions (Schedule I) . . . . 29(b) 446.00	29	
30	Taxable income (subtract line 29 from line 28)	30	8,750.00

Tax

31	TOTAL TAX (Schedule J)	31	1,750.00
32	Credits: (a) Overpayment from 1977 allowed as a credit . . .		
	(b) 1978 estimated tax payments		
	(c) Less refund of 1978 estimated tax applied for on Form 4466 . ( )		
	(d) Tax deposited: Form 7004 .... Form 7005 (attach)......... Total ▶		
	(e) Credit from regulated investment companies (attach Form 2439)		
	(f) U.S. tax on special fuels, nonhighway gas and lubricating oil (attach Form 4136) . .	32	
33	TAX DUE (subtract line 32 from line 31). See instruction G for depositary method of payment .	33	1,750.00
	(Check ▶ ☐ if Form 2220 is attached. See page 3 of instructions.) ▶ $..................		
34	OVERPAYMENT (subtract line 31 from line 32)	34	
35	Enter amount of line 34 you want: Credited to 1979 estimated tax ▶ .... Refunded ▶	35	

Please Sign Here

Under penalties of perjury, I declare that I have examined this return, including accompanying schedules and statements, and to the best of my knowledge and belief, it is true, correct, and complete. Declaration of preparer (other than taxpayer) is based on all information of which preparer has any knowledge.

▶ Signature of officer	Date	▶ Title

Paid Preparer's Information

Preparer's signature ▶		Preparer's social security no.	Check if self-employed ▶ ☐
Firm's name (or yours, if self-employed), address and ZIP code ▶		E.I. No. ▶	
		Date ▶	

263-104-1

99

Schedule A   Cost of Goods Sold (See instruction 2)

1 Inventory at beginning of year . . . .
2 Merchandise bought for manufacture or sale . . . .
3 Salaries and wages . . . .
4 Other costs (attach schedule) . . . .
5 Total . . . .
6 Less: Inventory at end of year . . . .
7 Cost of goods sold—Enter here and on line 2, page 1 . . . .
8 (a) Check valuation method(s) used for total closing inventory:
      ☐ Cost   ☐ Lower of cost or market   ☐ Other (if "other," attach explanation)
   (b) Check if this is the first year LIFO inventory method was adopted and used. (If checked, attach Form 970.). . . . . . ☐
   (c) If the LIFO inventory method was used for this taxable year, enter percentage (or amounts) of closing in-
      ventory computed under LIFO . . . .
   (d) Is the corporation engaged in manufacturing activities? . . . . ☐ Yes ☐ No
      If "Yes," are inventories valued under Regulations section 1.471–11 (full absorption accounting method)? . ☐ Yes ☐ No
   (e) Was there any substantial change in determining quantities, cost, or valuations between opening and closing inventory? . . . ☐ Yes ☐ No
      If "Yes," attach explanation.

Schedule C   Dividends (See instruction 4)

1 Domestic corporations subject to 85% deduction **525.00**
2 Certain preferred stock of public utilities . . . .
3 Foreign corporations subject to 85% deduction . . . .
4 Dividends from wholly-owned foreign subsidiaries subject to 100% deduction (section 245(b)) . . . . .
5 Other dividends from foreign corporations . . . .
6 Includable income from controlled foreign corporations under subpart F (attach Forms 3646) . . . . .
7 Foreign dividend gross-up (section 78) . . . .
8 Qualifying dividends received from affiliated groups and subject to the 100% deduction (section 243(a)(3)) .
9 Taxable dividends from a DISC or former DISC not included in line 1 (section 246(d)) . . . .
10 Other dividends . . . .
11 Total—Enter here and on line 4, page 1 . . . .   **525.00**

Schedule E   Compensation of Officers (See instruction 12)

1. Name of officer	2. Social security number	3. Time devoted to business	Percent of corporation stock owned		6. Amount of compensation	7. Expense account allowances
			4. Common	5. Preferred		
GEOFFREY FOURMYLE	000-00-0000	ALL	100		25,000.00	

Total compensation of officers—Enter here and on line 12, page 1 . . . . .   **25,000.00**

Schedule F   Bad Debts—Reserve Method (See instruction 15)

1. Year	2. Trade notes and accounts receivable outstanding at end of year	3. Sales on account	Amount added to reserve		6. Amount charged against reserve	7. Reserve for bad debts at end of year
			4. Current year's provision	5. Recoveries		
1973						
1974						
1975						
1976						
1977						
1978						

Schedule I   Special Deductions

1 (a) 85% of Schedule C, line 1 . . . .   **446.00**
   (b) 60.208% of Schedule C, line 2 . . . .
   (c) 85% of Schedule C, line 3 . . . .
   (d) 100% of Schedule C, line 4 . . . .
2 Total—See instructions for limitation . . . .
3 100% of Schedule C, line 8 . . . .
4 Dividends paid on certain preferred stock of public utilities (see instructions) . . . .
5 Western Hemisphere trade corporations (see instructions) . . . .
6 Total special deductions—Add lines 2 through 5. Enter here and on line 29(b), page 1 . . . .   **446.00**

100

Form 1120 (1978)   **Schedule J**   Tax Computation   Page **3**

(Fiscal year corporations, omit lines 1 through 8 and enter on line 9, the amount from Form 1120–FY (1978–79), line 5, Part III)

1 Taxable income (line 30, page 1)	**8,750.00**
2 Enter line 1 or $25,000, whichever is less. (Members of a controlled group enter one-half of surtax allocation, see instructions) .	**8,750.00**
3 Subtract line 2 from line 1	**0**
4 Enter line 3 or $25,000, whichever is less. (Members of a controlled group enter one-half of surtax allocation, see instructions) .	**0**
5 Subtract line 4 from line 3	**0**
6 20% of line 2	**1,750.00**
7 22% of line 4	**0**
8 48% of line 5	**0**
9 Income tax (Sum of lines 6, 7 and 8 or alternative tax from separate Schedule D, whichever is less)	**1,750.00**
10 (a) Foreign tax credit (attach Form 1118)	
(b) Investment credit (attach Form 3468)	
(c) Work incentive (WIN) credit (attach Form 4874)	
(d) New jobs credit (attach Form 5884)	
11 Total of lines 10(a), (b), (c), and (d)	**0**
12 Subtract line 11 from line 9	**1,750.00**
13 Personal holding company tax (attach Schedule PH (Form 1120))	
14 Tax from recomputing a prior year investment credit (attach Form 4255)	
15 Tax from recomputing a prior year WIN credit (see instructions—attach computation) . . .	
16 Minimum tax on tax preference items (see instructions—attach Form 4626)	
17 Total tax—Add lines 12 through 16. Enter here and on line 31, page 1	**1,750.00**

Schedule K   Record of Federal Tax Deposits Tax Class Number 503

(List deposits in order of date made—See instruction G)

Date of deposit	Amount	Date of deposit	Amount	Date of deposit	Amount

---

G (1) Did you claim a deduction for expenses connected with: **Yes | No**

(a) Entertainment facility (boat, resort, ranch, etc.)? . . .   ✓ No

(b) Living accommodations (except for employees on business)? . . . .   ✓ No

(c) Employee's families at conventions or meetings? . . .   ✓ No

If "Yes," were any of these conventions or meetings outside the United States or its possessions? . . . . . .   ✓ No

(d) Employee or family vacations not reported on Form W–2? .   ✓ No

(2) Enter total amount claimed on Form 1120 for entertainment, entertainment facilities, gifts, travel, and conventions of the type for which substantiation is required under section 274(d). (See instruction Y.) ▶ ....

H (1) Did you at the end of the taxable year own, directly or indirectly, 50% or more of the voting stock of a domestic corporation? (For rules of attribution, see section 267(c).) . . .

If "Yes," attach a schedule showing: (a) name, address, and identifying number; (b) percentage owned; (c) taxable income or (loss) (e.g., if a Form 1120: from Form 1120, line 28, page 1) of such corporation for the taxable year ending with or within your taxable year; (d) highest amount owed by you to such corporation during the year; and (e) highest amount owed to you by such corporation during the year.

(2) Did any individual, partnership, corporation, estate or trust at the end of the taxable year own, directly or indirectly, 50% or more of your voting stock? (For rules of attribution, see section 267(c).) If "Yes," complete (a) through (e) . . .   ✓

(a) Attach a schedule showing name, address, and identifying number; (b) Enter percentage owned ▶ _100_

(c) Was the owner of such voting stock a person other than a U.S. person? (See instruction S.) . . . . . .   ✓ No

If "Yes," enter owner's country ▶ ....

(d) Enter highest amount owed by you to such owner during the year ▶

(e) Enter highest amount owed to you by such owner during the year ▶   **Yes | No**

(Note: For purposes of H(1) and H(2), "highest amount owed" includes loans and accounts receivable/payable.)

I Did you ever declare a stock dividend? . . . .   ✓ No

J Taxable income or (loss) from Form 1120, line 28, page 1, for your taxable year beginning in:

1975 ...., 1976 ...., 1977 ....

K Were you a member of a controlled group subject to the provisions of section 1561? If "Yes," check the type of relationship . .   ✓ No

(1) ☐ parent-subsidiary   (2) ☐ brother-sister

(3) ☐ combination of (1) and (2) (See section 1563.)

L Refer to page 8 of instructions and state the principal:

Business activity ....

Product or service _ENGINEERING_ ....

M Did you file all required Forms 1087, 1096 and 1099?   _N/A._

N Were you a U.S. shareholder of any controlled foreign corporation? (See sections 951 and 957.) If "Yes," attach Form 3646 for each such corporation . . . .

O Did you, at any time during the taxable year, have an interest in or signature or other authority over a bank, securities or other financial account in a foreign country (see instruction V)? . .   ✓ No

P Were you the grantor of, or transferor to, a foreign trust during any taxable year, which foreign trust was in being during the current taxable year, whether or not you have any beneficial interest in such trust? If "Yes," you may be required to file Forms 3520, 3520–A, or 926 . . . .   ✓ No

Q During this taxable year, did you pay dividends (other than stock dividends and distributions in exchange for stock) in excess of your current and accumulated earnings and profits? (See sections 301 and 316.) . . . .   ✓ No

If "Yes," file Form 5452. If this is a consolidated return, answer here for parent corporation and on Form 851, Affiliation Schedule, for each subsidiary.

263–104–2

101

Schedule L　Balance Sheets

ASSETS	Beginning of taxable year (A) Amount	(B) Total	End of taxable year (C) Amount	(D) Total
1 Cash		7,000.00		17,000.00
2 Trade notes and accounts receivable . . .				
(a) Less allowance for bad debts				
3 Inventories				
4 Gov't obligations: (a) U.S. and instrumentalities .				
(b) State, subdivisions thereof, etc.				
5 Other current assets (attach schedule)		4,000.00		6,000.00
6 Loans to stockholders				
7 Mortgage and real estate loans				
8 Other investments (attach schedule) (STOCK)		10,000.00		12,000.00
9 Buildings and other fixed depreciable assets . .	5,000.00		5,000.00	
(a) Less accumulated depreciation	5,000.00	5,000.00	500.00	4,500.00
10 Depletable assets				
(a) Less accumulated depletion				
11 Land (net of any amortization)				
12 Intangible assets (amortizable only)				
(a) Less accumulated amortization				
13 Other assets (attach schedule)		2,250.00		10,500.00
14 Total assets		28,250.00		50,000.00
LIABILITIES AND STOCKHOLDERS' EQUITY				
15 Accounts payable		8,250.00		10,000.00
16 Mtges., notes, bonds payable in less than 1 yr. .				
17 Other current liabilities (attach schedule) . . .				7,000.00
18 Loans from stockholders				2,804.00
19 Mtges., notes, bonds payable in 1 yr. or more . .				
20 Other liabilities (attach schedule)				
21 Capital stock: (a) Preferred stock				
(b) Common stock	10,000.00	10,000.00		10,000.00
22 Paid-in or capital surplus		10,000.00		10,000.00
23 Retained earnings—Appropriated (attach sch.) . .				
24 Retained earnings—Unappropriated				9,196.00
25 Less cost of treasury stock		( )		( )
26 Total liabilities and stockholders' equity . . .		28,250.00		50,000.00

Schedule M-1　Reconciliation of Income Per Books With Income Per Return

1 Net income per books	9,196.00	7 Income recorded on books this year not included in this return (itemize)	
2 Federal income tax		(a) Tax-exempt interest $	
3 Excess of capital losses over capital gains . . .			
4 Income subject to tax not recorded on books this year (itemize)			
		8 Deductions in this tax return not charged against book income this year (itemize)	
5 Expenses recorded on books this year not deducted in this return (itemize)		(a) Depreciation . . $	
(a) Depreciation . . . $		(b) Depletion . . . $	
(b) Depletion . . . . $			
		9　Total of lines 7 and 8	
6　Total of lines 1 through 5	9,196.00	10 Income (line 28, page 1)—line 6 less 9 .	9,196.00

Schedule M-2　Analysis of Unappropriated Retained Earnings Per Books (line 24 above)

1 Balance at beginning of year	—	5 Distributions: (a) Cash	
2 Net income per books	9,196.00	(b) Stock	
3 Other increases (itemize)		(c) Property	
		6 Other decreases (itemize)	
		7　Total of lines 5 and 6 . . .	
4　Total of lines 1, 2, and 3	9,196.00	8 Balance at end of year (line 4 less 7) . . .	9,196.00

☆ U.S. GOVERNMENT PRINTING OFFICE : 1978—O-263-104　　　　　　　　263-104-1

Department of the Treasury—Internal Revenue Service

U.S. Individual Income Tax Return 19**78**

| For Privacy Act Notice, see page 3 of Instructions | For the year January 1–December 31, 1978, or other tax year beginning | , 1978, ending | , 19 |

Use IRS label. Otherwise, please print or type.	Your first name and initial (if joint return, also give spouse's name and initial)	Last name	Your social security number
	GEOFFREY	FOURMYLE	000 00 0000
	Present home address (Number and street, including apartment number, or rural route)		Spouse's social security no.
	5217 CERES BOULEVARD		
	City, town or post office, State and ZIP code		Your occupation
	SAN FRANCISCO CA 94701		ENGINEER

Do you want $1 to go to the Presidential Election Campaign Fund? ✓ Yes ☐ No
If joint return, does your spouse want $1 to go to this fund? . . ☐ Yes ☐ No

Note: Checking Yes will not increase your tax or reduce your refund.

Spouse's occupation

Filing Status

Check only one box.

1 ✓ Single
2 ☐ Married filing joint return (even if only one had income)
3 ☐ Married filing separate return. If spouse is also filing, give spouse's social security number in the space above and enter full name here ▶
4 ☐ Unmarried head of household. Enter qualifying name ▶ _____ . See page 6 of Instructions.
5 ☐ Qualifying widow(er) with dependent child (Year spouse died ▶ 19). See page 6 of Instructions.

Exemptions

Always check the box labeled Yourself. Check other boxes if they apply.

6a ✓ Yourself ☐ 65 or over ☐ Blind

b ☐ Spouse ☐ 65 or over ☐ Blind

c First names of your dependent children who lived with you ▶ _____

Enter number of boxes checked on 6a and b ▶ **1**

Enter number of children listed ▶ ☐

d Other dependents:

(1) Name	(2) Relationship	(3) Number of months lived in your home	(4) Did dependent have income of $750 or more?	(5) Did you provide more than one-half of dependent's support?

Enter number of other dependents ▶ ☐

Add numbers entered in boxes above ▶ **1**

7 Total number of exemptions claimed . . . .

Income

Please attach Copy B of your Forms W–2 here.

If you do not have a W–2, see page 5 of Instructions.

8 Wages, salaries, tips, and other employee compensation . . . . | 8 | 25,000 | 00
9 Interest income (If over $400, attach Schedule B) . . . . | 9 |
10a Dividends (If over $400, attach Schedule B) . . . ., 10b Exclusion . . . .
10c Subtract line 10b from line 10a . . . . | 10c |
11 State and local income tax refunds (does not apply unless refund is for year you itemized deductions) . . . . | 11 |
12 Alimony received . . . . | 12 |
13 Business income or (loss) (attach Schedule C) . . . . | 13 |
14 Capital gain or (loss) (attach Schedule D) . . . . | 14 |
15 Taxable part of capital gain distributions not reported on Schedule D (see page 9 of Instructions) . . | 15 |
16 Net gain or (loss) from Supplemental Schedule of Gains and Losses (attach Form 4797) . . . . | 16 |

Please attach check or money order here.

17 Fully taxable pensions and annuities not reported on Schedule E . . . . | 17 |
18 Pensions, annuities, rents, royalties, partnerships, estates or trusts, etc. (attach Schedule E) . . . . | 18 |
19 Farm income or (loss) (attach Schedule F) . . . . | 19 |
20 Other income (state nature and source—see page 10 of Instructions) ▶ _____ | 20 |

21 Total income. Add lines 8, 9, and 10c through 20 . . . . ▶ | 21 | 25,000 | 00

Adjustments to Income

22 Moving expense (attach Form 3903) . . . . | 22 |
23 Employee business expenses (attach Form 2106) . . | 23 |
24 Payments to an IRA (see page 10 of Instructions) . . . . . | 24 |
25 Payments to a Keogh (H.R. 10) retirement plan . . . | 25 |
26 Interest penalty due to early withdrawal of savings | 26 |
27 Alimony paid (see page 10 of Instructions) . . . . | 27 |
28 Total adjustments. Add lines 22 through 27 . . . . ▶ | 28 | 0 |

Adjusted Gross Income

29 Subtract line 28 from line 21 . . . . | 29 | 25,000 | 00
30 Disability income exclusion (attach Form 2440) . . . . | 30 | 0 |
31 Adjusted gross income. Subtract line 30 from line 29. If this line is less than $8,000, see page 2 of Instructions. If you want IRS to figure your tax, see page 4 of Instructions . . . . ▶ | 31 | 25,000 | 00

☆ U.S. GOVERNMENT PRINTING OFFICE: 1978—O-263-303 13-2587299

Form 1040 (1978)

Tax Compu- tation	32 Amount from line 31	32	25,000	00
	33 If you do not itemize deductions, enter zero . . . . } If you itemize, complete Schedule A (Form 1040) and enter the amount from Schedule A, line 41 . . . . }	33	O	

	Caution: If you have unearned income and can be claimed as a dependent on your parent's return, check here ▶ ☐ and see page 11 of the instructions. Also see page 11 of the Instructions if:
	    • You are married filing a separate return and your spouse itemizes deductions, OR
	    • You file Form 4563, OR
	    • You are a dual-status alien.			

	34 Subtract line 33 from line 32. Use the amount on line 34 to find your tax from the Tax Tables, or to figure your tax on Schedule TC, Part I . . . .
	    Use Schedule TC, Part I, and the Tax Rate Schedules ONLY if:
	    • The amount on line 34 is more than $20,000 ($40,000 if you checked Filing Status Box 2 or 5), OR
	    • You have more exemptions than those covered in the Tax Table for your filing status, OR
	    • You use any of these forms to figure your tax: Schedule D, Schedule G, or Form 4726.
	    Otherwise, you MUST use the Tax Tables to find your tax.
		34	25,000	00

	35 Tax. Enter tax here and check if from ☐ Tax Tables or ☑ Schedule TC . . . . ▶	35	5,830	00
	36 Additional taxes. (See page 11 of Instructions.) Enter total and check if from ☐ Form 4970, } ☐ Form 4972, ☐ Form 5544, ☐ Form 5405, or ☐ Section 72(m)(5) penalty tax . . . }	36	O	
	37 Total. Add lines 35 and 36 . . . . ▶	37	5,830	00
Credits	38 Credit for contributions to candidates for public office . .	38		
	39 Credit for the elderly (attach Schedules R&RP)	39		
	40 Credit for child and dependent care expenses (attach Form 2441) .	40		
	41 Investment credit (attach Form 3468)	41		
	42 Foreign tax credit (attach Form 1116)	42		
	43 Work Incentive (WIN) Credit (attach Form 4874)	43		
	44 New jobs credit (attach Form 5884)	44		
	45 Residential energy credits (see page 12 of instructions, attach Form 5695) . .	45		
	46 Total credits. Add lines 38 through 45 . . . . ▶	46		
	47 Balance. Subtract line 46 from line 37 and enter difference (but not less than zero) . ▶	47		
Other Taxes	48 Self-employment tax (attach Schedule SE)	48		
	49 Minimum tax. Check here ▶ ☐ and attach Form 4625	49		
	50 Tax from recomputing prior-year investment credit (attach Form 4255)	50		
	51 Social security (FICA) tax on tip income not reported to employer (attach Form 4137) . .	51		
	52 Uncollected employee FICA and RRTA tax on tips (from Form W-2)	52		
	53 Tax on an IRA (attach Form 5329)	53		
	54 Total tax. Add lines 47 through 53 . . . . ▶	54		
Payments Attach Forms W-2, W-2G, and W-2P to front.	55 Total Federal income tax withheld	55		
	56 1978 estimated tax payments and credit from 1977 return .	56		
	57 Earned income credit. If line 31 is under $8,000, see page 2 of Instructions. If eligible, enter child's name ▶................	57		
	58 Amount paid with Form 4868	58		
	59 Excess FICA and RRTA tax withheld (two or more employers)	59		
	60 Credit for Federal tax on special fuels and oils (attach Form 4136) .	60		
	61 Regulated Investment Company credit (attach Form 2439)	61		
	62 Total. Add lines 55 through 61 . . . . ▶	62		
Refund or Due	63 If line 62 is larger than line 54, enter amount OVERPAID . . . . ▶	63		
	64 Amount of line 63 to be REFUNDED TO YOU . . . . ▶	64		
	65 Amount of line 63 to be credited on 1979 estimated tax . ▶	65		
	66 If line 54 is larger than line 62, enter BALANCE DUE. Attach check or money order for full amount payable to "Internal Revenue Service." Write your social security number on check or money order . . ▶ (Check ▶ ☐ if Form 2210 (2210F) is attached. See page 14 of instructions.) ▶ $	66		

104

1040 U.S. Individual Income Tax Return 1978

Department of the Treasury—Internal Revenue Service

For Privacy Act Notice, see page 3 of Instructions	For the year January 1–December 31, 1978, or other tax year beginning	, 1978, ending	, 19 .

Use IRS label. Otherwise, please print or type.

Your first name and initial (if joint return, also give spouse's name and initial) GEOFFREY

Last name FOURMYLE

Present home address (Number and street, including apartment number, or rural route) 5217 CERES BOULEVARD

City, town or post office, State and ZIP code SAN FRANCISCO CA 94701

Your social security number 000 00 0000

Spouse's social security no.

Your occupation ENGINEER

Spouse's occupation

Do you want $1 to go to the Presidential Election Campaign Fund? ✔Yes / No
If joint return, does your spouse want $1 to go to this fund? . . Yes / No

Note: Checking Yes will not increase your tax or reduce your refund.

Filing Status

Check only one box.

1 ✔ Single
2 ☐ Married filing joint return (even if only one had income)
3 ☐ Married filing separate return. If spouse is also filing, give spouse's social security number in the space above and enter full name here ▶...
4 ☐ Unmarried head of household. Enter qualifying name ▶................. See page 6 of Instructions.
5 ☐ Qualifying widow(er) with dependent child (Year spouse died ▶ 19). See page 6 of Instructions.

Exemptions

Always check the box labeled Yourself. Check other boxes if they apply.

6a ✔ Yourself ☐ 65 or over ☐ Blind } Enter number of boxes checked on 6a and b ▶ 1

b ☐ Spouse ☐ 65 or over ☐ Blind

c First names of your dependent children who lived with you ▶-- } Enter number of children listed ▶

d Other dependents: (1) Name	(2) Relationship	(3) Number of months lived in your home	(4) Did dependent have income of $750 or more?	(5) Did you provide more than one-half of dependent's support?

Enter number of other dependents ▶

7 Total number of exemptions claimed . . . . Add numbers entered in boxes above ▶ 1

Income

Please attach Copy B of your Forms W–2 here.

If you do not have a W–2, see page 5 of Instructions.

Please attach check or money order here.

8	Wages, salaries, tips, and other employee compensation	8	
9	Interest income (If over $400, attach Schedule B)	9	
10a	Dividends (If over $400, attach Schedule B).525. 00 , 10b Exclusion .100 00		
10c	Subtract line 10b from line 10a	10c	425 00
11	State and local income tax refunds (does not apply unless refund is for year you itemized deductions)	11	
12	Alimony received	12	
13	Business income or (loss) (attach Schedule C)	13	34,421 00
14	Capital gain or (loss) (attach Schedule D)	14	
15	Taxable part of capital gain distributions not reported on Schedule D (see page 9 of Instructions) . .	15	
16	Net gain or (loss) from Supplemental Schedule of Gains and Losses (attach Form 4797)	16	
17	Fully taxable pensions and annuities not reported on Schedule E	17	
18	Pensions, annuities, rents, royalties, partnerships, estates or trusts, etc. (attach Schedule E)	18	
19	Farm income or (loss) (attach Schedule F)	19	
20	Other income (state nature and source—see page 10 of Instructions) ▶-------------------- ---	20	
21	Total income. Add lines 8, 9, and 10c through 20 . . . . ▶	21	34,486 00

Adjustments to Income

22	Moving expense (attach Form 3903)	22
23	Employee business expenses (attach Form 2106) . .	23
24	Payments to an IRA (see page 10 of Instructions)	24
25	Payments to a Keogh (H.R. 10) retirement plan . . .	25
26	Interest penalty due to early withdrawal of savings	26
27	Alimony paid (see page 10 of Instructions)	27

28	Total adjustments. Add lines 22 through 27 . . . . ▶	28	0

Adjusted Gross Income

29	Subtract line 28 from line 21	29	34,486 00
30	Disability income exclusion (attach Form 2440)	30	0
31	Adjusted gross income. Subtract line 30 from line 29. If this line is less than $8,000, see page 2 of Instructions. If you want IRS to figure your tax, see page 4 of Instructions . . . . ▶	31	34,486 00

☆ U.S. GOVERNMENT PRINTING OFFICE: 1978—O-263-303 13-2567299

Form 1040 (1978)

Tax Compu- tation	32 Amount from line 31	32	34,486 00
	33 If you do not itemize deductions, enter zero . . . . } If you itemize, complete Schedule A (Form 1040) and enter the amount from Schedule A, line 41	33	O
	Caution: If you have unearned income and can be claimed as a dependent on your parent's return, check here ▶ ☐ and see page 11 of the Instructions. Also see page 11 of the Instructions if: • You are married filing a separate return and your spouse itemizes deductions, OR • You file Form 4563, OR • You are a dual-status alien.		
	34 Subtract line 33 from line 32. Use the amount on line 34 to find your tax from the Tax Tables, or to figure your tax on Schedule TC, Part I . . . . Use Schedule TC, Part I, and the Tax Rate Schedules ONLY if: • The amount on line 34 is more than $20,000 ($40,000 if you checked Filing Status Box 2 or 5), OR • You have more exemptions than those covered in the Tax Table for your filing status, OR • You use any of these forms to figure your tax: Schedule D, Schedule G, or Form 4726. Otherwise, you MUST use the Tax Tables to find your tax.	34	34,486 00
	35 Tax. Enter tax here and check if from ☐ Tax Tables or ☑ Schedule TC	35	9,901 20
	36 Additional taxes. (See page 11 of Instructions.) Enter total and check if from ☐ Form 4970, } ☐ Form 4972, ☐ Form 5544, or ☐ Section 72(m)(5) penalty tax . . .	36	O
	37 Total. Add lines 35 and 36 . . . . ▶	37	

Credits	38 Credit for contributions to candidates for public office . .	38		
	39 Credit for the elderly (attach Schedules R&RP)	39		
	40 Credit for child and dependent care expenses (attach Form 2441) .	40		
	41 Investment credit (attach Form 3468)	41		
	42 Foreign tax credit (attach Form 1116)	42		
	43 Work Incentive (WIN) Credit (attach Form 4874)	43		
	44 New jobs credit (attach Form 5884)	44		
	45 Residential energy credits (see page 12 of Instructions, attach Form 5695) . .	45		
	46 Total credits. Add lines 38 through 45	46	O
	47 Balance. Subtract line 46 from line 37 and enter difference (but not less than zero) . ▶	47	9,901 20

Other Taxes	48 Self-employment tax (attach Schedule SE)	48	1,433 70
	49 Minimum tax. Check here ▶ ☐ and attach Form 4625	49	
	50 Tax from recomputing prior-year investment credit (attach Form 4255)	50	
	51 Social security (FICA) tax on tip income not reported to employer (attach Form 4137) . .	51	
	52 Uncollected employee FICA and RRTA tax on tips (from Form W–2)	52	
	53 Tax on an IRA (attach Form 5329)	53	
	54 Total tax. Add lines 47 through 53 . . . . ▶	54	11,334 90

Payments Attach Forms W–2, W–2G, and W–2P to front.	55 Total Federal income tax withheld	55		
	56 1978 estimated tax payments and credit from 1977 return .	56		
	57 Earned income credit. If line 31 is under $8,000, see page 2 of Instructions. If eligible, enter child's name ▶.............	57		
	58 Amount paid with Form 4868	58		
	59 Excess FICA and RRTA tax withheld (two or more employers)	59		
	60 Credit for Federal tax on special fuels and oils (attach Form 4136) .	60		
	61 Regulated Investment Company credit (attach Form 2439) .	61		
	62 Total. Add lines 55 through 61 . . . . ▶	62	

Refund or Due	63 If line 62 is larger than line 54, enter amount OVERPAID . . . . ▶	63	
	64 Amount of line 63 to be REFUNDED TO YOU . . . . ▶	64	
	65 Amount of line 63 to be credited on 1979 estimated tax. ▶	65	
	66 If line 54 is larger than line 62, enter BALANCE DUE. Attach check or money order for full amount payable to "Internal Revenue Service." Write your social security number on check or money order . . ▶ (Check ▶ ☐ if Form 2210 (2210F) is attached. See page 14 of instructions.) ▶ $	66	

Under penalties of perjury, I declare that I have examined this return, including accompanying schedules and statements, and to the best of my knowledge and belief, it is true, correct, and complete. Declaration of preparer (other than taxpayer) is based on all information of which preparer has any knowledge.

Please Sign Here	Your signature	Date	Spouse's signature (if filing jointly, BOTH must sign even if only one had income)
	Paid Preparer's Information	Preparer's signature ▶	Preparer's social security no.	Check if self-employed ▶ ☐
		Firm's name (or yours, if self-employed), address and ZIP code ▶	E.I. No. ▶
			Date ▶

Profit or (Loss) From Business or Profession
(Sole Proprietorship)
Partnerships, Joint Ventures, etc., Must File Form 1065.
► Attach to Form 1040. ► See Instructions for Schedule C (Form 1040).

1978

Name of proprietor	Social security number of proprietor
GEOFFREY FOURMYLE	000 00 0000

A Main business activity (see Instructions) ► ENGINEER ; product ►
B Business name ► GEOFFREY FOURMYLE
C Employer identification number ► 00-0000000
D Business address (number and street) ► 5217 CERES BOULEVARD

C

City, State and ZIP code ► SAN FRANCISCO CA 94701
E Accounting method: (1) ☑ Cash (2) ☐ Accrual (3) ☐ Other (specify) ►
F Method(s) used to value closing inventory:
(1) ☐ Cost (2) ☐ Lower of cost or market (3) ☐ Other (if other, attach explanation)

	Yes	No
G Was there any major change in determining quantities, costs, or valuations between opening and closing inventory? . . If "Yes," attach explanation.		✔
H Does this business activity involve oil or gas, movies or video tapes, or leasing personal (section 1245) property to others? (See page 25 of the Instructions.)	✔	
I Did you deduct expenses for an office in your home?		✔

Part I Income

1 a Gross receipts or sales	1a		
b Returns and allowances	1b		
c Balance (subtract line 1b from line 1a)	1c		
2 Cost of goods sold and/or operations (Schedule C-1, line 8)	2		
3 Gross profit (subtract line 2 from line 1c)	3		
4 Other income (attach schedule)	4	45,000	00
5 Total income (add lines 3 and 4) . . . . ►	5	45,000	00

Part II Deductions

			28 Telephone	489	00
6 Advertising			28 Telephone	489	00
7 Amortization			29 Travel and entertainment . . .	250	00
8 Bad debts from sales or services .			30 Utilities	240	00
9 Bank charges			31 a Wages . . .		
10 Car and truck expenses			b New Jobs Credit .		
11 Commissions			c Subtract line 31b from line 31a .		
12 Depletion			32 Other expenses (specify):		
13 Depreciation (explain in Schedule C-2)	500	00	a		
14 Dues and publications	100	00	b		
15 Employee benefit programs . . .			c		
16 Freight (not included on Schedule C-1)			d		
17 Insurance			e		
18 Interest on business indebtedness			f		
19 Laundry and cleaning			g		
20 Legal and professional services .			h		
21 Office supplies			i		
22 Pension and profit-sharing plans .	6,000	00	j		
23 Postage			k		
24 Rent on business property . . .	3,000	00	l		
25 Repairs			m		
26 Supplies (not included on Schedule C-1)			n		
27 Taxes			o		
			p		
			q		
			r		

33 Total deductions (add amounts in columns for lines 6 through 32r) . . . . ►	33	10,579	00
34 Net profit or (loss) (subtract line 33 from line 5). Enter here and on Form 1040, line 13. ALSO enter on Schedule SE (Form 1040), line 5a. (For "at risk" provisions, see page 25 of Instructions.) . . . . ►	34	34,421	00

263-056-2

SCHEDULE C-1.—Cost of Goods Sold and/or Operations (See Schedule C Instructions for Part I, Line 2)

1 Inventory at beginning of year (if different from last year's closing inventory, attach explanation) .	**1**	
2 a Purchases	**2a**	
b Cost of items withdrawn for personal use	**2b**	
c Balance (subtract line 2b from line 2a)	**2c**	
3 Cost of labor (do not include salary paid to yourself)	**3**	
4 Materials and supplies	**4**	
5 Other costs (attach schedule)	**5**	
6 Add lines 1, 2c, and 3 through 5	**6**	
7 Inventory at end of year	**7**	
8 Cost of goods sold and/or operations (subtract line 7 from line 6). Enter here and on Part I, line 2. ▶	**8**	

SCHEDULE C-2.—Depreciation (See Schedule C Instructions for line 13)
If you need more space, please use Form 4562.

Description of property (a)	Date acquired (b)	Cost or other basis (c)	Depreciation allowed or allowable in prior years (d)	Method of computing depreciation (e)	Life or rate (f)	Depreciation for this year (g)
1 Total additional first-year depreciation (do not include in items below)——▶						
2 Other depreciation:						
Buildings						
Furniture and fixtures	1 1 78	5,000.00	—	STRAIGHT LINE	10 YRS	500 00
Transportation equipment . .						
Machinery and other equipment .						
Other (Specify)						
3 Totals		5,000.00			**3**	500 00
4 Depreciation claimed in Schedule C-1					**4**	
5 **Balance** (subtract line 4 from line 3). Enter here and on Part II, line 13 . . . . ▶					**5**	500 00

SCHEDULE C-3.—Expense Account Information (See Schedule C Instructions for Schedule C-3)

Enter information for yourself and your five highest paid employees. In determining the five highest paid employees, add expense account allowances to the salaries and wages. However, you don't have to provide the information for any employee for whom the combined amount is less than $25,000, or for yourself if your expense account allowance plus line 34, page 1, is less than $25,000.

Name (a)	Expense account (b)	Salaries and Wages (c)
Owner		
1		
2		
3		
4		
5		

Did you claim a deduction for expenses connected with:	Yes	No
A Entertainment facility (boat, resort, ranch, etc.)?		
B Living accommodations (except employees on business)?		
C Employees' families at conventions or meetings?		
If "Yes," were any of these conventions or meetings outside the U.S. or its possessions? (See page 26 of Instructions) . .		
D Vacations for employees or their families not reported on Form W-2?		

☆ U.S. GOVERNMENT PRINTING OFFICE : 1978—O-263-056   263-056-1

Computation of Social Security Self-Employment Tax

1978

▶ Each self-employed person must file a Schedule SE. ▶ Attach to Form 1040.
▶ See Instructions for Schedule SE (Form 1040).

● If you had wages, including tips, of $17,700 or more that were subject to social security or railroad retirement taxes, do not fill in this schedule (unless you are eligible for the Earned Income Credit). See Instructions.

● If you had more than one business, combine profits and losses from all your businesses and farms on this Schedule SE.

Important.—The self-employment income reported below will be credited to your social security record and used in figuring social security benefits.

NAME OF SELF-EMPLOYED PERSON (AS SHOWN ON SOCIAL SECURITY CARD)	Social security number of self-employed person ▶
GEOFFREY FOURMYLE	000 00 0000

● If you have only farm income complete Parts I and III. ● If you have only nonfarm income complete Parts II and III.
● If you have both farm and nonfarm income complete Parts I, II, and III.

Part I Computation of Net Earnings from FARM Self-Employment

You may elect to compute your net farm earnings using the OPTIONAL METHOD, line 3, instead of using the Regular Method, line 2, if your gross profits are: (1) $2,400 or less, or (2) more than $2,400 and net profits are less than $1,600. However, lines 1 and 2 must be completed even if you elect to use the FARM OPTIONAL METHOD.

REGULAR METHOD	a Schedule F, line 58 (cash method), or line 76 (accrual method) .	**1a**	
1 Net profit or (loss) from:	b Farm partnerships	**1b**	
2 Net earnings from farm self-employment (add lines 1a and b)		**2**	
FARM OPTIONAL METHOD 3 If gross profits from farming ¹ are:	a Not more than $2,400, enter two-thirds of the gross profits . .		
	b More than $2,400 and the net farm profit is less than $1,600, enter $1,600	**3**	

¹ Gross profits from farming are the total gross profits from Schedule F, line 32 (cash method), or line 74 (accrual method), plus the distributive share of gross profits from farm partnerships (Schedule K-1 (Form 1065), line 3) as explained in Instructions for Schedule SE.

4 Enter here and on line 12a, the amount on line 2, or line 3 if you elect the farm optional method . | **4** |

Part II Computation of Net Earnings from NONFARM Self-Employment

	a Schedule C, line 34. (Enter combined amount if more than one business.) .	**5a**	34,421 00
	b Partnerships, joint ventures, etc. (other than farming)	**5b**	
REGULAR METHOD 5 Net profit or (loss) from:	c Service as a minister, member of a religious order, or a Christian Science practitioner. (Include rental value of parsonage or rental allowance furnished.) If you filed Form 4361 and have not revoked that exemption, check here ▶ ☐ and enter zero on this line	**5c**	
	d Service with a foreign government or international organization	**5d**	
	e Other—Specify ▶...	**5e**	

6 Total (add lines 5a through e) . . . . | **6** | 34,421 00 |
7 Enter adjustments if any (attach statement, see page 27 of instructions) . . . . | **7** | |
8 Adjusted net earnings or (loss) from nonfarm self-employment (line 6, as adjusted by line 7) . . | **8** | 34,421 00 |

If line 8 is $1,600 or more **OR** if you do not elect to use the Nonfarm Optional Method, skip lines 9 through 11 and enter amount from line 8 on line 12b, Part III.

Note: You may use the nonfarm optional method (line 9 through line 11) only if line 8 is less than $1,600 and less than two-thirds of your gross nonfarm profits,¹ and you had actual net earnings from self-employment of $400 or more for at least 2 of the 3 following years: 1975, 1976, and 1977. The nonfarm optional method can only be used for 5 tax years.

NONFARM OPTIONAL METHOD

9 a Maximum amount reportable, under both optional methods combined (farm and nonfarm) . . | **9a** | $1,600 00 |
  b Enter amount from line 3. (If you did not elect to use the farm optional method, enter zero) . | **9b** | |
  c Balance (subtract line 9b from line 9a) . . . . | **9c** | |
10 Enter two-thirds of gross nonfarm profits ² or $1,600, whichever is smaller . . . . | **10** | |
11 Enter here and on line 12b, the amount on line 9c or line 10, whichever is smaller . . . . | **11** | |

² Gross profits from nonfarm business are the total gross profits from Schedule C, line 3, plus the distributive share of gross profits from nonfarm partnerships (Schedule K-1 (Form 1065), line 15(a)) as explained in Instructions for Schedule SE. Also, include gross profits from services reported on line 5c, d, and e, as adjusted by line 7.

Part III Computation of Social Security Self-Employment Tax

12 Net earnings or (loss): a From farming (from line 4) . . . . | **12a** | |
  b From nonfarm (from line 8, or line 11 if you elect to use the Nonfarm Optional Method) . . . | **12b** | 34,421 00 |
13 Total net earnings or (loss) from self-employment reported on lines 12a and 12b. (If line 13 is less than $400, you are not subject to self-employment tax. Do not fill in rest of schedule.) . . . . | **13** | 34,421 00 |
14 The largest amount of combined wages and self-employment earnings subject to social security or railroad retirement taxes for 1978 is . . . . | **14** | $17,700 00 |
15 a Total "FICA" wages (from Forms W-2) and "RRTA" compensation . . . | **15a** | |
  b Unreported tips subject to FICA tax from Form 4137, line 9 or to RRTA . . | **15b** | |
  c Add lines 15a and b . . . . | **15c** | 0 |
16 Balance (subtract line 15c from line 14) . . . . | **16** | 34,421 00 |
17 Self-employment income—line 13 or 16, whichever is smaller . . . . | **17** | 34,421 00 |
18 Self-employment tax. (If line 17 is $17,700, enter $1,433.70; if less, multiply the amount on line 17 by .081.) Enter here and on Form 1040, line 48 . . . . | **18** | 1,433 70 |

☆ U.S. GOVERNMENT PRINTING OFFICE : 1978—O-263-062

263-062-1

SE

109

Form **1120**	U.S. Corporation Income Tax Return	**1978**

Department of the Treasury
Internal Revenue Service

For calendar year 1978 or other taxable year beginning
.... , 1978, ending .... , 19......

Check if a—
A Consolidated return ☐
B Personal Holding Co. ☐
C Business Code No. (See Page 8 of instructions)
8599

Use IRS label. Otherwise please print or type.

Name TIFFANY FIELD + Co., INC.

Number and street 795 FIFTH AVENUE

City or town, State, and ZIP code NEW YORK, NY 10021

D Employer identification number (see instruction W)
00-0000000

E Date incorporated 1/1/78

F Enter total assets (see instruction X)
$50,000.00

Gross Income

1 Gross receipts or gross sales.................Less: Returns and allowances...........	1	
2 Less: Cost of goods sold (Schedule A) and/or operations (attach schedule)	2	
3 Gross profit	3	
4 Dividends (Schedule C)	4	2,000.00
5 Interest on obligations of the United States and U.S. instrumentalities	5	
6 Other interest	6	
7 Gross rents	7	
8 Gross royalties	8	
9 (a) Capital gain net income (attach separate Schedule D)	9(a)	
(b) Net gain or (loss) from Form 4797, line 11, Part II (attach Form 4797)	9(b)	
10 Other income (see instructions—attach schedule)	10	70,000.00
11 TOTAL income—Add lines 3 through 10	11	72,000.00

Deductions

12 Compensation of officers (Schedule E)	12	30,000.00
13 (a) Salaries and wages........................ 13(b) Less new jobs credit........................ Balance ▶	13(c)	
14 Repairs (see instructions)	14	
15 Bad debts (Schedule F if reserve method is used)	15	
16 Rents	16	
17 Taxes	17	
18 Interest	18	
19 Contributions (not over 5% of line 30 adjusted per instructions—attach schedule)	19	500.00
20 Amortization (attach schedule)	20	
21 Depreciation from Form 4562 (attach Form 4562) ...., less depreciation claimed in Schedule A and elsewhere on return ...., Balance ▶	21	500.00
22 Depletion	22	
23 Advertising	23	
24 Pension, profit-sharing, etc. plans (see instructions) (enter number of plans ▶ ....1........) .	24	7,500.00
25 Employee benefit programs (see instructions)	25	
26 Other deductions (attach schedule)	26	17,000.00
27 TOTAL deductions—Add lines 12 through 26	27	55,500.00
28 Taxable income before net operating loss deduction and special deductions (subtract line 27 from line 11) .	28	16,500.00
29 Less: (a) Net operating loss deduction (see instructions—attach schedule) . . 29(a)		
(b) Special deductions (Schedule I) . . . . 29(b) 1,700.00	29	1,700.00
30 Taxable income (subtract line 29 from line 28)	30	14,800.00

Tax

31 TOTAL TAX (Schedule J)	31	2,960.00
32 Credits: (a) Overpayment from 1977 allowed as a credit . . .		
(b) 1978 estimated tax payments		
(c) Less refund of 1978 estimated tax applied for on Form 4466 . ( )		
(d) Tax deposited: Form 7004........... Form 7005 (attach)........... Total ▶		
(e) Credit from regulated investment companies (attach Form 2439) .		
(f) U.S. tax on special fuels, nonhighway gas and lubricating oil (attach Form 4136) . .	32	
33 TAX DUE (subtract line 32 from line 31). See instruction G for depositary method of payment .	33	
(Check ▶ ☐ if Form 2220 is attached. See page 3 of instructions.) ▶ $..................		
34 OVERPAYMENT (subtract line 31 from line 32) . . . . Refunded ▶	34	
35 Enter amount of line 34 you want: Credited to 1979 estimated tax ▶ Refunded ▶	35	

Please Sign Here

Under penalties of perjury, I declare that I have examined this return, including accompanying schedules and statements, and to the best of my knowledge and belief, it is true, correct, and complete. Declaration of preparer (other than taxpayer) is based on all information of which preparer has any knowledge.

▶ Signature of officer .... Date ▶ Title ....

Paid Preparer's Information

Preparer's signature ▶	Preparer's social security no.	Check if self-employed ▶ ☐
Firm's name (or yours, if self-employed), address and ZIP code ▶	E.I. No. ▶	
	Date ▶	

263–104–1

110

Schedule A   Cost of Goods Sold (See instruction 2)

1 Inventory at beginning of year . . . .
2 Merchandise bought for manufacture or sale . . . .
3 Salaries and wages . . . .
4 Other costs (attach schedule) . . . .
5 Total . . . .
6 Less: Inventory at end of year . . . .
7 Cost of goods sold—Enter here and on line 2, page 1 . . . .
8 (a) Check valuation method(s) used for total closing inventory:
   ☐ Cost   ☐ Lower of cost or market   ☐ Other (if "other," attach explanation)
   (b) Check if this is the first year LIFO inventory method was adopted and used. (If checked, attach Form 970.) . . . . . . ☐
   (c) If the LIFO inventory method was used for this taxable year, enter percentage (or amounts) of closing inventory computed under LIFO . . . .
   (d) Is the corporation engaged in manufacturing activities? . . . .   ☐ Yes ☐ No
   If "Yes," are inventories valued under Regulations section 1.471–11 (full absorption accounting method)? .   ☐ Yes ☐ No
   (e) Was there any substantial change in determining quantities, cost, or valuations between opening and closing inventory? . . .   ☐ Yes ☐ No
   If "Yes," attach explanation.

Schedule C   Dividends (See instruction 4)

1 Domestic corporations subject to 85% deduction 2,000.00
2 Certain preferred stock of public utilities . . . .
3 Foreign corporations subject to 85% deduction . . . .
4 Dividends from wholly-owned foreign subsidiaries subject to 100% deduction (section 245(b)) . . . . .
5 Other dividends from foreign corporations . . . .
6 Includable income from controlled foreign corporations under subpart F (attach Forms 3646) . . . . .
7 Foreign dividend gross-up (section 78) . . . .
8 Qualifying dividends received from affiliated groups and subject to the 100% deduction (section 243(a)(3)) .
9 Taxable dividends from a DISC or former DISC not included in line 1 (section 246(d)) . . . .
10 Other dividends . . . .
11 Total—Enter here and on line 4, page 1 . . . .   2,000.00

Schedule E   Compensation of Officers (See instruction 12)

| 1. Name of officer | 2. Social security number | 3. Time devoted to business | Percent of corporation stock owned | | 6. Amount of compensation | 7. Expense account allowances |
			4. Common	5. Preferred		
TIFFANY FIELD	000-00-0000	ALL	100		30,000.00	
Total compensation of officers—Enter here and on line 12, page 1	30,000.00	

Schedule F   Bad Debts—Reserve Method (See instruction 15)

| 1. Year | 2. Trade notes and accounts receivable outstanding at end of year | 3. Sales on account | Amount added to reserve | | 6. Amount charged against reserve | 7. Reserve for bad debts at end of year |
			4. Current year's provision	5. Recoveries		
1973						
1974						
1975						
1976						
1977						
1978						

Schedule I   Special Deductions

1 (a) 85% of Schedule C, line 1 . . . .   1,700.00
  (b) 60.208% of Schedule C, line 2 . . . .
  (c) 85% of Schedule C, line 3 . . . .
  (d) 100% of Schedule C, line 4 . . . .
2 Total—See instructions for limitation . . . .
3 100% of Schedule C, line 8 . . . .
4 Dividends paid on certain preferred stock of public utilities (see instructions) . . . .
5 Western Hemisphere trade corporations (see instructions) . . . .
6 Total special deductions—Add lines 2 through 5. Enter here and on line 29(b), page 1 . . . .   1,700.00

263–104–2

111

(Fiscal year corporations, omit lines 1 through 8 and enter on line 9, the amount from Form 1120—FY (1978–79), line 5, Part III)

1 Taxable income (line 30, page 1)	14,800.00
2 Enter line 1 or $25,000, whichever is less. (Members of a controlled group enter one-half of surtax allocation, see instructions) .	14,800.00
3 Subtract line 2 from line 1	0
4 Enter line 3 or $25,000, whichever is less. (Members of a controlled group enter one-half of surtax allocation, see instructions) .	0
5 Subtract line 4 from line 3	0
6 20% of line 2	2,960.00
7 22% of line 4	0
8 48% of line 5	0
9 Income tax (Sum of lines 6, 7 and 8 or alternative tax from separate Schedule D, whichever is less)	2,960.00

10 (a) Foreign tax credit (attach Form 1118)		
(b) Investment credit (attach Form 3468)		
(c) Work incentive (WIN) credit (attach Form 4874)		
(d) New jobs credit (attach Form 5884)		

11 Total of lines 10(a), (b), (c), and (d)	0
12 Subtract line 11 from line 9	2,960.00
13 Personal holding company tax (attach Schedule PH (Form 1120))	
14 Tax from recomputing a prior year investment credit (attach Form 4255)	
15 Tax from recomputing a prior year WIN credit (see instructions—attach computation)	
16 Minimum tax on tax preference items (see instructions—attach Form 4626)	
17 Total tax—Add lines 12 through 16. Enter here and on line 31, page 1	2,960.00

Schedule K Record of Federal Tax Deposits Tax Class Number 503
(List deposits in order of date made—See Instruction G)

Date of deposit	Amount	Date of deposit	Amount	Date of deposit	Amount

G (1) Did you claim a deduction for expenses connected with: **Yes No**
  (a) Entertainment facility (boat, resort, ranch, etc.)? . . .   ✓
  (b) Living accommodations (except for employees on business)? . . . .   ✓
  (c) Employee's families at conventions or meetings? . . .   ✓
  If "Yes," were any of these conventions or meetings outside the United States or its possessions? . . . . . .   ✓
  (d) Employee or family vacations not reported on Form W-2? .   ✓
(2), Enter total amount claimed on Form 1120 for entertainment, entertainment facilities, gifts, travel, and conventions of the type for which substantiation is required under section 274(d). (See instruction Y.) ▶ ....

H (1) Did you at the end of the taxable year own, directly or indirectly, 50% or more of the voting stock of a domestic corporation? (For rules of attribution, see section 267(c).) . .
  If "Yes," attach a schedule showing: (a) name, address, and identifying number; (b) percentage owned; (c) taxable income or (loss) (e.g., if a Form 1120: from Form 1120, line 28, page 1) of such corporation for the taxable year ending with or within your taxable year; (d) highest amount owed by you to such corporation during the year; and (e) highest amount owed to you by such corporation during the year.
(2) Did any individual, partnership, corporation, estate or trust at the end of the taxable year own, directly or indirectly, 50% or more of your voting stock? (For rules of attribution, see section 267(c).) If "Yes," complete (a) through (e) . . .   ✓
  (a) Attach a schedule showing name, address, and identifying number; (b) Enter percentage owned ▶ **100**
  (c) Was the owner of such voting stock a person other than a U.S. person? (See Instruction S.) . . . .   ✓
  If "Yes," enter owner's country ▶ ....
  ....
  (d) Enter highest amount owed by you to such owner during the year ▶

  (e) Enter highest amount owed to you by such owner during the year ▶   **Yes No**
  (Note: For purposes of H(1) and H(2), "highest amount owed" includes loans and accounts receivable/payable.)
I Did you ever declare a stock dividend? . . . .   ✓
J Taxable income or (loss) from Form 1120, line 28, page 1, for your taxable year beginning in:
  1975 ...., 1976 ...., 1977 ....
K Were you a member of a controlled group subject to the provisions of section 1561? If "Yes," check the type of relationship . .
  (1) ☐ parent-subsidiary   (2) ☐ brother-sister
  (3) ☐ combination of (1) and (2) (See section 1563.)
L Refer to page 8 of instructions and state the principal:
  Business activity ....
  Product or service ... **DESIGNING** ....
M Did you file all required Forms 1087, 1096 and 1099? . **N/A**
N Were you a U.S. shareholder of any controlled foreign corporation? (See sections 951 and 957.) If "Yes," attach Form 3646 for each such corporation . . . .
O Did you, at any time during the taxable year, have an interest in or signature or other authority over a bank, securities or other financial account in a foreign country (see instruction V)? . .   ✓
P Were you the grantor of, or transferor to, a foreign trust during any taxable year, which foreign trust was in being during the current taxable year, whether or not you have any beneficial interest in such trust? If "Yes," you may be required to file Forms 3520, 3520–A, or 926 . . . .   ✓
Q During this taxable year, did you pay dividends (other than stock dividends and distributions in exchange for stock) in excess of your current and accumulated earnings and profits? (See sections 301 and 316.) . . . .   ✓
  If "Yes," file Form 5452. If this is a consolidated return, answer here for parent corporation and on Form 851, Affiliation Schedule, for each subsidiary.

263–104–2

112

Schedule L — Balance Sheets

ASSETS	Beginning of taxable year		End of taxable year	
	(A) Amount	(B) Total	(C) Amount	(D) Total
1 Cash		7,000.00		17,000.00
2 Trade notes and accounts receivable				
(a) Less allowance for bad debts				
3 Inventories				
4 Gov't obligations: (a) U.S. and instrumentalities .				
(b) State, subdivisions thereof, etc.				
5 Other current assets (attach schedule)		4,000.00		6,000.00
6 Loans to stockholders				
7 Mortgage and real estate loans				
8 Other investments (attach schedule) (STOCK)		10,000.00		12,000.00
9 Buildings and other fixed depreciable assets . .	5,000.00		5,000.00	
(a) Less accumulated depreciation		5,000.00	500.00	4,500.00
10 Depletable assets				
(a) Less accumulated depletion				
11 Land (net of any amortization)				
12 Intangible assets (amortizable only)				
(a) Less accumulated amortization				
13 Other assets (attach schedule)		2,250.00		10,500.00
14 Total assets		28,250.00		50,000.00
LIABILITIES AND STOCKHOLDERS' EQUITY				
15 Accounts payable		8,250.00		6,500.00
16 Mtges., notes, bonds payable in less than 1 yr. . .				
17 Other current liabilities (attach schedule) . . .				7,000.00
18 Loans from stockholders				
19 Mtges., notes, bonds payable in 1 yr. or more . .				
20 Other liabilities (attach schedule)				
21 Capital stock: (a) Preferred stock				
(b) Common stock	10,000.00	10,000.00	10,000.00	10,000.00
22 Paid-in or capital surplus		10,000.00		10,000.00
23 Retained earnings—Appropriated (attach sch.) . .				
24 Retained earnings—Unappropriated				16,500.00
25 Less cost of treasury stock		( )		( )
26 Total liabilities and stockholders' equity . . .				50,000.00

Schedule M-1 Reconciliation of Income Per Books With Income Per Return

1 Net income per books	16,500.00	7 Income recorded on books this year not in-	
2 Federal income tax		cluded in this return (itemize)	
3 Excess of capital losses over capital gains . . .		(a) Tax-exempt interest $	
4 Income subject to tax not recorded on books this year			
(itemize)			
		8 Deductions in this tax return not charged	
5 Expenses recorded on books this year not deducted in		against book income this year (itemize)	
this return (itemize)		(a) Depreciation . . $	
(a) Depreciation . . . $		(b) Depletion . . . $	
(b) Depletion . . . . $			
		9 Total of lines 7 and 8	
6 Total of lines 1 through 5	16,500.00	10 Income (line 28, page 1)—line 6 less 9 .	16,500.00

Schedule M-2 Analysis of Unappropriated Retained Earnings Per Books (line 24 above)

1 Balance at beginning of year	—	5 Distributions: (a) Cash	
2 Net income per books	16,500.00	(b) Stock	
3 Other increases (itemize)		(c) Property	
		6 Other decreases (itemize)	
		7 Total of lines 5 and 6	
4 Total of lines 1, 2, and 3	16,500.00	8 Balance at end of year (line 4 less 7) . . .	16,500.00

Form 1040 — U.S. Individual Income Tax Return 1978

Department of the Treasury—Internal Revenue Service

For the year January 1–December 31, 1978, or other tax year beginning _____, 1978, ending _____, 19 ____.

For Privacy Act Notice, see page 3 of Instructions

Use IRS label. Otherwise, please print or type.

Your first name and initial (if joint return, also give spouse's name and initial): **TIFFANY**
Last name: **FIELD**

Present home address (Number and street, including apartment number, or rural route): **795 FIFTH AVENUE**

City, town or post office, State and ZIP code: **NEW YORK NY 10021**

Your social security number: **000 00 0000**

Spouse's social security no.:

Your occupation: **DESIGNER**

Spouse's occupation:

Do you want $1 to go to the Presidential Election Campaign Fund? [✓] Yes [ ] No
If joint return, does your spouse want $1 to go to this fund? . . [ ] Yes [ ] No

Note: Checking Yes will not increase your tax or reduce your refund.

Filing Status

Check only one box.

1. [✓] Single
2. [ ] Married filing joint return (even if only one had income)
3. [ ] Married filing separate return. If spouse is also filing, give spouse's social security number in the space above and enter full name here ▶ _____
4. [ ] Unmarried head of household. Enter qualifying name ▶ _____ . See page 6 of Instructions.
5. [ ] Qualifying widow(er) with dependent child (Year spouse died ▶ 19 ____). See page 6 of Instructions.

Exemptions

Always check the box labeled Yourself. Check other boxes if they apply.

6a [✓] Yourself [ ] 65 or over [ ] Blind
b [ ] Spouse [ ] 65 or over [ ] Blind

Enter number of boxes checked on 6a and b ▶ **1**

c First names of your dependent children who lived with you ▶ _____

Enter number of children listed ▶

d Other dependents: (1) Name	(2) Relationship	(3) Number of months lived in your home	(4) Did dependent have income of $750 or more?	(5) Did you provide more than one-half of dependent's support?

Enter number of other dependents ▶

Add numbers entered in boxes above ▶ **1**

7 Total number of exemptions claimed . . . .

Income

Please attach Copy B of your Forms W–2 here.

If you do not have a W–2, see page 5 of Instructions.

Please attach check or money order here.

8 Wages, salaries, tips, and other employee compensation	8	30,000	00
9 Interest income (If over $400, attach Schedule B)	9		
10a Dividends (If over $400, attach Schedule B) _____, 10b Exclusion _____			
10c Subtract line 10b from line 10a	10c		
11 State and local income tax refunds (does not apply unless refund is for year you itemized deductions)	11		
12 Alimony received	12		
13 Business income or (loss) (attach Schedule C)	13		
14 Capital gain or (loss) (attach Schedule D)	14		
15 Taxable part of capital gain distributions not reported on Schedule D (see page 9 of Instructions) . .	15		
16 Net gain or (loss) from Supplemental Schedule of Gains and Losses (attach Form 4797)	16		
17 Fully taxable pensions and annuities not reported on Schedule E	17		
18 Pensions, annuities, rents, royalties, partnerships, estates or trusts, etc. (attach Schedule E)	18		
19 Farm income or (loss) (attach Schedule F)	19		
20 Other income (state nature and source—see page 10 of Instructions) ▶ _____	20		
21 Total income. Add lines 8, 9, and 10c through 20 . . . . ▶	21	30,000	00

Adjustments to Income

22 Moving expense (attach Form 3903)	22			
23 Employee business expenses (attach Form 2106) . .	23			
24 Payments to an IRA (see page 10 of Instructions) . .	24			
25 Payments to a Keogh (H.R. 10) retirement plan . . .	25			
26 Interest penalty due to early withdrawal of savings	26			
27 Alimony paid (see page 10 of Instructions)	27			
28 Total adjustments. Add lines 22 through 27 . . . . ▶		28	0	

Adjusted Gross Income

29 Subtract line 28 from line 21	29	30,000	00
30 Disability income exclusion (attach Form 2440)	30	0	
31 Adjusted gross income. Subtract line 30 from line 29. If this line is less than $8,000, see page 2 of Instructions. If you want IRS to figure your tax, see page 4 of Instructions . . . . ▶	31	30,000	00

Form 1040 (1978)

114

Tax Compu- tation	32 Amount from line 31	32	30,000	00
	33 If you do not itemize deductions, enter zero . . . . }	33	0	
	If you itemize, complete Schedule A (Form 1040) and enter the amount from Schedule A, line 41			
	Caution: If you have unearned income and can be claimed as a dependent on your parent's return, check here ▶ ☐ and see page 11 of the Instructions. Also see page 11 of the Instructions if:			
	• You are married filing a separate return and your spouse itemizes deductions, OR			
	• You file Form 4563, OR			
	• You are a dual-status alien.			
	34 Subtract line 33 from line 32. Use the amount on line 34 to find your tax from the Tax Tables, or to figure your tax on Schedule TC, Part I . . . . Use Schedule TC, Part I, and the Tax Rate Schedules ONLY if:	34	30,000	00
	• The amount on line 34 is more than $20,000 ($40,000 if you checked Filing Status Box 2 or 5), OR			
	• You have more exemptions than those covered in the Tax Table for your filing status, OR			
	• You use any of these forms to figure your tax: Schedule D, Schedule G, or Form 4726.			
	Otherwise, you MUST use the Tax Tables to find your tax.			
	35 Tax. Enter tax here and check if from ☐ Tax Tables or ☑ Schedule TC	35	7,882	50
	36 Additional taxes. (See page 11 of Instructions.) Enter total and check if from ☐ Form 4970, } ☐ Form 4972, ☐ Form 5544, or ☐ Section 72(m)(5) penalty tax . . .)	36	0	
	37 Total. Add lines 35 and 36 . . . . ▶	37	7,882	50
Credits	38 Credit for contributions to candidates for public office . .	38		
	39 Credit for the elderly (attach Schedules R&RP)	39		
	40 Credit for child and dependent care expenses (attach Form 2441) .	40		
	41 Investment credit (attach Form 3468)	41		
	42 Foreign tax credit (attach Form 1116)	42		
	43 Work Incentive (WIN) Credit (attach Form 4874)	43		
	44 New jobs credit (attach Form 5884)	44		
	45 Residential energy credits (see page 12 of Instructions, attach Form 5695) . .	45		
	46 Total credits. Add lines 38 through 45	46		
	47 Balance. Subtract line 46 from line 37 and enter difference (but not less than zero) . ▶	47		
Other Taxes	48 Self-employment tax (attach Schedule SE)	48		
	49 Minimum tax. Check here ▶ ☐ and attach Form 4625	49		
	50 Tax from recomputing prior-year Investment credit (attach Form 4255)	50		
	51 Social security (FICA) tax on tip income not reported to employer (attach Form 4137) . .	51		
	52 Uncollected employee FICA and RRTA tax on tips (from Form W-2)	52		
	53 Tax on an IRA (attach Form 5329)	53		
	54 Total tax. Add lines 47 through 53 . . . . ▶	54		
Payments Attach Forms W-2, W-2G, and W-2P to front.	55 Total Federal income tax withheld	55		
	56 1978 estimated tax payments and credit from 1977 return .	56		
	57 Earned income credit. If line 31 is under $8,000, see page 2 of Instructions. If eligible, enter child's name ▶..............................	57		
	58 Amount paid with Form 4868	58		
	59 Excess FICA and RRTA tax withheld (two or more employers)	59		
	60 Credit for Federal tax on special fuels and oils (attach Form 4136) .	60		
	61 Regulated Investment Company credit (attach Form 2439)	61		
	62 Total. Add lines 55 through 61 . . . . ▶	62		
Refund or Due	63 If line 62 is larger than line 54, enter amount OVERPAID . . . . ▶	63		
	64 Amount of line 63 to be REFUNDED TO YOU . . . . . . ▶	64		
	65 Amount of line 63 to be credited on 1979 estimated tax . ▶	65		
	66 If line 54 is larger than line 62, enter BALANCE DUE. Attach check or money order for full amount payable to "Internal Revenue Service." Write your social security number on check or money order . . ▶ (Check ▶ ☐ if Form 2210 (2210F) is attached. See page 14 of instructions.) ▶ $	66		

Please Sign Here

Under penalties of perjury, I declare that I have examined this return, including accompanying schedules and statements, and to the best of my knowledge and belief, it is true, correct, and complete. Declaration of preparer (other than taxpayer) is based on all information of which preparer has any knowledge.

▶ Your signature	Date	▶ Spouse's signature (if filing jointly, BOTH must sign even if only one had income)	

Paid Preparer's Information	Preparer's signature ▶	Preparer's social security no.	Check if self- employed ▶ ☐
	Firm's name (or yours, if self-employed), address and ZIP code ▶	E.I. No. ▶	
		Date ▶	

115

Department of the Treasury—Internal Revenue Service
U.S. Individual Income Tax Return 19**78**

| For Privacy Act Notice, see page 3 of Instructions | For the year January 1–December 31, 1978, or other tax year beginning | , 1978, ending | , 19 . |

Use IRS label. Other- wise, please print or type.	Your first name and initial (if joint return, also give spouse's name and initial) TIFFANY	Last name FIELD	Your social security number 000 00 0000
	Present home address (Number and street, including apartment number, or rural route) 795 FIFTH AVENUE		Spouse's social security no.
	City, town or post office, State and ZIP code NEW YORK NY 10021		Your occupation DESIGNER

Do you want $1 to go to the Presidential Election Campaign Fund? ✔Yes ☐No
If joint return, does your spouse want $1 to go to this fund? . . ☐Yes ☐No

Note: Checking Yes will not increase your tax or reduce your refund.

Spouse's occupation

Filing Status
Check only one box.

1 ✔ Single
2 ☐ Married filing joint return (even if only one had income)
3 ☐ Married filing separate return. If spouse is also filing, give spouse's social security number in the space above and enter full name here ▶
4 ☐ Unmarried head of household. Enter qualifying name ▶_____. See page 6 of Instructions.
5 ☐ Qualifying widow(er) with dependent child (Year spouse died ▶ 19). See page 6 of Instructions.

Exemptions
Always check the box labeled Yourself. Check other boxes if they apply.

6a ✔ Yourself ☐ 65 or over ☐ Blind — Enter number of boxes checked on 6a and b ▶ |1|
b ☐ Spouse ☐ 65 or over ☐ Blind
c First names of your dependent children who lived with you ▶_____ — Enter number of children listed ▶

d Other dependents: (1) Name	(2) Relationship	(3) Number of months lived in your home	(4) Did depend- ent have income of $750 or more?	(5) Did you provide more than one-half of dependent's support?	Enter number of other dependents ▶

Add numbers entered in boxes above ▶ |1|

7 Total number of exemptions claimed . . . . |8|

Income

Please attach Copy B of your Forms W–2 here.

If you do not have a W–2, see page 5 of Instructions.

8	Wages, salaries, tips, and other employee compensation	8	
9	Interest income (If over $400, attach Schedule B)	9	
10a	Dividends (If over $400, attach Schedule B). 2,000 00 , 10b Exclusion 100 00		
10c	Subtract line 10b from line 10a	10c	1,900 00
11	State and local income tax refunds (does not apply unless refund is for year you itemized deductions)	11	
12	Alimony received	12	
13	Business income or (loss) (attach Schedule C)	13	45,000 00
14	Capital gain or (loss) (attach Schedule D)	14	
15	Taxable part of capital gain distributions not reported on Schedule D (see page 9 of Instructions) . .	15	
16	Net gain or (loss) from Supplemental Schedule of Gains and Losses (attach Form 4797)	16	
17	Fully taxable pensions and annuities not reported on Schedule E	17	
18	Pensions, annuities, rents, royalties, partnerships, estates or trusts, etc. (attach Schedule E)	18	
19	Farm income or (loss) (attach Schedule F)	19	
20	Other income (state nature and source—see page 10 of Instructions) ▶_____	20	
21	Total income. Add lines 8, 9, and 10c through 20 . . . . ▶	21	46,900 00

Please attach check or money order here.

Adjustments to Income

22	Moving expense (attach Form 3903)	22			
23	Employee business expenses (attach Form 2106) . .	23			
24	Payments to an IRA (see page 10 of Instructions)	24			
25	Payments to a Keogh (H.R. 10) retirement plan . . .	25			
26	Interest penalty due to early withdrawal of savings	26			
27	Alimony paid (see page 10 of Instructions)	27			
28	Total adjustments. Add lines 22 through 27 . . . . ▶		28	0

Adjusted Gross Income

29	Subtract line 28 from line 21	29	46,900 00
30	Disability income exclusion (attach Form 2440)	30	0
31	Adjusted gross income. Subtract line 30 from line 29. If this line is less than $8,000, see page 2 of Instructions. If you want IRS to figure your tax, see page 4 of Instructions . . . . ▶	31	46,900 00

☆ U.S. GOVERNMENT PRINTING OFFICE: 1978—O-263-303 13-2687299

Form 1040 (1978)

Tax Computation	32 Amount from line 31	32	46,900	00
	33 If you do not itemize deductions, enter zero . . . . } If you itemize, complete Schedule A (Form 1040) and enter the amount from Schedule A, line 41 . . . . .)	33	0	
	Caution: If you have unearned income and can be claimed as a dependent on your parent's return, check here ▶ ☐ and see page 11 of the Instructions. Also see page 11 of the Instructions if: • You are married filing a separate return and your spouse itemizes deductions, OR • You file Form 4563, OR • You are a dual-status alien.			
	34 Subtract line 33 from line 32. Use the amount on line 34 to find your tax from the Tax Tables, or to figure your tax on Schedule TC, Part I . . . . Use Schedule TC, Part I, and the Tax Rate Schedules ONLY if: • The amount on line 34 is more than $20,000 ($40,000 if you checked Filing Status Box 2 or 5), OR • You have more exemptions than those covered in the Tax Table for your filing status, OR • You use any of these forms to figure your tax: Schedule D, Schedule G, or Form 4726. Otherwise, you MUST use the Tax Tables to find your tax.	34	46,900	00
	35 Tax. Enter tax here and check if from ☐ Tax Tables or ☑ Schedule TC	35	16,178	46
	36 Additional taxes. (See page 11 of Instructions.) Enter total and check if from ☐ Form 4970, } ☐ Form 4972, ☐ Form 5544, ☐ Form 5405, or ☐ Section 72(m)(5) penalty tax . . .)	36		
	37 Total. Add lines 35 and 36 . . . . ▶	37	16,178	46
Credits	38 Credit for contributions to candidates for public office . .	38			
	39 Credit for the elderly (attach Schedules R&RP)	39		
	40 Credit for child and dependent care expenses (attach Form 2441) .	40		
	41 Investment credit (attach Form 3468)	41		
	42 Foreign tax credit (attach Form 1116)	42		
	43 Work Incentive (WIN) Credit (attach Form 4874)	43		
	44 New jobs credit (attach Form 5884)	44		
	45 Residential energy credits (see page 12 of Instructions, attach Form 5695) . .	45		
	46 Total credits. Add lines 38 through 45	46	0	
	47 Balance. Subtract line 46 from line 37 and enter difference (but not less than zero) . ▶	47	16,178	46
Other Taxes	48 Self-employment tax (attach Schedule SE)	48	1,433	70
	49 Minimum tax. Check here ▶ ☐ and attach Form 4625	49		
	50 Tax from recomputing prior-year investment credit (attach Form 4255)	50		
	51 Social security (FICA) tax on tip income not reported to employer (attach Form 4137) . .	51		
	52 Uncollected employee FICA and RRTA tax on tips (from Form W–2)	52		
	53 Tax on an IRA (attach Form 5329)	53		
	54 Total tax. Add lines 47 through 53 . . . . ▶	54	17,612	16
Payments Attach Forms W–2, W–2G, and W–2P to front.	55 Total Federal income tax withheld	55			
	56 1978 estimated tax payments and credit from 1977 return . .	56		
	57 Earned income credit. If line 31 is under $8,000, see page 2 of Instructions. If eligible, enter child's name ▶	57		
	58 Amount paid with Form 4868	58		
	59 Excess FICA and RRTA tax withheld (two or more employers) .	59		
	60 Credit for Federal tax on special fuels and oils (attach Form 4136) .	60		
	61 Regulated Investment Company credit (attach Form 2439)	61		
	62 Total. Add lines 55 through 61 . . . . ▶	62		
Refund or Due	63 If line 62 is larger than line 54, enter amount OVERPAID . . . . ▶	63		
	64 Amount of line 63 to be REFUNDED TO YOU . . . . ▶	64		
	65 Amount of line 63 to be credited on 1979 estimated tax. ▶	65		
	66 If line 54 is larger than line 62, enter BALANCE DUE. Attach check or money order for full amount payable to "Internal Revenue Service." Write your social security number on check or money order . . ▶ (Check ▶ ☐ if Form 2210 (2210F) is attached. See page 14 of instructions.) ▶ $	66		

Please Sign Here

Under penalties of perjury, I declare that I have examined this return, including accompanying schedules and statements, and to the best of my knowledge and belief, it is true, correct, and complete. Declaration of preparer (other than taxpayer) is based on all information of which preparer has any knowledge.

Your signature	Date	Spouse's signature (if filing jointly, BOTH must sign even if only one had income)

Paid Preparer's Information	Preparer's signature ▶	Preparer's social security no.	Check if self-employed ▶ ☐
	Firm's name (or yours, if self-employed), address and ZIP code ▶	E.I. No. ▶	
		Date ▶	

117

Profit or (Loss) From Business or Profession
(Sole Proprietorship)
Partnerships, Joint Ventures, etc., Must File Form 1065.
▶ Attach to Form 1040. ▶ See Instructions for Schedule C (Form 1040).

1978

Name of proprietor	Social security number of proprietor
TIFFANY FIELD	000 : 00 : 0000

A Main business activity (see Instructions) ▶ DESIGNER ....; product ▶ ....

B Business name ▶ TIFFANY FIELD ....

C Employer identification number ▶ 00-0000000 ....

D Business address (number and street) ▶ 795 FIFTH AVENUE ....

City, State and ZIP code ▶ NEW YORK NY 10021 ....

E Accounting method: (1) ☑ Cash (2) ☐ Accrual (3) ☐ Other (specify) ▶ ....

F Method(s) used to value closing inventory:
(1) ☐ Cost (2) ☐ Lower of cost or market (3) ☐ Other (if other, attach explanation)

	Yes	No
G Was there any major change in determining quantities, costs, or valuations between opening and closing inventory? . . If "Yes," attach explanation.		✔
H Does this business activity involve oil or gas, movies or video tapes, or leasing personal (section 1245) property to others? (See page 25 of the Instructions.)		✔
I Did you deduct expenses for an office in your home?		✔

Part I Income

1 a Gross receipts or sales	1a			
b Returns and allowances	1b			
c Balance (subtract line 1b from line 1a)		1c		
2 Cost of goods sold and/or operations (Schedule C–1, line 8) . .		2		
3 Gross profit (subtract line 2 from line 1c)		3		
4 Other income (attach schedule)		4	70,000	00
5 Total income (add lines 3 and 4) . . . . ▶		5	70,000	00

Part II Deductions

			28 Telephone	2,500	00
6 Advertising			29 Travel and entertainment . . .	4,000	00
7 Amortization			30 Utilities	1,000	00
8 Bad debts from sales or services .			31 a Wages . . .		
9 Bank charges			b New Jobs Credit .		
10 Car and truck expenses . . .			c Subtract line 31b from 31a . .		
11 Commissions			32 Other expenses (specify):		
12 Depletion			a		
13 Depreciation (explain in Schedule C–2)	500	00	b		
14 Dues and publications . . .	1,500	00	c		
15 Employee benefit programs . . .			d		
16 Freight (not included on Schedule C–1)			e		
17 Insurance			f		
18 Interest on business indebtedness			g		
19 Laundry and cleaning			h		
20 Legal and professional services .			i		
21 Office supplies	1,000	00	j		
22 Pension and profit-sharing plans .	7,500	00	k		
23 Postage + X Boxing . . .	1,000	00	l		
24 Rent on business property . . .	6,000	00	m		
25 Repairs			n		
26 Supplies (not included on Schedule C–1)			o		
27 Taxes			p		
			q		
			r		

33 Total deductions (add amounts in columns for lines 6 through 32r) . . . . ▶ | 33 | 25,000 | 00 |

34 Net profit or (loss) (subtract line 33 from line 5). Enter here and on Form 1040, line 13. ALSO enter on Schedule SE (Form 1040), line 5a. (For "at risk" provisions, see page 25 of Instructions). . . . ▶ | 34 | 45,000 | 00 |

118

SCHEDULE C–1.—Cost of Goods Sold and/or Operations (See Schedule C Instructions for Part I, Line 2)

1 Inventory at beginning of year (if different from last year's closing inventory, attach explanation) .	**1**	
2 a Purchases **2a**		
b Cost of items withdrawn for personal use **2b**		
c Balance (subtract line 2b from line 2a)	**2c**	
3 Cost of labor (do not include salary paid to yourself)	**3**	
4 Materials and supplies	**4**	
5 Other costs (attach schedule)	**5**	
6 Add lines 1, 2c, and 3 through 5	**6**	
7 Inventory at end of year	**7**	
8 **Cost of goods sold and/or operations** (subtract line 7 from line 6). Enter here and on Part I, line 2 . ▶	**8**	

SCHEDULE C–2.—Depreciation (See Schedule C Instructions for line 13)
If you need more space, please use Form 4562.

Description of property (a)	Date acquired (b)	Cost or other basis (c)	Depreciation allowed or allowable in prior years (d)	Method of computing depreciation (e)	Life or rate (f)	Depreciation for this year (g)
1 Total additional first-year depreciation (do not include in items below)————————▶						
2 Other depreciation:						
Buildings						
Furniture and fixtures	1/1/78	5,000.00	—	STRAIGHT LINE	10 YRS	500 00
Transportation equipment . .						
Machinery and other equipment .						
Other (Specify)						
3 Totals		5,000.00			**3**	500 00
4 Depreciation claimed in Schedule C–1					**4**	0
5 **Balance** (subtract line 4 from line 3). Enter here and on Part II, line 13 . . . . ▶					**5**	500 00

SCHEDULE C–3.—Expense Account Information (See Schedule C Instructions for Schedule C–3)

Enter information for yourself and your five highest paid employees. In determining the five highest paid employees, add expense account allowances to the salaries and wages. However, you don't have to provide the information for any employee for whom the combined amount is less than $25,000, or for yourself if your expense account allowance plus line 34, page 1, is less than $25,000.

Name (a)	Expense account (b)	Salaries and Wages (c)
Owner		
1		
2		
3		
4		
5		

Did you claim a deduction for expenses connected with:	Yes	No
A Entertainment facility (boat, resort, ranch, etc.)?		
B Living accommodations (except employees on business)?		
C Employees' families at conventions or meetings?		
If "Yes," were any of these conventions or meetings outside the U.S. or its possessions? (See page 26 of Instructions.) .		
D Vacations for employees or their families not reported on Form W–2?		

Computation of Social Security Self-Employment Tax

► Each self-employed person must file a Schedule SE. ► Attach to Form 1040.
► See Instructions for Schedule SE (Form 1040).

1978

● If you had wages, including tips, of $17,700 or more that were subject to social security or railroad retirement taxes, do not fill in this schedule (unless you are eligible for the Earned Income Credit). See Instructions.

● If you had more than one business, combine profits and losses from all your businesses and farms on this Schedule SE.

Important.—The self-employment income reported below will be credited to your social security record and used in figuring social security benefits.

NAME OF SELF-EMPLOYED PERSON (AS SHOWN ON SOCIAL SECURITY CARD)	Social security number of self-employed person ►
TIFFANY FIELD	000 00 0000

● If you have only farm income complete Parts I and III. ● If you have only nonfarm income complete Parts II and III.
● If you have both farm and nonfarm income complete Parts I, II, and III.

Part I Computation of Net Earnings from FARM Self-Employment

You may elect to compute your net farm earnings using the OPTIONAL METHOD, line 3, instead of using the Regular Method, line 2, if your gross profits are: (1) $2,400 or less, or (2) more than $2,400 and net profits are less than $1,600. However, lines 1 and 2 must be completed even if you elect to use the FARM OPTIONAL METHOD.

REGULAR METHOD	**a** Schedule F, line 58 (cash method), or line 76 (accrual method) .	1a	
1 Net profit or (loss) from: {b Farm partnerships		1b	
2 Net earnings from farm self-employment (add lines 1a and b)		2	
FARM OPTIONAL METHOD **a** Not more than $2,400, enter two-thirds of the gross profits . .			
3 If gross profits from farming [1] are: **b** More than $2,400 and the net farm profit is less than $1,600, enter $1,600		3	

[1] Gross profits from farming are the total gross profits from Schedule F, line 32 (cash method), or line 74 (accrual method), plus the distributive share of gross profits from farm partnerships (Schedule K-1 (Form 1065), line 3) as explained in Instructions for Schedule SE.

4 Enter here and on line 12a, the amount on line 2, or line 3 if you elect the farm optional method .	4	

Part II Computation of Net Earnings from NONFARM Self-Employment

	a Schedule C, line 34. (Enter combined amount if more than one business.) .	5a	45,000 00
	b Partnerships, joint ventures, etc. (other than farming)	5b	
REGULAR METHOD	**c** Service as a minister, member of a religious order, or a Christian Science practitioner. (Include rental value of parsonage or rental allowance furnished.) If you filed Form 4361 and have not revoked that exemption, check here ► ☐ and enter zero on this line	5c	
5 Net profit or (loss) from:	**d** Service with a foreign government or international organization . . .	5d	
	e Other—Specify ►	5e	
6 Total (add lines 5a through e)		6	45,000 00
7 Enter adjustments if any (attach statement, see page 27 of instructions)		7	0
8 Adjusted net earnings or (loss) from self-employment (line 6, as adjusted by line 7) . .		8	45,000 00

If line 8 is $1,600 or more **OR** if you do not elect to use the Nonfarm Optional Method, skip lines 9 through 11 and enter amount from line 8 on line 12b, Part III.

Note: You may use the nonfarm optional method (line 9 through line 11) only if line 8 is less than $1,600 and less than two-thirds of your gross nonfarm profits,[2] and you had actual net earnings from self-employment of $400 or more for at least 2 of the 3 following years: 1975, 1976, and 1977. The nonfarm optional method can only be used for 5 tax years.

SE

NONFARM OPTIONAL METHOD

9 **a** Maximum amount reportable, under both optional methods combined (farm and nonfarm) .	9a	$1,600 00
b Enter amount from line 3. (If you did not elect to use the farm optional method, enter zero.)	9b	
c Balance (subtract line 9b from line 9a)	9c	
10 Enter two-thirds of gross nonfarm profits [2] or $1,600, whichever is smaller	10	
11 Enter here and on line 12b, the amount on line 9c or line 10, whichever is smaller	11	

[2] Gross profits from nonfarm profits are the total of the gross profits from Schedule C, line 3, plus the distributive share of gross profits from nonfarm partnerships (Schedule K-1 (Form 1065), line 15(a)) as explained in Instructions for Schedule SE. Also, include gross profits from services reported on line 5c, d, and e, as adjusted by line 7.

Part III Computation of Social Security Self-Employment Tax

12 Net earnings or (loss): **a** From farming (from line 4)	12a	
b From nonfarm (from line 8, or line 11 if you elect to use the Nonfarm Optional Method) . . .	12b	45,000 00
13 Total net earnings or (loss) from self-employment reported on lines 12a and 12b. (If line 13 is less than $400, you are not subject to self-employment tax. Do not fill in rest of schedule.)	13	45,000 00
14 The largest amount of combined wages and self-employment earnings subject to social security or railroad retirement taxes for 1978 is	14	$17,700 00
15 **a** Total "FICA" wages (from Forms W–2) and "RRTA" compensation . . [15a]		
b Unreported tips subject to FICA tax from Form 4137, line 9 or to RRTA . . [15b]		
c Add lines 15a and b	15c	0
16 Balance (subtract line 15c from line 14)	16	45,000 00
17 Self-employment income—line 13 or 16, whichever is smaller	17	45,000 00
18 Self-employment tax. (If line 17 is $17,700, enter $1,433.70; if less, multiply the amount on line 17 by .081.) Enter here and on Form 1040, line 48	18	1,433 70

☆U.S. GOVERNMENT PRINTING OFFICE: 1978— 263-328

23-188-5979

Form **4726**	**Maximum Tax on Personal Service Income**	**1978**
Department of the Treasury Internal Revenue Service	▶ Attach to Form 1040 (or Form 1041).	

Name(s) as shown on Form 1040 (or Form 1041) TIFFANY   FIELD

Identifying number 000-00-0000

Do not complete this form if—(a) Taxable income or personal service taxable income is:
$40,200 or less, and on Form 1040, you checked box 1 or box 4,
$55,200 or less, and on Form 1040, you checked box 2 or box 5,
$26,000 or less and this is an Estate or Trust return (Form 1041);
(b) You elected income averaging; or
(c) On Form 1040, you checked box 3.

A—Personal Service Income	B—Deductions Against Personal Service Income
Total personal service income **45,000.00**	Total deductions against personal service income . . **0**

1	Personal service net income—Subtract total amount in column B from total amount in column A . .	1	**45,000.00**
2	Enter your adjusted gross income (see instructions)	2	**46,900.00**
3	Divide the amount on line 1 by the amount on line 2. Enter percentage result here, but not more than 100%. Round to nearest 4 numbers (see instructions)	3	**9595%**
4	Enter your taxable income (see instructions)	4	**46,150.00**
5	Multiply the amount on line 4 by the percentage on line 3	5	**44,280.93**
6	Enter the total of your 1978 tax preference items (see instructions)	6	**0**
7	Personal service taxable income. Subtract line 6 from line 5 (see instructions)	7	**44,280.93**
8	If: on Form 1040, you checked box 1 or box 4, enter $40,200 . . . . on Form 1040, you checked box 2 or box 5, enter $55,200 . . . . Estate or Trust, enter $26,000	8	**40,200.00**
9	Subtract line 8 from line 7 (if zero or less, do not complete rest of form)	9	**4,080.93**
10	Enter 50% of line 9	10	**2,040.47**
11	Tax on amount on line 4	11	16,562.50	
12	Tax on amount on line 7	12	15,534.51	
13	Subtract line 12 from line 11	13	**1,027.99**
14	If the amount on line 8 is: $40,200, enter $13,290 ($12,240 if unmarried head of household) . . $55,200, enter $18,060 . . . . $26,000, enter $9,030	14	**13,290.00**
15	Add lines 10, 13, and 14. This is your maximum tax (see instructions)	15	**16,358.46**

Computation of Alternative Tax

16	Amount from line 4 . . . . -	16	
17	Enter amount reportable on Schedule D (Form 1040), line 26 or Schedule D (Form 1041), line 20° .	17	
18	Subtract line 17 from line 16	18	
	Note: If Schedule D (Form 1040), line 15; Form 4798, line 7; or Schedule D (Form 1041), line 17(e) or 31 is not more than $50,000, skip lines 19 through 23.		
19	Enter amount reportable on Schedule D (Form 1040), line 28 or Schedule D (Form 1041), line 22 . .	19	
20	Add lines 18 and 19	20	
21	Enter amount from line 11	21	
22	Tax on amount on line 20	22	
23	Subtract line 22 from line 21	23	
24	Tax on amount on line 18. **Caution:** If line 7 is more than line 18, enter instead, amount on line 12 less 50% of the excess of line 7 over line 18	24	
25	Subtract line 24 from line 11	25	
26	Subtract line 25 from line 15	26	
27	Enter 25% of Schedule D (Form 1040), line 15; Form 4798, line 7; or Schedule D (Form 1041), line 17(e) or 31, but not more than $12,500	27	
28	Add lines 23 (if applicable), 26 and 27	28	

°If you reported capital gain distributions but did not use Schedule D (Form 1040), enter on line 17 the amount shown on Form 1040, line 15.

263–165–1

Form **4726** (1978)

14

Retire with the Biggest Tax Break Possible

When you retire, you will be liquidating your corporation, which has served you well all these years, and distributing all the assets and liabilities to the stockholders in exchange for all the stock. The excess of the value of the assets over the liabilities and investment in the stock is treated as a capital gain. In effect, you are converting ordinary earned income into capital gains, which are taxed as follows under the Revenue Act of 1978: 60 percent of capital gains each year is not taxed at all. The remaining 40 percent is taxed at your normal tax rate, which could be as high as 28 percent, if your normal rate is 70 percent. To the extent to which you haven't declared corporate dividends, which would be taxed to you at ordinary income-tax rates, you can turn those dividends into capital gains if you can wait until you liquidate your corporation.

You don't necessarily have to sell the stock in your corporate portfolio either. You can distribute in cash or in kind: you give your stock back to the corporation, and the corporation gives you its assets—its stock portfolio, and anything else it owns.

In this case, you'd have to send the corporation's stock to the transfer agent so that it can be reissued in your name alone.

You would also have to notify the IRS 30 days after adopting your plan of liquidation. You would have to have a meeting of the board of directors which, as you know by now, can be just you, while you're watching "M.A.S.H."

Liquidation of your corporation is treated by the IRS as a sale because essentially it's a sale of your stock. You can choose from among three forms of liquidation: the lump-sum method (§331), the installment method (§453), or the 30-day method of sale (§333). To understand how these differ, let's take the same corporation through the three liquidation options.

Example: The XYZ Corporation liquidates on June 30, 1980. It has fixed assets valued at $10,000, receivables of $30,000, and inventory of $10,000. The stockholder's basis in his stock is $20,000.

§331 — Lump-Sum Method

The lump-sum method is a complete liquidation. There is no time requirement, as there is with §333, the one-month liquidation. With this method, each asset takes a basis to its value at the date of liquidation:

Total assets	$50,000
Less basis in stock	−20,000
Capital gain	$30,000

The stockholder pays no tax on $18,000 (60 percent of $30,000) and is taxed only on $12,000 (40 percent of $30,000). The maximum tax on the liquidation of the corporation would be $8,400.

To elect the lump-sum method of liquidation, your corporation would file IRS Form 966.

§453 — *Installment Method*

Like the lump-sum method, the installment method doesn't require a time frame. If you don't receive more than 30 percent of the sale price in the year of the sale, you can spread the gain over the period in which the payments are received. You could have a very protracted liquidation and spread the payments over 10 or 20 years, which might make sense if the corporation's assets were $250,000 or more. The only problem in protracted liquidations is convincing the IRS that the payments are made in liquidation, as opposed to ordinary distributions of an ongoing company. You would have to establish a status of liquidation, proving that your company had closed up shop.

There are many ways to do this. Although an adoption of a plan of liquidation by the board of directors of your corporation will suffice, if you can add some concrete proofs—dropping membership in unions or professional societies, disconnecting the corporation's answering service, and the like—so much the better.

The installment method of sale receives preferential capital-gains treatment, but, in essence, you are income-averaging your gain. Under the Revenue Act of 1978, only 40 percent of your gain is taxed, replacing the maximum 25 percent capital-gains tax provision of the Tax Reform Act of 1976. This change benefits all but the highest-bracket taxpayers, whose capital-gains tax is now 28 percent (40 percent of 70 percent), 3 percent higher.

Fortunately, in addition to the capital-gains rate changes, the Revenue Act of 1978 removed capital gains from the list of tax-preference items. Thus, investors are no longer penalized by the effective 7½ percent surtax on capital gains in addition to the normal income tax on capital gains.

Thus, to the extent that you can average capital gains on the installment basis, you can minimize the new minimum tax you will be liable for.

Let's return to XYZ Corporation to see how the installment method works.

First, the gross profit percentage is calculated by dividing the gross profit (total assets less the stockholder's basis) by the contract price (total assets):

$$\$30,000 \div \$50,000 = 60\%$$

Thus, the gross profit percentage is 60 percent. Therefore, only 60 percent of each annual installment is taxed at capital-gains rates; the remaining 40 percent is treated as a return of capital and is therefore not taxed.

If your stockholder takes 30 percent in 1980—the year of the sale—as his first installment, the calculations look like this:

$15,000	installment payment
− 6,000	return of capital
$ 9,000	gain—taxed at capital-gains rates

In the remaining 7 years—from 1981 through 1987—if 10 percent is paid out each year, the calculations for each year look like this:

$5,000	installment payment
−2,000	return of capital
$3,000	gain—taxed at capital-gains rates

Once again, it's important to note that you must make sure that your corporation is in liquidation status during this entire time. Of course, you could close down the corporation and still work in semiretirement as a sole proprietor; many people do.

To elect the installment method of liquidation, your corporation would file IRS Form 966.

§331 vs. §453

Even if you have no basis in the corporation's stock (a concept that will be explained a few pages later), so that all the corporation's assets become your capital gain, the lump-sum method and the installment method of liquidation are still equally attractive. Here are some of the trade-offs:

(1) The quickness of the wrap-up.

(2) Do you need/want the money all at once?

(3) The future value of money—a slow payout of constant dollars is almost certain to diminish your purchasing power.

If you're a cynic, you may want to choose lump-sum liquidation, take all the money, and invest it yourself to beat inflation.

Your tax bracket may also be a factor. The lump-sum payment may push you into too high a tax bracket and force you to choose the installment method.

In part, too, it's a question of financial life-style, similar to the discussion of whether to choose the 25 percent money-purchase plan or the 10 percent money-purchase plan combined with the 15 percent profit-sharing plan. If you feel that you can manage all your money at once, you may prefer the lump-sum method of liquidation; if, on the other hand, you feel more secure with payments being made to you every year for a number of years, you may prefer the installment method.

But what if your corporation has no fixed assets or inventory, you may say. Many corporations have no fixed assets or inventory and, in planning for liquidation, may have let their clients know 30 days in advance so that there are no accounts receivable; everything has been collected. All your corporation may have is a portfolio of stocks. In this case, you would still choose among the lump-sum method, the installment method, and the one-month liquidation method, which I have reserved for last because it is not recommended for small corporations where personal services are the material income-producing factor.

§333 — One-Month Liquidation Method

Under the one-month liquidation method, you postpone any tax on the appreciation of the assets you have received in exchange for the stock until you sell the assets. If you elect this method, all the assets must be distributed within *one calendar month* (e.g., July, not July 15–August 15). The IRS must be notified by the corporation's filing IRS Form 966 and your filing IRS Form 964, so that you become a qualified electing stockholder. Then, within one calendar month, all the assets must be distributed to the shareholders. You take the assets and substitute your investment in the stock for the assets. The assets take the place of the stock and become stock in your hands. Thus, you defer tax on the appreciation of the assets until you sell them.

Let's go back to XYZ Corporation. The basis in the assets is determined as follows: Each asset is divided by the total assets and then multiplied by the stockholder's basis in his stock:

$$\text{Fixed assets} = (\$10,000 \div \$50,000) \times \$20,000 = \$4,000$$
$$\text{Inventory} = (\$10,000 \div \$50,000) \times \$20,000 = \$4,000$$
$$\text{Receivables} = (\$30,000 \div \$50,000) \times \$20,000 = \underline{\$12,000}$$
$$\$20,000 \text{ basis}$$

There is no immediate tax, but when the assets are sold, the tax is based on the difference between the proceeds and the stockholder's new basis. For example, on receivables, when the stockholder collected the $30,000, he'd pay tax only on $18,000, which is the difference between the $30,000 and the $12,000 basis.

The trade-off is that in normal liquidation (lump-sum or installment methods) there is a capital gain for the excess of the value of the assets over the liabilities plus the investment in the stock. But under the one-month liquidation method, the assets in the stockholder's hands have a tax basis equal to the fair market value when distributed. Any tax on the appreciation is postponed until these assets are sold.

The one-month liquidation is a nice alternative to the installment method: you can regulate the time of picking up the appreciation in your corporate assets by timing your selling of them. Thus, this is another way of deferring taxes and of spreading the gain.

Why Choose §333?

The one-month liquidation is designed for companies with no inventory or receivables. If you elect the one-month liquidation and take the assets at a low basis, you do not get capital-gains treatment when you collect these ordinary-income assets two or three months down the road. This liquidation option is designed for companies with fixed assets—e.g., real estate—where the shareholders contemplate holding the assets as investments for a long period of time after liquidation. Other fixed assets might be antiques, art, stamp or coin collections, jewelry, a portfolio of stocks. In fact, the shareholders might not sell these assets at all, but might defer taxes permanently by leaving them to beneficiaries in their wills.

Raising the Basis of Your Stock

This is a good time to discuss the basis of your stock: what it is and how to raise it. The basis of your stock is a dollar figure which consists of the assets (property, etc.) that the shareholder contributes to the corporation both at its inception and throughout its life. Even if your corporation is a service corporation, you can still make contributions to it: at its inception, you might give the corporation some office equipment and furniture and a library. These items are valued at cost, not present value, since the IRS considers current or replacement value irrelevant.

Assets you contribute to your corporation will increase the basis of your stock. They increase the value of the outstanding shares pro rata; they do not increase the value of any ESOP shares. Depending on when the shares are issued, you may have shares at varying bases, just as though you had bought stock at varying prices.

Why do you want to increase the basis of your stock? You want to make your basis as high as possible so that when you liquidate the corporation, as much money as possible is considered a return of capital and exempt from taxes. Thus, if your stock had a basis of $10,000 and you liquidated a corporation with assets of $100,000, the $10,000 would be considered a return of capital; you would subtract it from the $100,000 and start your calculations with $90,000.

If your corporation deals in services, you can still contribute to the corporation during its life. Attractive contributions would be in areas where corporations get preferential treatment, as opposed to individuals: either cash, with which the corporation could buy stocks, or the stocks themselves, since as soon as the stocks were transferred to the corporation, their dividends would be 85 percent tax-free. But remember: once you give the cash or stock to the corporation, you cannot use the dividends yourself or take the money out of the corporation without declaring a distribution and being taxed on it.

You could also buy paintings and other works of art or antiques for your corporation to raise the basis of your stock, but you would have to use your own funds to do so. While you are increasing the basis of the stock, you are increasing the assets of your corporation at the same time; in a sense, you are adding the same quantity to both sides of a balance, so that there is actually no net change. It would be far more desirable to give the corporation money to purchase stocks or the stocks themselves, since corporations are able to shelter 85 percent of dividends from taxes and individuals are not, as explained above. If you do transfer stock to the corporation, remember that you must use your cost—and not the current market price—as the basis.

In this connection, a 60-year-old professional could incorporate and turn over his stock portfolio to his corporation, at which point his dividends would be 85 percent tax-exempt. As long as his earned income constituted 40 percent or more of his total annual income, he would not be held to be a personal holding corporation. He could then retire at 65 or 70 with lots of tax-free dividend accumulation and a fairly high basis on his stock, so that when his corporation was liquidated, a good part of the assets would be considered a return of capital and therefore be tax-free.

Your Pension

But liquidating your corporation is only half the story; the other half is drawing your pension. Like corporate assets, retirement-fund assets can be either converted to cash or distributed in kind. If the shareholder elects lump-sum distribution (the entire balance of the retirement fund within one taxable year), which has several favorable tax advantages, the occasion must be either (1) separation from the employer; (2) reaching the age of 59½; or (3) disability. Lump-sum distributions cannot be taken because the plan has been terminated.

Workaholics will be delighted to know that there is no maximum age for retirement.

If the shareholder/employee is less than 59½ years old, there is an unresolved problem: What comes first as the triggering event in a one-person corporation—separation from the employer or termination of the plan, since it is a one-person corporation? These events cannot be simultaneous.

There is a fairly easy way to resolve this problem. The shareholder/employee can make his separation from service a little earlier than the termination of his plan by going on a one-month terminal leave and then liquidating the corporation.

When you liquidate your pension plan, your gain is calculated as the value of its assets in excess of any amounts you may have contributed to it yourself. (This is the 6 percent Voluntary Contribution mentioned in Chapter 9, "All About ERISA.") Similar to the §453 installment method of liquidation, your pension gain is subject to a special 10-year averaging computation, so that taxes are minimized.

In order to perform the calculation, reduce the gain by the minimum distribution allowance. The minimum distribution allowance is equal to the lesser of [$10,000] or [½ the distribution] − (⅕ the distributions in excess of $20,000).

Let's look at some examples:

If your pension is $25,000 and your contribution is $0, your gain is $25,000. The minimum distribution allowance is equal to

$$\$10,000 - \tfrac{1}{5} \ (\$25,000 - \$20,000)$$
$$\$10,000 - \tfrac{1}{5} \ (\$5,000)$$
$$\$10,000 - \$1,000 = \$9,000$$

Thus your minimum distribution allowance is $9,000, and the net value of your pension is $16,000.

As you can see, the smaller the distribution is, the higher the minimum distribution allowance will be. On pensions smaller than $20,000, the minimum distribution allowance is the full $10,000; the benefits of the minimum distribution allowance are completely phased out when the distribution is $70,000 or more:

$$\$10,000 - \frac{1}{5} \, (\$70,000 - \$20,000)$$
$$\$10,000 - \frac{1}{5} \, (\$50,000)$$
$$\$10,000 - \$10,000 = \$0$$

Although the $25,000 in the first example (taxed as $16,000) or the $70,000 in the second example (taxed as $70,000) is received as a lump sum, the distribution is taxed as though it were received over a period of 10 years. The tax is paid all in one year, but the tax rate is the low income-averaging rate. In a sense, this lump-sum pension distribution is analogous to the lump-sum liquidation of the corporation's assets under §331.

There is no pension-distribution plan analogous to §333, the one-month liquidation.

There is, however, a pension-distribution plan analogous to the installment-method liquidation of the corporation under §453. In this case, the pension distribution is taken down as an annuity and would be taxed under the annuity rules, which are the same as the installment rules.

Thus, you are left with two choices: taking your pension as a lump sum or as an annuity. Since both the lump-sum and the annuity options are treated similarly by the IRS, which should you take? Essentially, it's a question of life-style. Some people are happier with a lump sum; some people need that lump sum; some people need to have their money doled out to them because they're spendthrifts. But, since taxes in the aggregate are higher with the annuity option, it may be wisest for even the spendthrifts to take the lump sum, pay the taxes on it, and then buy a mutual fund which will send them a check every month or every quarter.

15

If You Should Die First—Planning for Your Heirs

In the old days (before December 31, 1976), using the example of XYZ Corporation in the preceding chapter, your heirs could use your stock's value on the date of your death as the adjusted cost. Thus, instead of your basis of $20,000, your heirs could use the new stepped-up figure of $50,000. Then, when they liquidated the corporation at $50,000, they would not have to pay any capital-gains taxes, since under the law there was no gain ($50,000 − $50,000 = $0).

The Tax Reform Act of 1976 has closed that loophole, but on a deferred basis which may or may not take effect on January 1, 1980. (Remember: that's an election year!) If it does take effect, your estate will have to take what is called the carry-over basis of your stock subject to certain minor adjustments for estate taxes paid. In effect, the estate will step into your shoes and carry over that $20,000 basis in your stock and be in the same position as you would have been if you had lived and liquidated the corporation yourself. The $30,000 gain will be preserved, and taxes will have to be paid on it.

Your heirs will be able to choose the same liquidation options—§331, §333, or §453—as you would have had, but alas, at *your* basis, not the stepped-up basis formerly permitted.

If the distribution (either pension or the liquidation of the corporation) is taken as a lump sum by your beneficiaries, it is included in your estate. However, if the distribution is taken as an annuity, it will bypass the estate and not be subject to estate taxes. Therefore, the shortest length of annuity that will satisfy the IRS would seem to be an ideal way to save paying estate taxes.

Incorporation permits another estate-planning feature: deferred compensation, which is not available to sole proprietors. Deferred compensation defers current income to the individual and provides future benefit. A deferred-compensation agreement can even designate your choice of beneficiary.

But deferred compensation is a good idea for you, as well as in planning for your heirs. A deferred-compensation agreement can fund your retirement and provide security for the future.

If you defer some of your salary, you are not subject to current taxes because you have not received this income. The corporation is the stakeholder: the deferred compensation is an asset of the corporation and becomes a benefit to the corporation because it can be carried as an asset, as a balance-sheet item.

Deferred-compensation plans offer an advantage to the corporation. If the corporation puts $200,000 into your deferred-compensation plan, it has an expense of $200,000. But if the $200,000 grows to $300,000, depending on the terms of the deferred-compensation agreement, the corporation can either pay out the $300,000 and write off an expense of $300,000, or pay out the $200,000, write off $200,000, and keep $100,000 as an asset.

However, there is a disadvantage to deferred-compensation plans: if the corporation goes bankrupt, the assets of the plan can be attached by creditors.

Deferred-compensation plans are not for the average employee because he or she needs current income. Plans could be set up for $50 a month, and many state and city employees and employees of large corporations participate in such plans. But deferred compensation really becomes very advantageous to the higher-paid employee who doesn't need all that current income. Instead of taking $60,000 a year, the employee may take a salary of $40,000 and defer $20,000.

In order to do this, a deferred-compensation agreement must be drawn up by a lawyer, setting up the amount or percentage of salary to be deferred, the number of years the funds will be deferred, and the terms of the payout. The agreement can be drawn flexibly enough so that the employee agrees to defer his bonus which, in a one-person corporation, he controls completely. The cost of drawing up a deferred-compensation agreement varies; if you find a lawyer who's done many of these and is familiar with them, the bill should be for no more than two or three hours of his time.

The deferred-compensation agreement must be a valid plan, in writing. It must impose reasonable obligations on the corporation to pay the deferred compensation, and it must anticipate that at the end of the time period, the money will be paid to the employee. The deferred-compensation agreement can't be a sham, where at the end of 10 years, the corporation throws the money away and can't pay. The corporation must intend to repay the funds.

Now: what happens to the deferred-compensation funds? The corporation carries them as an asset. There is no current write-off to the corporation, but there is no income to the employee, either.

Because deferred-compensation plans are not qualified under Section 401 of the Internal Revenue Code, the corporation can make use of these assets, borrow against them, use them as collateral, etc. The corporation can fund the plan any way it wants to. It doesn't even have to fund the plan: it can just pay the employee the agreed-upon sum at the end of the time period. The deferred-compensation plan permits the corporation to accumulate money in a special fund—without regard to the $150,000 limitation—because it's for a valid business purpose and therefore not subject to the accumulated earnings tax discussed in Chapter 1, "So You Want to Be a Corporation."

Thus, deferred compensation is not only a way for an individual to avoid paying taxes on a salary he does not need, but it's also a way for his corporation to accumulate funds in excess of $150,000 without being subjected to the accumulated earnings tax.

Deferred compensation can also work for smaller amounts of money. It can work for amounts as small as $5,000 or $10,000 a year or for a one-shot lump sum, as in the case of a prizefighter or an author who signs a contract for a large advance. In these cases, a deferred-compensation plan could be drawn up along with the contract.

Deferred compensation isn't for everyone, but if you think it may be for you, consult your lawyer and your accountant.

There you have the basic tax-planning options: for your heirs' liquidation of your corporation, for their being paid your pension benefits, and for your own deferred compensation. Hopefully the first two won't be needed, and you can enjoy the third for many, many years.

State Requirements for General Business and Professional Corporations

State	Professions Covered by P. C. Act	*Title and No. of* *P. C. Act*
Alabama	All licensed professions	Professional Corp. Act No. 260
Alaska	All licensed professions	Alaska Statute 10.45
Arizona	Accountants, doctors, lawyers	Arizona Revised Statute 10-908
Arkansas	All licensed professions	Act 155 of 1963
California	Accountants, chiropractors, clinical social workers, dentists, doctors, lawyers, marriage, family & child counselors, optometrists, osteopaths, physical therapists, podiatrists, psychologists, shorthand reporters, speech pathologists	Part 4, Division 3, Title 1, California Corps. Code
Colorado	Accountants, architects, chiropractors, dentists, doctors, lawyers, optometrists, veterinarians	Title 12
Connecticut	All licensed professions	Professional Service Corps. Chap. 594a
Delaware	Accountants, architects, chiropodists, chiropractors, dentists, doctors, en- gineers, lawyers, optometrists, os- teopaths, veterinarians	Chapter 6, General Corp. Law

Min. No. of Share-holders	Title of Form to Be Filed	Address	Filing Fee
1	Charter	Judge of Probate of County	N/A– Annual fee $10
1	Duplicate Originals of Articles of Incorporation	Dept. of Commerce & Economic Development Pouch D Juneau, Alaska 99811	$30
1	Articles of Incorporation	Sec'y of State 2222 West Encanto Blvd. Phoenix, Arizona 85009	$50
1	N/A	Sec'y of State Corporation Dept. State Capitol Bldg. Little Rock, Arkansas 72201	$15 min.
1	Articles of Incorporation *	Sec'y of State 111 Capitol Mall Sacramento, California 95814	$265
Not given	Articles of Incorporation	Sec'y of State 1575 Sherman Denver, Colorado 80203	$24.75 min.
1	Certificate of Incorpo-ration	Sec'y of State P. O. Box 846 30 Trinity St. Hartford, Connecticut 06115	$91 min.
1	Certificate of Incorpo-ration	**	N/A

N/A—not available

*After incorporation, application is made to the proper licensing board of the profession for a Certificate of Authority which, when granted, legally permits the corporation to practice the profession.

** Corporation must have registered office with registered agent in state. Certificate must be filed through registered agent.

State	Professions Covered by P. C. Act	Title and No. of P. C. Act
Florida	Accountants, architects, chiropodists, chiropractors, dentists, doctors, lawyers, life insurance agents, osteopaths, podiatrists, veterinarians	Professional Corp. Act Chap. 621
Georgia	Accountants, architects, chiropractors, dentists, doctors, engineers, land surveyors, lawyers, optometrists, osteopaths, podiatrists, psychologists (applied), veterinarians	Georgia Professional Corp. Act. No. 943
Hawaii	Accountants, chiropractors, dentists, doctors, lawyers and district court practitioners, naturopaths, opticians, optometrists, osteopaths, pharmacists, veterinarians	Part VIII of Chap. 416, Hawaii Revised Statutes
Idaho	All licensed professions	Title 30, Chap. 13
Illinois	All licensed professions	Professional Service Corp. Act
Indiana	All licensed professions	Professional Corp. Acts IC 23
Iowa	Accountants, architects, chiropractors, dentists, doctors, engineers, land surveyors, lawyers, optometrists, osteopaths, podiatrists, veterinarians	Professional Corp. Act 496C
Kansas	All licensed professions	Professional Corp. Law of Kansas Chap. 17
Kentucky	All licensed professions	Professional Service Corps., Kentucky Revised Statutes Chap. 274

Min. No. of Share- holders	Title of Form to Be Filed	Address	Filing Fee
1	Articles of Incorporation	Charter Section Sec'y of State Tallahassee, Florida 32304	$63
1	Articles of Incorporation	Sec'y of State 225 Peachtree St., N. E. Atlanta, Georgia 30303	$93
1	Articles of Incorporation and Affidavits of Officers	Dept. of Regulatory Agencies 1010 Richards St. Honolulu, Hawaii 96813	$50 min.
1	None	Division of Corporations Boise, Idaho	$20 min.
1	Articles of Incorporation	Sec'y of State Corporation Division Springfield, Illinois	$75 filing fee $25 min. initial franchise
1	Articles of Incorporation	Corporations Division #155 State House Indianapolis, Indiana 46204	$36 min.
1	Articles of Incorporation	Sec'y of State Corporation Division Des Moines, Iowa 50319	$20 min.
1	Articles of Incorporation	Sec'y of State Corporation Division Topeka, Kansas 66612	$50
1	No standard form for public use	Sec'y of State #150 Capitol Bldg. Frankfort, Kentucky 40601	$25 min.

State	Professions Covered by P. C. Act	Title and No. of P. C. Act
Louisiana	Accountants, chiropractors, dentists, doctors, lawyers	Louisiana Revised Statutes 12:8, 9, 11, 12, 14
Maine	Accountants, architects, chiropodists, chiropractors, dentists, doctors, lawyers, life insurance agents, osteopaths, podiatrists	Professional Service Corp. Act Chap. 22
Maryland	Accountants, doctors, lawyers, veterinarians. Architects and engineers can choose P. C.s or general business corporations.	Title 5, Maryland Code
Massachusetts	Accountants, chiropractors, dentists, doctors, electrologists, engineers, lawyers, optometrists, physical therapists, podiatrists, psychologists, veterinarians	Professional Corps., Chap. 156A
Michigan	All licensed professions	Act 192, P. A. of 1962, as amended
Minnesota	Accountants, chiropractors, dentists, doctors, lawyers, optometrists, osteopaths, podiatrists, psychologists, veterinarians	Minnesota Professional Corps. Act, Minn. Stat. 319A
Mississippi	All licensed professions	Mississippi Professional Corp. Law
Missouri	Accountants, architects, chiropodists, chiropractors, dentists, doctors, engineers, lawyers, optometrists, osteopaths, podiatrists, veterinarians	Title XXIII, Chap. 356 Revised Statutes of Missouri 1969, as amended

Min. No. of Shareholders	Title of Form to Be Filed	Address	Filing Fee
1	No forms available	Sec'y of State Corporations Division P. O. Box 44125 Baton Rouge, Louisiana	$25 min.
1	Articles of Incorporation	Sec'y of State Augusta, Maine 04333	$60 min.
1	Form No. 1 Form No. 25 (every year)	Dept. of Assessments and Taxation 301 West Preston St. Baltimore, Maryland 21201	$40 min.
1	Articles of Organization	Sec'y of the Commonwealth Corporation Division One Ashburton Place Boston, Massachusetts 02108	$125 min.
1	Articles of Incorporation Form C&S 101	Michigan Dept. of Commerce Corporation Division Box 30054 Lansing, Michigan 48909	$35 min.
1	Articles of Incorporation	Sec'y of State Corporation Division 180 State Office Bldg. St. Paul, Minnesota 55155	$75.50 min.
1	Articles of Incorporation	Sec'y of State P. O. Box 136 Jackson, Mississippi 39205	$25 min.
1	Articles of Incorporation Corp. Form #41	Sec'y of State Jefferson City, Missouri 65101	$53

State	Professions Covered by P. C. Act	Title and No. of P. C. Act
Montana	Accountants, architects, chiropodists, chiropractors, dentists, doctors, engineers, lawyers, nurses, optometrists, osteopaths, pharmacists, physical therapists, veterinarians	Professional Service Corp. Act, Chap. 21, Title 15, Revised Codes of Montana
Nebraska	All registered professions	Nebraska Professional Corp. Act, Chap. 21, Article 22
Nevada	All licensed professions	Professional Corps. and Associations Act
New Hampshire	Accountants, architects, chiropractors, dentists, doctors, engineers, nurses, optometrists, pharmacists, psychologists, veterinarians	Revised Statutes Annotated–Chap. 294-A, Professional Assns.
	INFORMATION UNAVAILABLE AT PRESS TIME	
New Jersey	All licensed professions	Professional Service Corp. Act NJSA 14A:17–1 et seq.
New Mexico	All licensed professions	Professional Corp. Act Sections 51-22-1 to 51-22-13 NMSA 1953 Compilation
New York	All licensed professions	Business Corp. Law Article 15
North Carolina	Accountants, architects, chiropractors, dentists, doctors, engineers, landscape architects, lawyers, optometrists, osteopaths, podiatrists, psychologists, surveyors, veterinarians	Professional Corp. Act Chap. 55B
North Dakota	All licensed professions	Professional Corp. Act Chap. 10-13

Min. No. of Share-holders	Title of Form to Be Filed	Address	Filing Fee
1	Forms not prescribed or furnished by state	Sec'y of State Capitol Helena, Montana 59601	$70 min.
1	Articles of Incorporation	Sec'y of State Corporation Division #2304 State Capitol Bldg. Lincoln, Nebraska 68509	$20 min.
1	Articles of Incorporation	Sec'y of State Corporation Division Carson City, Nevada	$50 min.
1	Record of Organization	Sec'y of State Concord, New Hampshire	$60 min.

INFORMATION UNAVAILABLE AT PRESS TIME

1	Certificate of Incorporation	New Jersey Department of State Commercial Recording Bureau Corporate Filing Section P. O. Box 1330 Trenton, New Jersey 08625	$60
1	Articles of Incorporation	State Corporation Commission Corporation & Franchise Tax Depts. P. O. Drawer 1269 Santa Fe, New Mexico 87501	$50 min.
1	Certificate of Incorporation	New York State Division of Corporations 162 Washington Avenue Albany, New York 12231	$60
1	Articles of Incorporation; Certification of Eligibility to Practice from licensing board	Sec'y of State Corporations Division 116 West Jones St. Raleigh, North Carolina 27603	$45 min.
1	Duplicate Originals of Articles of Incorporation	Sec'y of State Division of Corporations Bismarck, North Dakota 58505	$100

State	Professions Covered by P. C. Act	Title and No. of P. C. Act
Ohio	All licensed professions	Chap. 1785, Ohio Revised Code
Oklahoma	Accountants, architects, chiropodists, chiropractors, dentists, doctors, nurses, optometrists, osteopaths, physical therapists, podiatrists, psychologists, veterinarians	Professional Corp. Act Title 18
Oregon	All licensed professions	Chap. 58, Professional Corps.
Pennsylvania	Accountants, architects, auctioneers, chiropractors, dentists, doctors, engineers, funeral directors, landscape architects, lawyers, nurses, optometrists, osteopaths, pharmacists, podiatrists, psychologists, veterinarians	Pennsylvania Corp. Law—Act 160 of 1970
Rhode Island	Accountants, architects, chiropodists, chiropractors, dentists, doctors, engineers, nurses, optometrists, veterinarians	Title 7, Chap. 5.1 Professional Service Corps.
South Carolina	All licensed professions	South Carolina Professional Association Act
South Dakota	Accountants, chiropractors, dentists, doctors, lawyers, optometrists, veterinarians	SDCL Chapter 47-11 through 47-138-18
Tennessee	All licensed professions	Title 48, Chap. 20, Tennessee Code Annotated (Tennessee Professional Corp. Act)

Min. No. of Shareholders	Title of Form to Be Filed	Address	Filing Fee
1	Articles of Incorporation	Sec'y of State Division of Corporations 30 East Broad St. Columbus, Ohio 43215	$75
1	Duplicate Originals of Articles of Incorporation	Sec'y of State Rm. 101 Oklahoma State Capitol Bldg. Oklahoma City, Oklahoma 73105	$11 min.
1	Duplicate Originals of Professional Corp. Articles of Incorporation 11-P	Corporation Commissioner Commerce Bldg. Salem, Oregon 97310	$20 min.
1	Articles of Incorporation—Domestic Professional Corp.	Commonwealth of Pennsylvania Corporation Bureau Harrisburg, Pennsylvania	$75 min.
1	Duplicate Originals of Articles of Incorporation	Sec'y of State Providence, Rhode Island	$110
1	Articles of Association	Register of Mesne Conveyance Richland County Court House Columbia, South Carolina 29202	Sliding scale
1	Articles of Incorporation	Sec'y of State State Capitol Pierre, South Dakota 57501	$40 min.
1	Corporation Charter	Sec'y of State Corporation Division Nashville, Tennessee 37219	$10 min.

State	*Professions Covered by P. C. Act*	*Title and No. of P. C. Act*
Texas	Accountants, dentists, doctors, nurses, optometrists, osteopaths, podiatrists, psychologists, surveyors, veterinarians	Texas Professional Corp. Act
Utah	All licensed professions	Title 16, Chap. 11, Professional Corp. Act
Vermont	Architects, doctors, lawyers	Title 11
Virginia	All licensed professions	Chap. 7, Professional Corps.
Washington	All licensed professions	RCW 18.100
West Virginia	All licensed professions	Under general corporation laws
Wisconsin	All licensed professions	Service Corp. Law, Wisconsin Statute 180.99
Wyoming	Not specifically covered by statute	Sections 17-49.1 and 17.49-2 Wyoming Statutes 1957

Min. No. of Shareholders	Title of Form to Be Filed	Address	Filing Fee
1	Articles of Incorporation	Sec'y of State Corporation Division Sam Houston State Office Bldg. Austin, Texas 78711	$100
1	Application for a Certificate of Authority; Articles of Incorporation	Room 203 State Capitol Bldg. Salt Lake City, Utah 84114	$50 min.
2	DCI Articles of Association with proof of profession attached	Sec'y of State Montpelier, Vermont 05602	$20 min.
1	Articles of Incorporation	State Corporation Commissioner Box 1197 Richmond, Virginia 23209	$25 min.
1	Forms not supplied	Corporations Division Sec'y of State Legislative Bldg. Olympia, Washington 98501	$100 min.
1	Form 101, Articles of Incorporation	Sec'y of State Corporation Division Charleston, West Virginia 25305	$20 min.
1	Articles of Incorporation, Form 2	Sec'y of State Corporation Division State Capitol Bldg. Madison, Wisconsin 53702	$55 min.
No provision for minimum	No forms are furnished	Sec'y of State Division of Corporations Cheyenne, Wyoming	$27.50 min.*

*Bill to increase fees pending in legislature.

State	Title and No. of General Business Corp. Act	Min. No. of Shareholders	Title of Form to Be Filed	Address	Filing Fee
Alabama	Title 10, 1958 Recompiled Code	1	Charter	Judge of Probate of County	N/A
Alaska	Alaska Statute 10.05	1	Duplicate Originals of Articles of Incorporation	Dept. of Commerce and Economic Development Pouch D Juneau, Alaska 99811	$30
Arizona	Arizona Revised Statutes 10-050—10-149	1	Articles of Incorporation	Sec'y of State 2222 West Encanto Blvd. Phoenix, Arizona 85009	$50
Arkansas	Act 576 of 1965	1	Articles of Incorporation	Sec'y of State Corporation Dept. State Capitol Bldg. Little Rock, Arkansas 72201	$15 min.
California	Title 1, Division 1, Calif. Corps. Code	1	Articles of Incorporation	Sec'y of State 111 Capitol Mall Sacramento, California 95814	$265
Colorado	Title 7, Volume 3	Not given	Articles of Incorporation	Sec'y of State 1575 Sherman Denver, Colorado 80203	$24.75 min.

State	Title and No. of General Business Corp. Act	Min. No. of Shareholders	Title of Form to Be Filed	Address	Filing Fee
Connecticut	Stock Corporation Act Chap. 599	1	Certificate of Incorporation	Sec'y of State P. O. Box 846 30 Trinity St. Hartford, Connecticut 06115	$91 min.
Delaware	Title 8, General Corp. Law	1	Certificate of Incorporation	*	N/A
Florida	General Corp. Act Chap. 607	1	Articles of Incorporation	Charter Section Sec'y of State Tallahassee, Florida 32304	$63
Georgia	Georgia Title 22—Corporations	1	Articles of Incorporation	Sec'y of State 225 Peachtree St., N. E. Atlanta, Georgia 30303	$93
Hawaii	Chap. 416, Hawaii Revised Statutes	1	Articles of Incorporation and Affidavits of Officers	Dept. of Regulatory Agencies 1010 Richards Street Honolulu, Hawaii 96813	$50 min.
Idaho	Title 30, Chap. 1	1	None	Division of Corporations Boise, Idaho	$20 min.
Illinois	Business Corp. Act	1	Articles of Incorporation	Sec'y of State Corporation Division Springfield, Illinois	$75 filing fee $25 min. initial franchise

N/A—not available

*Corporation must have registered office with registered agent in state. Certificate must be filed through registered agent.

State	Title and No. of General Business Corp. Act	Min. No. of Shareholders	Title of Form to Be Filed	Address	Filing Fee
Indiana	Indiana General Corp. Act IC 23	1	Articles of Incorporation	Corporations Division #155 State House Indianapolis, Indiana 46204	$36 min.
Iowa	Iowa Business Corp. Act Chap. 496A	1	Articles of Incorporation	Sec'y of State Corporation Division Des Moines, Iowa 50319	$20 min.
Kansas	Kansas General Corp. Code Chap. 17	1	Articles of Incorporation	Sec'y of State Corporation Division Topeka, Kansas 66612	$50
Kentucky	Kentucky Business Corp. Act, Kentucky Revised Statutes Chap. 271A	1	No standard form for public use	Sec'y of State #150 Capitol Bldg. Frankfort, Kentucky 40601	$25 min.

State	Title and No. of General Business Corp. Act	Min. No. of Shareholders	Title of Form to Be Filed	Address	Filing Fee
Louisiana	Louisiana Revised Statutes 12:1, 2, 3	1	No standard form	Sec'y of State Corporations Division P. O. Box 44125 Baton Rouge, Louisiana 70804	$25 min.
Maine	Maine Business Corp. Act Title 13-A	1	Articles of Incorporation	Sec'y of State Augusta, Maine 04333	$60 min.
Maryland	Corps. and Assns. Article of Annotated Code of Maryland	1	Form 1	Dept. of Assessments and Taxation 301 West Preston St. Baltimore, Maryland 21201	$40 min.
Massachusetts	Business Corps. Chap. 156B	1	Articles of Organization	Sec'y of the Commonwealth Corporation Division One Ashburton Place Boston, Massachusetts 02108	$125 min.

State	Title and No. of General Business Corp. Act	Min. No. of Shareholders	Title of Form to Be Filed	Address	Filing Fee
Michigan	Act 284, P. A. of 1972, as amended	1	Articles of Incorporation Form C&S 101	Michigan Dept. of Commerce Corporation Division Box 30054 Lansing, Michigan 48909	$35 min.
Minnesota	Minn. Stat. 301	1	Articles of Incorporation	Sec'y of State Corporation Division 180 State Office Bldg. St. Paul, Minnesota 55155	$75.50 min.
Mississippi	Mississippi Business Corp. Law	2	Articles of Incorporation	Sec'y of State P. O. Box 136 Jackson, Mississippi 39205	$25 min.
Missouri	Title XXIII, Chap. 351 Revised Statutes of Missouri 1969, as amended	1	Articles of Incorporation Corp. Form #41	Sec'y of State Jefferson City, Missouri 65101	$53
Montana	Montana Business Corp. Act, Chap. 22, Title 15, Revised Code of Montana	1	Not prescribed or furnished by state	Sec'y of State Capitol Helena, Montana 59601	$70 min.
Nebraska	Nebraska Business Corp. Act, Chap. 21, Article 20	1	Articles of Incorporation	Sec'y of State Corporation Division #2304 State Capitol Bldg. Lincoln, Nebraska 68509	$20 min.

State	Title and No. of General Business Corp. Act	Min. No. of Shareholders	Title of Form to Be Filed	Address	Filing Fee
Nevada	Private Corps. Chap. 78	3	Articles of Incorporation	Sec'y of State Corporation Division Carson City, Nevada	$50 min.
New Hampshire	Revised Statutes Annotated (1955) Chap. 294, Business Corps.	1	Record of Organization	Sec'y of State Concord, New Hampshire	$60 min.
New Jersey	New Jersey Business Corp. Act NJSA 14:A 1-1 et seq.	1	Certificate of Incorporation	New Jersey Department of State Commercial Recording Bureau Corporate Filing Section P. O. Box 1330 Trenton, New Jersey 08625	$60
New Mexico	Business Corp. Act Sections 51-24-1—51-31-11, NMSA 1953 Compilation	1	Articles of Incorporation	State Corporation Commission Corporation and Franchise Tax Depts. P. O. Drawer 1269 Santa Fe, New Mexico 87501	$50 min.
New York	Business Corp. Law	1	Certificate of Incorporation	New York State Division of Corporations 162 Washington Avenue Albany, New York 12231	$60

State	Title and No. of General Business Corp. Act	Min. No. of Shareholders	Title of Form to Be Filed	Address	Filing Fee
North Carolina	Business Corp. Act Chap. 55	1	Articles of Incorporation	Sec'y of State Corporations Division 116 West Jones Street Raleigh, North Carolina 27603	$45 min.
North Dakota	North Dakota Business Act	3	Duplicate Originals of Articles of Incorporation	Sec'y of State Division of Corporations Bismarck, North Dakota 58505	$100 min.
Ohio	Chap. 1701, Ohio Revised Code	1	Articles of Incorporation	Sec'y of State Division of Corporations 30 East Broad Street Columbus, Ohio 43215	$75
Oklahoma	General Business Corp. Act Title 18	3	Duplicate Originals of Articles of Incorporation	Sec'y of State Rm. 101 Oklahoma State Capitol Bldg. Oklahoma City, Oklahoma 73105	$11 min.
Oregon	Chap. 57, Private Corporations	1	Duplicate Originals of Articles of Incorporation 11-B	Corporation Commissioner Commerce Bldg. Salem, Oregon 97310	$20 min.

State	Title and No. of General Business Corp. Act	Min. No. of Shareholders	Title of Form to Be Filed	Address	Filing Fee
Pennsylvania	P. L. 364	1	Articles of Incorporation—Domestic Business Corp.; Registry Statement (triplicate)	Commonwealth of Pennsylvania Corporation Bureau Harrisburg, Pennsylvania	$75 min.
Rhode Island	Title 7, Corporations, Associations and Partnerships	1	Duplicate Originals of Articles of Incorporation	Sec'y of State Providence, Rhode Island	$110
South Carolina	Chap. 1 of 1962 Code—Vol. 3	1	Articles of Incorporation	Sec'y of State Box 11350 Columbia, South Carolina 29201	$45 min.
South Dakota	SDCL 47-1—47-31	1	Articles of Incorporation	Sec'y of State State Capitol Pierre, South Dakota 57501	$40 min.
Tennessee	Title 48, Tennessee Code Annotated (Tennessee General Corp. Act)	1	Corporation Charter	Sec'y of State Corporate Division Nashville, Tennessee 37219	$10 min.

State	Title and No. of General Business Corp. Act	Min. No. of Shareholders	Title of Form to Be Filed	Address	Filing Fee
Texas	Texas Business Corp. Act	1	Articles of Incorporation	Sec'y of State Corporation Division Sam Houston State Office Bldg. Austin, Texas 78711	$100
Utah	Title 16, Chap. 10	1	Application for Certificate of Authority; Articles of Incorporation	Room 203 State Capitol Bldg. Salt Lake City, Utah 84114	$50 min.
Vermont	Title 11	1	DCI—Articles of Association	Sec'y of State Montpelier, Vermont 05602	$20 min.
Virginia	Virginia Stock Corp. Act	1	Articles of Incorporation	State Corporation Commission Box 1197 Richmond, Virginia 23209	$25 min.
Washington	RCW 23A	1	Forms not supplied	Corporations Division Sec'y of State Legislative Bldg. Olympia, Washington 98501	$100 min.

State	Title and No. of General Business Corp. Act	Min. No. of Shareholders	Title of Form to Be Filed	Address	Filing Fee
West Virginia	Chap. 31 Article 1	1	Articles of Incorporation	Sec'y of State Corporation Division Charleston, West Virginia 25305	$20 min.
Wisconsin	Wisconsin Business Corp. Law, Chap. 180	1	Articles of Incorporation, Form 2	Sec'y of State Corporation Division State Capitol Bldg. Madison, Wisconsin 53702	$55 min.
Wyoming	Section 17-36.1—Section 17-36.128 Wyoming Statutes 1957	No provision for minimum	No forms are furnished	Sec'y of State Division of Corporations Cheyenne, Wyoming	$27.50 min.*

*Bill to increase fees pending in legislature.

Sample Minutes and Bylaws for a Small Corporation

(FOR USE IF THERE IS ONE INCORPORATOR)

MINUTES OF ORGANIZATION MEETING OF
(NAME OF YOUR CORPORATION)

The undersigned, being the sole incorporator of this corporation, held an organization meeting at the date and place set forth below, at which meeting the following action was taken:

It was resolved that a copy of the Certificate of Incorporation together with the receipt issued by the Department of State showing payment of the statutory organization tax and the date and payment of the fee for filing the original Certificate of Incorporation be appended to these minutes.

Bylaws regulating the conduct of the business and affairs of the corporation, as prepared by _____ _____, counsel for the corporation, were adopted and ordered appended hereto.

The persons whose names appear below were named as directors.

The board of directors was authorized to issue all of the unsubscribed shares of the corporation at such time and in such amounts as determined by the board and to accept in payment money or other property, tangible or intangible, actually received or labor or services actually performed for the corporation or for its benefit or in its formation.

The principal office of the corporation was fixed at

Dated at
this   day of   19   _____
                                          Sole Incorporator

The undersigned accept their nomination as directors:

_____   _____
    Type director's name   Signature

_____   _____

_____   _____

The following are appended to the minutes of this meeting:

    Copy of Certificate of Incorporation, filed on
    Receipt of Department of State
    Bylaws

(FOR USE IF THERE IS MORE THAN ONE INCORPORATOR)

MINUTES OF ORGANIZATION MEETING OF
(NAME OF YOUR CORPORATION)

The organization meeting of the incorporators was held at
on the   day of   19   at   o'clock   M.
The following were present:

being a quorum and all of the incorporators.

One of the incorporators called the meeting to order. Upon motion duly made, seconded, and carried, _____ was duly elected chairman of the meeting and _____ duly elected secretary thereof. They accepted their respective offices and proceeded with the discharge of their duties.

A written Waiver of Notice of this meeting signed by all the incorporators was submitted, read by the secretary, and ordered appended to these minutes.

The secretary then presented and read to the meeting a copy of the Certificate of Incorporation of the corporation and reported that on the   day of   , 19   , the original thereof was duly filed by the Department of State.

Upon motion duly made, seconded, and carried, said report was adopted and the secretary was directed to append to these minutes a copy of the Certificate of Incorporation, together with the original receipt issued by the Department of State, showing payment of the statutory organization tax, the filing fee, and the date of filing of the certificate.

The chairman stated that the election of directors was then in order.

The following were nominated as directors:

Upon motion duly made, seconded, and carried, it was unanimously

RESOLVED, that each of the abovenamed nominees be and hereby is elected a director of the corporation.

Upon motion duly made, seconded, and carried, and by the affirmative vote of all present, it was

RESOLVED, that the board of directors be and it is hereby authorized to issue all of the unsubscribed shares of the corporation at such time and in such amounts as determined by the board, and to accept in payment money or other property, tangible or intangible, actually received or labor or other services actually performed for the corporation or for its benefit or in its formation.

The chairman presented and read, article by article, the proposed bylaws for the conduct and regulation of the business and affairs of the corporation as prepared by _____ _____, counsel for the corporation.

Upon motion duly made, seconded, and carried, they were adopted and in all respects, ratified, confirmed and approved, as and for the bylaws of this corporation.

The secretary was directed to cause them to be inserted in the minute book immediately following the receipt of the Department of State.

Upon motion duly made, seconded, and carried, the principal office of the corporation was fixed at_____, County of _____, State of New York.

Upon motion duly made, seconded, and carried, and by the affirmative vote of all present, it was

RESOLVED, that the signing of these minutes shall constitute full ratification thereof and Waiver of Notice of the Meeting by the signatories.

There being no further business before the meeting, the same was, on motion, duly adjourned.

Dated this   day of   , 19 .

_____

Secretary of meeting

_____
_____

Chairman of meeting

_____
_____
_____

The following are appended to the minutes of this meeting:

Waiver of Notice of organization meeting
Copy of Certificate of Incorporation, filed on
Receipt of Department of State
Bylaws

WAIVER OF NOTICE OF ORGANIZATION MEETING
OF
(NAME OF YOUR CORPORATION)

We, the undersigned, being all the incorporators named in the Certificate of Incorporation of the above corporation, hereby agree and consent that the organization meeting thereof be held on the date and at the time and place stated below and hereby waive all notice of such meeting and of any adjournment thereof.

Place of meeting:
Date of meeting:
Time of meeting:

_____
Incorporator

_____
Incorporator

_____
Incorporator

Dated:

BYLAWS
OF
(NAME OF YOUR CORPORATION)

ARTICLE I — Offices

The principal office of the corporation shall be in the   of
, County of   , State of New York. The corporation may
also have offices at such other places within or without the State of
New York as the board may from time to time determine or the business of the corporation may require.

ARTICLE II — Shareholders

1. *Place of Meetings.* Meetings of shareholders shall be held at
the principal office of the corporation or at such place within or
without the State of New York as the board shall authorize.

2. *Annual Meeting.* The annual meeting of the shareholders shall
be held on the   day of   at   M. in each year if not a
legal holiday, and, if a legal holiday, then on the next business day
following at the same hour, when the shareholders shall elect a
board and transact such other business as may properly come before
the meeting.

3. *Special Meetings.* Special meetings of the shareholders may be
called by the board or by the president and shall be called by the
president or the secretary at the request in writing of a majority of
the board or at the request in writing by shareholders owning a majority in amount of the shares issued and outstanding. Such request
shall state the purpose or purposes of the proposed meeting. Business transacted at a special meeting shall be confined to the purposes stated in the notice.

4. *Fixing Record Date.* For the purpose of determining the shareholders entitled to notice of or to vote at any meeting of shareholders or any adjournment thereof, or to express consent to or dissent from any proposal without a meeting, or for the purpose of

determining shareholders entitled to receive payment of any dividend or the allotment of any rights, or for the purpose of any other action, the board shall fix, in advance, a date as the record date for any such determination of shareholders. Such date shall not be more than fifty nor less than ten days before the date of such meeting, nor more than fifty days prior to any other action. If no record date is fixed, it shall be determined in accordance with the provisions of law.

5. *Notice of Meetings of Shareholders.* Written notice of each meeting of shareholders shall state the purpose or purposes for which the meeting is called, the place, date, and hour of the meeting, and unless it is the annual meeting, shall indicate that it is being issued by or at the direction of the person or persons calling the meeting. Notice shall be given either personally or by mail to each shareholder entitled to vote at such meeting, not less than ten nor more than fifty days before the date of the meeting. If action is proposed to be taken that might entitle shareholders to payment for their shares, the notice shall include a statement of that purpose and to that effect. If mailed, the notice is given when deposited in the United States mail, with postage thereon prepaid, directed to the shareholder at his address as it appears on the record of shareholders, or, if he shall have filed with the secretary a written request that notices to him be mailed to some other address, then directed to him at such other address.

6. *Waivers.* Notice of meeting need not be given to any shareholder who signs a waiver of notice, in person or by proxy, whether before or after the meeting. The attendance of any shareholder at a meeting, in person or by proxy, without protesting prior to the conclusion of the meeting the lack of notice of such meeting, shall constitute a waiver of notice by him.

7. *Quorum of Shareholders.* Unless the Certificate of Incorporation provides otherwise, the holders of (a majority) (your own determination of a quorum, expressed either as a fraction or a percentage) of the shares entitled to vote thereat shall constitute a quorum at a meeting of shareholders for the transaction of any business, provided that when a specified item of business is required to be

voted on by a class or classes, the holders of (a majority) (your own determination of a quorum, expressed either as a fraction or a percentage) of the shares of such class or classes shall constitute a quorum for the transaction of such specified item of business.

When a quorum is once present to organize a meeting, it is not broken by the subsequent withdrawal of any shareholders.

The shareholders present may adjourn the meeting despite the absence of a quorum.

8. *Proxies.* Every shareholder entitled to vote at a meeting of shareholders or to express consent or dissent without a meeting may authorize another person or persons to act for him by proxy.

Every proxy must be signed by the shareholder or his attorney-in-fact. No proxy shall be valid after expiration of eleven months from the date thereof unless otherwise provided in the proxy. Every proxy shall be revocable at the pleasure of the shareholder executing it, except as otherwise provided by law.

9. *Qualification of Voters.* Every shareholder of record shall be entitled at every meeting of shareholders to one vote for every share standing in his name on the record of shareholders, unless otherwise provided in the Certificate of Incorporation.

10. *Vote of Shareholders.* Except as otherwise required by statute or by the Certificate of Incorporation:

(Create your own election requirements, or use the following:)

(a) directors shall be elected by a plurality of the votes cast at a meeting of shareholders by the holders of shares entitled to vote in the election;

(b) all other corporate action shall be authorized by a majority of the votes cast.

11. *Written Consent of Shareholders.* Any action that may be taken by vote may be taken without a meeting on written consent, setting forth the action so taken, signed by the holders of all the outstanding shares entitled to vote thereon or signed by such lesser number of holders as may be provided for in the Certificate of Incorporation.

ARTICLE III — Directors

1. *Board of Directors.* Subject to any provision in the Certificate of Incorporation, the business of the corporation shall be managed by its board of directors, each of whom shall be at least 18 years of age and (choose the number) be shareholders.

2. *Number of Directors.* The number of directors shall be ————. When all of the shares are owned by less than three shareholders, the number of directors may be less than three but not less than the number of shareholders.

3. *Election and Term of Directors.* At each annual meeting of shareholders, the shareholders shall elect directors to hold office until the next annual meeting. Each director shall hold office until the expiration of the term for which he is elected and until his successor has been elected and qualified, or until his prior resignation or removal.

4. *Newly Created Directorships and Vacancies.* Newly created directorships resulting from an increase in the number of directors and vacancies occurring in the board for any reason except the removal of directors without cause may be filled by a vote of a majority of the directors then in office, although less than a quorum exists, unless otherwise provided in the Certificate of Incorporation. Vacancies occurring by reason of the removal of directors without cause shall be filled by vote of the shareholders unless otherwise provided in the Certificate of Incorporation. A director elected to fill a vacancy caused by resignation, death, or removal shall be elected to hold office for the unexpired term of his predecessor.

5. *Removal of Directors.* Any or all of the directors may be removed for cause by vote of the shareholders or by action of the board. Directors may be removed without cause only by vote of the shareholders.

6. *Resignation.* A director may resign at any time by giving written notice to the board, the president, or the secretary of the corporation. Unless otherwise specified in the notice, the resignation shall take effect upon receipt thereof by the board or such officer,

and the acceptance of the resignation shall not be necessary to make it effective.

7. *Quorum of Directors.* Unless otherwise provided in the Certificate of Incorporation, (a majority) (your own determination of a quorum, expressed either as a fraction or a percentage) of the entire board shall constitute a quorum for the transaction of business or of any specified item of business.

8. *Action of the Board.* Unless otherwise required by law, the vote of (a majority) (your own determination of a quorum, expressed either as a fraction or a percentage) of directors present at the time of the vote, if a quorum is present at such time, shall be the act of the board. Each director present shall have one vote regardless of the number of shares, if any, which he may hold.

9. *Place and Time of Board Meetings.* The board may hold its meetings at the office of the corporation or at such other places, either within or without the State of New York, as it may from time to time determine.

10. *Regular Annual Meeting.* A regular annual meeting of the board shall be held immediately following the annual meeting of shareholders at the place of such annual meeting of shareholders.

11. *Notice of Meetings of the Board, Adjournment.*

(a) Regular meetings of the board may be held without notice at such time and place as it shall from time to time determine. Special meetings of the board shall be held upon notice to the directors and may be called by the president upon three days' notice to each director either personally or by mail or by wire; special meetings shall be called by the president or by the secretary in a like manner on written request of two directors. Notice of a meeting need not be given to any director who submits a Waiver of Notice whether before or after the meeting or who attends the meeting without protesting prior thereto or at its commencement, the lack of notice to him.

(b) A majority of the directors present, whether or not a quorum is present, may adjourn any meeting to another time and place. Notice of the adjournment shall be given all directors who were absent at the time of the adjournment and, unless such time and place are announced at the meeting, to the other directors.

12. *Chairman.* The president, or, in his absence, a chairman chosen by the board, shall preside at all meetings of the board.

13. *Executive and Other Committees.* By resolution adopted by a majority of the entire board, the board may designate from among its members an executive committee and other committees, each consisting of three or more directors. Each such committee shall serve at the pleasure of the board.

14. *Compensation.* No compensation, as such, shall be paid to directors for their services, but by resolution of the board, a fixed sum and expenses for actual attendance at each regular or special meeting of the board may be authorized. Nothing herein contained shall be construed to preclude any director from serving the corporation in any other capacity and receiving compensation therefor.

ARTICLE IV — Officers

1. *Offices, Election, Term.*

(a) Unless otherwise provided for in the Certificate of Incorporation, the board may elect or appoint a president, one or more vice-presidents, a secretary and a treasurer, and such other officers as it may determine, who shall have such duties, powers, and functions as hereinafter provided.

(b) All officers shall be elected or appointed to hold office until the meeting of the board following the annual meeting of shareholders.

(c) Each officer shall hold office for the term for which he is elected or appointed and until his successor has been elected or appointed and qualified.

2. *Removal, Resignation, Salary, Etc.*

(a) Any officer elected or appointed by the board may be removed by the board with or without cause.

(b) In the event of the death, resignation, or removal of an officer, the board in its discretion may elect or appoint a successor to fill the unexpired term.

(c) Unless there is only one shareholder, any two or more offices may be held by the same person, except the offices of president and secretary. If there is only one shareholder, all offices may be held by the same person.

(d) The salaries of all officers shall be fixed by the board.

(e) The directors may require any officer to give security for the faithful performance of his duties.

3. *President.* The president shall be the chief executive officer of the corporation; he shall preside at all meetings of the shareholders and of the board; he shall have the management of the business of the corporation and shall see that all orders and resolutions of the board are effected.

4. *Vice-presidents.* During the absence or disability of the president, the vice-president, or, if there are more than one, the executive vice-president, shall have all the powers and functions of the president. Each vice-president shall perform such other duties as the board shall prescribe.

5. *Secretary.* The secretary shall:

(a) attend all meetings of the board and of the shareholders;

(b) record all votes and minutes of all proceedings in a book to be kept for that purpose;

(c) give or cause to be given notice of all meetings of shareholders and of special meetings of the board;

(d) keep in safe custody the seal of the corporation and affix it to any instrument when authorized by the board;

(e) when required, prepare or cause to be prepared and available at each meeting of shareholders a certified list in alphabetical order of the names of shareholders entitled to vote thereat, indicating the number of shares of each respective class held by each;

(f) keep all the documents and records of the corporation as required by law or otherwise in a proper and safe manner;

(g) perform such other duties as may be prescribed by the board.

6. *Assistant Secretaries.* During the absence or disability of the secretary, the assistant secretary, or, if there are more than one, the one so designated by the secretary or by the board, shall have all the powers and functions of the secretary.

7. *Treasurer.* The treasurer shall:

(a) have the custody of the corporate funds and securities;

(b) keep full and accurate accounts of receipts and disbursements in the corporate books;

(c) deposit all money and other valuables in the name and to the credit of the corporation in such depositories as may be designated by the board;

(d) disburse the funds of the corporation as may be ordered or authorized by the board and preserve proper vouchers for such disbursements;

(e) render to the president and board at the regular meetings of the board, or whenever they require it, an account of all his transactions as treasurer and of the financial condition of the corporation;

(f) render a full financial report at the annual meeting of the shareholders if so requested;

(g) be furnished by all corporate officers and agents, at his request, with such reports and statements as he may require as to all financial transactions of the corporation;

(h) perform such other duties as are given to him by these bylaws or as from time to time are assigned to him by the board or the president.

8. *Assistant Treasurer.* During the absence or disability of the treasurer, the assistant treasurer, or, if there are more than one, the one so designated by the secretary or by the board, shall have all the powers and functions of the treasurer.

9. *Sureties and Bonds.* In case the board shall so require, any officer or agent of the corporation shall execute to the corporation a bond in such sum and with such surety or sureties as the board may direct, conditioned upon the faithful performance of his duties to the corporation and including responsibility for negligence and for the accounting for all property, funds, or securities of the corporation which may come into his hands.

ARTICLE V — Certificates for Shares

1. *Certificates.* The shares of the corporation shall be represented by certificates. They shall be numbered and entered in the books of the corporation as they are issued. They shall exhibit the holder's

name and the number of shares and shall be signed by the president or a vice-president and the treasurer or the secretary and shall bear the corporate seal.

2. *Lost or Destroyed Certificates.* The board may direct a new certificate or certificates to be issued in place of any certificate or certificates theretofore issued by the corporation, alleged to have been lost or destroyed, upon the making of an affidavit of that fact by the person claiming the certificate to be lost or destroyed. When authorizing such issue of a new certificate or certificates, the board may, in its discretion and as a condition precedent to the issuance thereof, require the owner of such lost or destroyed certificate or certificates, or his legal representative, to advertise the same in such manner as it shall require and/or give the corporation a bond in such sum and with such surety or sureties as it may direct as indemnity against any claim that may be made against the corporation with respect to the certificate alleged to have been lost or destroyed.

3. *Transfers of Shares.*

(a) Upon surrender to the corporation or the transfer agent of the corporation of a certificate for shares duly endorsed or accompanied by proper evidence of succession, assignment, or authority to transfer, it shall be the duty of the corporation to issue a new certificate to the person entitled thereto, and cancel the old certificate; every such transfer shall be entered in the transfer book of the corporation which shall be kept at its principal office. No transfer shall be made within ten days next preceding the annual meeting of shareholders.

(b) The corporation shall be entitled to treat the holder of record of any share as the holder in fact thereof and, accordingly, shall not be bound to recognize any equitable or other claim to or interest in such share on the part of any other person whether or not it shall have express or other notice thereof, except as expressly provided by the laws of the State of New York.

4. *Closing Transfer Books.* The board shall have the power to close the share transfer books of the corporation for a period of not more than ten days during the thirty-day period immediately preceding (1) any shareholders' meeting, or (2) any date upon which share-

holders shall be called upon to or have a right to take action without a meeting, or (3) any date fixed for the payment of a dividend or any other form of distribution, and only those shareholders of record at the time the transfer books are closed, shall be recognized as such for the purpose of (1) receiving notice of or voting at such meeting, or (2) allowing them to take appropriate action, or (3) entitling them to receive any dividend or other form of distribution.

ARTICLE VI — Dividends

Subject to the provisions of the Certificate of Incorporation and to applicable law, dividends on the outstanding shares of the corporation may be declared in such amounts and at such time or times as the board may determine. Before payment of any dividend, there may be set aside out of the net profits of the corporation available for dividends such sum or sums as the board from time to time in its absolute discretion deems proper as a reserve fund to meet contingencies, or for equalizing dividends, or for repairing or maintaining any property of the corporation, or for such other purpose as the board shall think conducive to the interests of the corporation, and the board may modify or abolish any such reserve.

ARTICLE VII — Corporate Seal

The seal of the corporation shall be circular in form and bear the name of the corporation, the year of its organization, and the words "Corporate Seal, New York." The seal may be used by causing it to be impressed directly on the instrument or writing to be sealed, or upon adhesive substance affixed thereto. The seal on the certificates for shares or on any corporate obligation for the payment of money may be a facsimile, engraved or printed.

ARTICLE VIII — Execution of Instruments

All corporate instruments and documents shall be signed or countersigned, executed, verified, or acknowledged by such officer or officers or other person or persons as the board may from time to time designate.

ARTICLE IX — Fiscal Year

This fiscal year shall begin the first day of (month) in each year.

ARTICLE X — References to Certificate of Incorporation

References to the Certificate of Incorporation in these bylaws shall include all amendments thereto or changes thereof unless specifically excepted.

ARTICLE XI — Bylaw Changes
Amendment, Repeal, Adoption, Election of Directors

(a) Except as otherwise provided in the Certificate of Incorporation, the bylaws may be amended, repealed, or adopted by vote of the holders of the shares at the time entitled to vote in the election of any directors. Bylaws may also be amended, repealed, or adopted by the board, but any bylaw adopted by the board may be amended by the shareholders entitled to vote thereon as hereinabove provided.

(b) If any bylaw regulating an impending election of directors is adopted, amended, or repealed by the board, there shall be set forth in the notice of the next meeting of shareholders for the election of directors the bylaw so adopted, amended, or repealed, together with a concise statement of the changes made.

MINUTES OF FIRST MEETING OF BOARD OF DIRECTORS
OF
(NAME OF YOUR CORPORATION)

The first meeting of the board was held at
on the   day of   , 19   at   o'clock   M.
The following were present:

being a quorum and all of the directors of the corporation.

_____ was nominated and elected temporary chairman and acted as such until relieved by the president.

_____ was nominated and elected temporary secretary, and acted as such until relieved by the permanent secretary.

The secretary then presented and read to the meeting a Waiver of Notice of Meeting, subscribed by all the directors of the corporation, and it was ordered that it be appended to the minutes of this meeting.

The following were duly nominated and, a vote having been taken, were unanimously elected officers of the corporation to serve for one year and until their successors are elected and qualified:

President:
Vice-President:
Secretary:
Treasurer:

The president and secretary thereupon assumed their respective offices in place and stead of the temporary chairman and the temporary secretary.

Upon motion duly made, seconded, and carried, it was

RESOLVED, that the seal now presented at this meeting, an impression of
which is directed to be made in the
margin of the minute book, be and the
same is hereby adopted as the seal of
this corporation, and further

RESOLVED, that the president and treasurer be and they
hereby are authorized to issue certificates for shares in the
form as submitted to this meeting, and further

RESOLVED, that the share and transfer book now presented at this meeting be and the same hereby is adopted as
the share and transfer book of the corporation. Upon motion
duly made, seconded, and carried, it was

RESOLVED, that the treasurer be and hereby is authorized
to open a bank account in behalf of the corporation with
(name of bank) located at (address) and a resolution for that
purpose on the printed form of said bank was adopted and
was ordered appended to the minutes of this meeting.

Upon motion duly made, seconded, and carried, it was

RESOLVED, that the corporation proceed to carry on the
business for which it was incorporated.

(The following is the appropriate form to be included here if a
proposal or offer for the sale, transfer, or exchange of property has
been made to the corporation:)

The secretary then presented to the meeting a written proposal
from _____ _____ to the corporation.

Upon motion duly made, seconded, and carried, the said proposal was ordered filed with the secretary, and he was requested to
spread the same at length upon the minutes, said proposal being as
follows:

(Insert proposal here.)

The proposal was taken up for consideration, and, on motion, the
following resolution was unanimously adopted:

WHEREAS, a written proposal has been made to this corporation in the form as set forth above in these minutes, and

WHEREAS, in the judgment of this board the assets proposed to be transferred to the corporation are reasonably worth the amount of the consideration demanded therefor, and that it is in the best interests of this corporation to accept the said offer as set forth in said proposal,

NOW, THEREFORE, IT IS RESOLVED, that said offer, as set forth in said proposal, be and the same hereby is approved and accepted, and that in accordance with the terms thereof, this corporation shall, as full payment for said property, issue to said offeror(s) or nominee(s) (number of shares) fully paid and nonassessable shares of this corporation, and it is

FURTHER RESOLVED, that upon the delivery to this corporation of said assets and the execution and delivery of such proper instruments as may be necessary to transfer and convey the same to this corporation, the officers of this corporation are authorized and directed to execute and deliver the certificate or certificates for such shares as are required to be issued and delivered on acceptance of said offer in accordance with the foregoing.

The chairman presented to the meeting a form of certificate required under Tax Law Section 275A to be filed in the office of the tax commission.

Upon motion duly made, seconded, and carried, it was

RESOLVED, that the proper officers of this corporation are hereby authorized and directed to execute and file such certificate forthwith. On motion duly made, seconded, and carried, it was

RESOLVED, that all of the acts taken and decisions made at the organization meeting be and they hereby are ratified, and it was

FURTHER RESOLVED, that the signing of these minutes shall constitute full ratification thereof and Waiver of Notice of the Meeting by the signatories.

There being no further business before the meeting, on motion duly made, seconded, and carried, the meeting was adjourned. Dated this   day of   , 19   .

_____

_____   Secretary

_____   _____

_____   Chairman

A true copy of each of the following documents referred to in the foregoing minutes is appended hereto.
Waiver of Notice of Meeting
Specimen certificate for shares
Resolution designating depository of funds

WAIVER OF NOTICE OF FIRST MEETING OF BOARD
OF
(NAME OF YOUR CORPORATION)

We, the undersigned, being all the directors of the above corporation, hereby agree and consent that the first meeting of the board be held on the date and at the time and place stated below for the purpose of electing officers and the transaction thereat of all such other business as may lawfully come before said meeting and hereby waive all notice of the meeting and of any adjournment thereof.

Place of meeting:
Date of meeting:
Time of meeting:

_____
Director

_____
Director

_____
Director

Dated:

MINUTES OF FIRST MEETING OF SHAREHOLDERS
OF
(NAME OF YOUR CORPORATION)

The first meeting of the shareholders was held at
on the   day of   , 19   at   o'clock   M.

The meeting was duly called to order by the president, who stated the object of the meeting.

The secretary then read the roll of the shareholders as they appear in the share record book of the corporation and reported that a quorum of the shareholders was present.

The secretary then read a Waiver of Notice of Meeting signed by all the shareholders and on motion duly made, seconded, and carried, it was ordered that the said waiver be appended to the minutes of this meeting.

The president then asked the secretary to read the minutes of the organization meeting and the minutes of the first meeting of the board.

On motion duly made, seconded, and unanimously carried, the following resolution was adopted:

WHEREAS, the minutes of the organization meeting and the minutes of the first meeting of the board have been read to this meeting, and

WHEREAS, at the organization meeting the bylaws of the corporation were adopted, it is

RESOLVED, that this meeting hereby approves, ratifies, and adopts the said bylaws as the bylaws of the corporation, and it is

FURTHER RESOLVED, that all of the acts taken and the decisions made at the organization meeting and at the first meeting of the board hereby are approved and ratified, and it is

FURTHER RESOLVED, that the signing of these minutes shall constitute full ratification thereof and Waiver of Notice of the Meeting by the signatories.

There being no further business, the meeting was adjourned.
Dates this   day of   , 19 .

_____
Secretary

_____
_____
_____

The following is appended hereto:
Waiver of Notice of Meeting

WAIVER OF NOTICE OF FIRST MEETING OF SHAREHOLDERS
OF
(NAME OF YOUR CORPORATION)

We, the undersigned, being all of the shareholders of the above corporation, hereby agree and consent that the first meeting of the shareholders be held on the date and at the time and place stated below for the purpose of electing officers and the transaction thereat of all such other business as may lawfully come before said meeting and hereby waive all notice of the meeting and of any adjournment thereof.

Place of meeting:
Date of meeting:
Time of meeting:

                                              _____
_____
_____

Dated:

Model Profit-Sharing Plan

(Under Section 401(a) of the
Internal Revenue Code)

(NAME OF YOUR CORPORATION)
PROFIT-SHARING PLAN

ARTICLE I — Purpose

The _____ (hereafter referred to as "Employer") establishes this plan to provide for the participation of its Employees in the Profits, to provide funds for their retirement, and to provide funds for their Beneficiaries in the event of death. The benefits provided in this Plan shall be paid from the Trust established by the Employer.

The Plan and the Trust forming a part hereof are established and shall be maintained for the exclusive benefit of eligible Employees and their Beneficiaries. Except as provided in Article XI, no part of the Trust funds shall revert to the Employer, or be used for or diverted to purposes other than the exclusive benefit of Employees or their Beneficiaries.

ARTICLE II — Definitions

As used in this Plan, the following words and phrases shall have the meanings set forth below, unless the context clearly indicates otherwise:

185

2.1 Allocation Date — The last day of each Plan Year.

2.2 Beneficiary — The person or persons designated in writing by the Participant or if (i) no such person is designated, (ii) all such persons predecease the Participant, or (iii) the Plan Administrator is unable to locate the designated beneficiary, the spouse followed by the Participant's descendants per stirpes (including adopted children), and lastly, the Participant's estate.

2.3 Compensation — A Participant's wages, salaries, and other amounts received for personal services rendered to the Employer as an Employee which are actually paid during the Limitation Year. This term shall not include deferred compensation, stock options, and other distributions which receive special Federal income tax benefit.

2.4 Disability — A physical or mental impairment which in the opinion of the Plan Administrator is of such permanence and degree that a Participant is unable because of such impairment to perform any gainful activity for which he/she is suited by virtue of his/her experience, training, or education. The permanence and degree of such impairment shall be supported by medical evidence.

2.5 Effective Date — The first day of the Plan Year for which the Employer adopts the Plan.

2.6 Employee — An individual who is employed by the Employer.

2.7 Employer — The person named in Article I.

2.8 Employer Contribution Account — A separate account maintained for a Participant consisting of his/her allocable share of Employer contributions and earnings of the Trust, plan forfeitures, and realized and unrealized gains and losses allocable to such account, less any amounts distributed to the Participant or his/her Beneficiary from such account.

2.9 Investment Adjustment — The fair market value of Trust assets determined as of the current Allocation Date, less all contributions made during the Plan Year, plus distributions made during the Plan Year, less the fair market value of the Trust assets as of the preceding Allocation Date. For purposes of this Section, the fair market value of assets as of an Allocation Date and contributions made during a Plan Year do not include amounts contributed for a Plan Year which are made after such Plan Year.

2.10 Limitation Year — A calendar year — unless any other

twelve-consecutive-month period is designated pursuant to a written resolution adopted by the Employer.

2.11 Nonforfeitable Interest — The unconditional and legally enforceable right to which the Participant or his/her Beneficiary (whichever is applicable) is entitled in the Participant's entire Voluntary Contribution Account balance and in that percentage of his/her Employer Contribution Account balance which has vested pursuant to Article VI.

2.12 Normal Retirement Date — The Participant's 65th birthday.

2.13 One-Year Break in Service — a twelve (12)-consecutive-month Period of Severance.

2.14 Period of Separation — A period of time commencing with the date an Employee separates from service and ending with the date such Employee resumes employment with the Employer.

2.15 Period of Service — For purposes of determining an Employee's initial or continued eligibility to participate in the Plan or his/her vested interest in his/her Employer Contribution Account, an Employee shall be credited for the time period commencing with his/her employment commencement date and ending on the date a Period of Severance begins. A Period of Service for these purposes includes a Period of Separation of less than twelve (12) consecutive months. In the case of an Employee who separates from service and later resumes employment with the Employer, the Period of Service prior to his/her resumption of employment shall be aggregated only if such Employee is a Reemployed Individual.

2.16 Period of Severance — A period of time commencing with the earlier of:

(a) the date an Employee separates from service by reason of quitting, retirement, death, or discharge, or

(b) the date twelve (12) months after the date an Employee separates from service,

and ending, in the case of an Employee who separates from service by reason other than death, with the date such Employee resumes employment with the Employer.

2.17 Participant — An Employee who satisfies the eligibility requirements of Article III.

2.18 Plan — This document, the provisions of the Trust Agreement, and any amendments to either.

2.19 Plan Administrator — The Employer or the person or persons designated by the Employer in Section 12.2(a) to administer the Plan in accordance with its provisions.

2.20 Plan Year — A twelve-consecutive-month period coinciding with the Limitation Year, including any such period completed before the Effective Date of the Plan.

2.21 Profits — Current and accumulated profits determined in accordance with generally accepted accounting principles.

2.22 Qualified Public Accountant — (i) A person who is a certified public accountant, certified by a regulatory authority of a state; (ii) a person who is a licensed public accountant, licensed by a regulatory authority of a state; or (iii) a person certified by the Secretary of Labor as a qualified public accountant.

2.23 Reemployed Individual — A person who, after having separated from service, resumes employment:

(a) with any Nonforfeitable Interest in his/her Employer Contribution Account, or

(b) with no such Nonforfeitable Interst, and who resumes such employment either (i) before a One-Year Break in Service, or (ii) after a One-Year Break in Service but before his/her latest Period of Severance equals or exceeds his/her Period of Service.

2.24 Suspense Account — An account established pursuant to Section 4.3.

2.25 Trust Agreement — The agreement between the Trustee and the Employer entered into for the purpose of holding, managing, and administering all property held by the Trustee for the exclusive benefit of the Participants and their Beneficiaries.

2.26 Trustee — The person designated by the Employer pursuant to Section 12.2 in accordance with the Trust Agreement and any successor who is appointed pursuant to the terms of that Section.

2.27 Voluntary Contribution Account — A separate account maintained for each Participant consisting of all Employee voluntary contributions and earnings of the Trust and adjustments for withdrawals, and realized and unrealized gains and losses attributable thereto.

ARTICLE III — Participation

3.1 Age and Service — Except as provided in Section 3.2, an Employee who has attained age twenty-four and one-half (24½) and has completed six months of employment will participate on the first day of the first Plan Year after such age and service requirements are satisfied.

3.2 Reemployed Individuals — A Reemployed Individual shall participate in the Plan on the later of the date he/she is reemployed by the Employer, or the date described in Section 3.1.

ARTICLE IV — Contributions and Allocations

4.1 Employer Contributions —

(a) The Employer shall contribute to the Trust for each Limitation Year that ends with or within the Employer's taxable year an amount determined annually by the Employer out of Profits. The contribution shall be made to the Trust at or shortly before the close of the Limitation Year or within a period of two and one-half (2½) months after the close of the Limitation Year. If the contribution is on account of the Employer's preceding taxable year, the contribution shall be accompanied by the Employer's signed statement to the Trustee that payment is on account of such taxable year. The amount of the contribution shall not be in excess of

(i) the sum of the amounts described in Section 4.5 for all Participants,

(ii) reduced by forfeitures arising under Section 4.3.

(b) In the case of the reinstatement of any amounts forfeited prior to a One-Year Break in Service under Section 6.6, the Employer shall contribute, within a reasonable time after the repayment described in Section 6.6, an amount sufficient when added to forfeitures to reinstate such amounts. Such contributions shall be made without regard to Profits.

4.2 Voluntary Contributions — At any time after an initial allocation is made on his/her behalf in accordance with Section 4.4(a), an

Employee who has satisfied the requirements of Section 3.1 and who is currently employed by the Employer may contribute to the Trust in respect of each Limitation Year an amount not to exceed six (6) percent of Compensation paid to him/her by the Employer during such Limitation Year. Voluntary Contributions under this Plan shall be credited to each Participant's Voluntary Contribution Account as of the date of receipt by the Trustee.

4.3 Forfeitures — Except as provided in Sections 7.2 and 7.3, a forfeiture with respect to a participant who separates from service shall arise as of

(a) the date such Participant received a distribution in the case of a Participant who received a distribution of any portion of his/her Employer Contribution Account pursuant to Section 9.3, or

(b) in the case of a Participant who elects to defer his/her benefit pursuant to Section 9.3, the date such Participant has completed a One-Year Break in Service.

Such forfeitures shall be credited to a Suspense Account to be utilized in a manner prescribed in Section 4.4(a).

4.4 Allocation of Contributions and Forfeitures —

(a) The aggregate limitation prescribed by Section 4.5 shall be determined for all Active Participants described in Subsection (d) as of each Allocation Date. If forfeitures that have arisen under Section 4.3 exceed the total amount so determined, then such total amount so determined shall be withdrawn from the Suspense Account and allocated in accordance with Sections 4.4(b) and (c). The amount by which such forfeitures exceed such total amount shall remain in the Suspense Account until the next succeeding Allocation Date as of which time any balance in the Suspense Account shall be treated as forfeitures arising under Section 4.3.

(b) Next, Employer contributions and forfeitures shall be allocated to the Employer Contribution Accounts of all Employees or Beneficiaries entitled to the reinstatement of any amounts forfeited prior to a One-Year Break in Service under Section 6.6, if the Participant has repaid the amount distributed to him/her on such separation from service as provided in Section 6.6. This amount shall be allocated in the proportion that the amount required for each en- titled Employee or Beneficiary bears to the amount required for all entitled Employees and Beneficiaries until all such amounts are fully allocated.

(c) Finally, any remaining Employer contributions and forfeitures shall be allocated to the Employer Contribution Account of each Par- ticipant employed on the Allocation Date in the proportion that each Participant's Compensation for the Limitation Year in which the Allo- cation Date falls bears to the Compensation of all Participants em- ployed on the Allocation Date for such Limitation Year. The alloca- tion for any Participant shall not exceed the amount prescribed by Section 4.5. If, after the first such allocation, any Employer contribu- tions and forfeitures remain, the remainder shall be allocated and reallocated in the following manner until exhausted. In each sub- sequent allocation, any remainder shall be allocated to the Employee Contribution Accounts of all Participants employed on the Allocation Date for whom the total allocation is then less than the amount prescribed in Section 4.5 in the proportion that each such Partici- pant's Compensation bears to the Compensation of all such Partici- pants employed on the Allocation Date for such Limitiation Year. The total allocation for any such Participant shall not exceed the amount prescribed in Section 4.5.

(d) Any Participant employed during the Limitation Year shall be entitled to an allocation of Employer contributions and forfeitures, if any, if he/she is employed on the Plan's Allocation Date, pursuant to Subsection (c).

(e) For purposes of this Section, Compensation earned before an Employee commences participation in accordance with Section 3.1 shall be disregarded.

4.5 Limitation on Allocation of Employer Contributions and For- feitures —

(a) In no case shall the amount allocated to a Participant's Em- ployer Contribution Account for the Limitation Year exceed the lesser of:

(i) the amount specified in Section 415(c)(1)(A) of the Internal

Revenue Code as adjusted annually for increases in the cost of living in accordance with Section 415(d) of the Code, as in effect on the last day of the Limitation Year, or

(ii) twenty-five (25) percent of the Participant's Compensation for such Limitation Year.

(b) Amounts contributed pursuant to Section 4.1(b) shall not be taken into account for purposes of Section 4.5(a).

ARTICLE V — Valuation of Accounts

As of each Allocation Date, all Plan assets held in the Trust shall be valued at fair market value and the Investment Adjustment shall be determined. Such Investment Adjustment shall be allocated among all account balances as of the current Allocation Date (after reduction for any forfeitures arising under Section 4.3) in the proportion each such account balance as of the immediately preceding Allocation Date bears to the total of all such account balances as of such immediately preceding Allocation Date, including any contributions made for the prior year which were made after such immediately preceding Allocation Date but allocated as of such date. For purposes of this Article, all account balances include (i) the account balances of all Participants and Beneficiaries who have account balances as of the current Allocation Date (including Beneficiaries who have acquired account balances since the immediately preceding Allocation Date) and (ii) the Suspense Account (prior to allocations to or from such account for the Limitation Year).

ARTICLE VI — Vesting

6.1 Normal Retirement — Notwithstanding Section 6.4, a Participant shall have a Nonforfeitable Interest in his/her entire Employer Contribution Account if he/she is employed on or after his/her Normal Retirement Date. No forfeiture shall thereafter arise under Section 4.3.

6.2 Voluntary Contribution Account — A Participant shall have a

Nonforfeitable Interest in his/her Voluntary Contribution Account at all times.

6.3 Termination, Partial Termination, or Complete Discontinuance of Employer Contributions — Notwithstanding any other provision of this Plan, in the event of a termination or partial termination of the Plan, or a complete discontinuance of Employer contributions under the Plan, all affected Participants shall have a Nonforfeitable Interest in their Employer Contribution Accounts determined as of the date of such event. The value of these accounts and their Voluntary Contribution Accounts shall be determined as of the date of such event. The value of these accounts and their Voluntary Contribution Accounts as of such date shall be determined in accordance with the method described in Article V as if such date were the Allocation Date for the Limitation Year in which the termination or complete discontinuance occurs.

6.4 Vesting of Employer Contributions — A Participant shall have a Nonforfeitable Interest in the percentage of his/her Employer Contribution Account determined pursuant to the following schedule:

Period of Service	Nonforfeitable Percentage
Less than 4 years	0
4	40
5	45
6	50
7	60
8	70
9	80
10	90
11 or more	100

Except as provided in Section 6.5, credit shall be given for the Period of Service described in Section 2.15 completed after the Participant commences employment with the Employer, including service before any One-Year Break in Service. In the event of a forfeiture, the percentage of a Participant's Employer Contribution Account which has not become nonforfeitable under this Section shall be forfeited in accordance with Section 4.3.

6.5 Vesting After a One-Year Break in Service — No Period of Service after a One-Year Break in Service shall be taken into account in determining the nonforfeitable percentage in a Participant's Employer Contribution Account accrued up to any such One-Year Break in Service.

6.6 Vesting After a Distribution Without a One-Year Break in Service — A Participant who separates from service of the Employer and receives a distribution of his/her Nonforfeitable Interest (of less than one hundred (100) percent) in his/her Employer Contribution Account in accordance with Section 7.4, shall forfeit amounts that are not nonforfeitable as of the Allocation Date following the distribution if he/she is not employed on such Allocation Date. However, if the Participant returns to the employment of the Employer before incurring a One-Year Break in Service, any amounts so forfeited shall be reinstated to the Participant's Employer Contribution Account within a reasonable time after repayment by the Participant of the amount of the distribution. Such repayment must be made before the earlier of:

(a) the date two years after the date of resumption of employment, or

(b) the conclusion of a One-Year Break in Service, after such resumption of employment.

ARTICLE VII — Benefits

7.1 Normal Retirement — Upon separation from service on or after his/her Normal Retirement Date, other than by reason of death, a Participant shall be entitled to a benefit based on the combined balance of his/her Employer and Voluntary Contribution Accounts distributed in a manner provided in Article X.

7.2 Disability — In the event that a Participant incurs a Disability before his/her Normal Retirement Date, either before or after he/she separates from service of the Employer, he/she shall be entitled to a Disability benefit based on the combined balance of his/her Employer and Voluntary Contribution Accounts distributed in the manner provided in Section 10.2.

7.3 Death — In the event of the death of a Participant prior to the commencement of a benefit described in Sections 7.1, 7.2, and 7.4, the Beneficiary shall be paid the combined balance in the Participant's Employer Contribution and Voluntary Contribution Accounts distributed in the manner provided in Section 10.2.

7.4 Termination of Service — In the event that a Participant separates from the service of the Employer prior to his/her Normal Retirement Date for any reason other than death or Disability, his/her Non-forfeitable Interest in his/her Employer Contribution Account determined pursuant to Article VI and the balance of his/her Voluntary Contribution Account shall be distributable to him/her in accordance with the election procedure provided in Section 9.3.

7.5 Valuation Date to Be Used for Computation of Benefits — if a Participant or Beneficiary becomes entitled to a benefit pursuant to Sections 7.1, 7.2, 7.3, or 7.4, the value of the account balances to be distributed shall be determined as of the Allocation Date immediately preceding or coinciding with the event giving rise to the distribution plus voluntary contributions made after such date less withdrawals made after such date. For purposes of Section 7.1, the event occasioning the benefit shall be the Participant's separation from service on or after his/her Normal Retirement Date other than by reason of death.

For purposes of Section 7.2, the event occasioning the benefit shall be the Employee's separation from service of the Employer on account of Disability. For purposes of Section 7.3, the event occasioning the benefit shall be the death of the Participant prior to the commencement of a benefit described in Sections 7.1, 7.2, or 7.4. For purposes of Section 7.4, if a Participant does not make the election described in Section 9.3 to defer the distribution of benefits, the event occasioning the benefit shall be the date he/she separates from service.

However, if a Participant does make the election described in Section 9.3 and payment is deferred, the event occasioning the benefit shall be the earlier of the Participant's death, Disability, or his/her attaining Normal Retirement Date.

ARTICLE VIII — Withdrawal of Voluntary Employee Contributions

At any time, upon written request to the Plan Administrator, an Employee may withdraw from his/her Voluntary Contribution Account an amount not to exceed the lesser of (i) his/her net voluntary contributions or (ii) his/her Voluntary Contribution Account balance. His/her net voluntary contributions shall equal the total amount of his/her voluntary contributions, less withdrawals.

ARTICLE IX — Commencement of Benefits

9.1 Benefits After Normal Retirement Date — Payments shall be made or commence within one hundred twenty (120) days after the Participant separates from service of the Employer (including separation by reason of death or Disability) on or after attaining his/her Normal Retirement Date.

9.2 Certain Benefits Before Nornal Retirement Date — Except as provided in Section 9.1, upon death, payment shall be made not later than one hundred twenty (120) days after receipt by the Plan Administrator of proof of death. Except as provided in Section 9.1, upon Disability, payment shall be made no earlier than the first day the Participant is absent from work on account of Disability and no later than the later of (i) one hundred twenty (120) days after the determination by the Plan Administrator that Disability exists or (ii) the first day the Participant is absent from work on account of Disability.

9.3 Termination of Service Before Normal Retirement Date — Upon separation from service before Normal Retirement Date other than by reason of death or Disability, any benefit to which a Participant is entitled under Section 7.4 shall be paid or commence not later than one hundred twenty (120) days after his/her separation from service unless he/she has previously irrevocably elected to defer such benefit until the earlier of his/her death or attainment of his/her Normal Retirement Date, to be paid within the time prescribed in Sections 9.1 or 9.2 (whichever is applicable) in the form prescribed in Section 10.2. A Participant may irrevocably elect by written notice to the Plan Administrator no later than thirty (30) days before his/her separation from service to defer payment of such benefit.

9.4 Commencement of Benefits — Notwithstanding anything in Sections 9.1, 9.2, and 9.3, payments of benefits shall be made or commence no more than sixty (60) days after the close of the Plan Year in which the Participant separates from service on or after his/her Normal Retirement Date.

ARTICLE X — Modes of Distribution of Benefits

10.1 Period Certain —

(a) Unless a Participant elects otherwise, as specified in Section 10.2, the Plan benefit to be distributed on account of separation from service other than by reason of death or Disability shall be paid in monthly installments over a period certain designated by the Participant not greater than 120 months. In the event that the Participant fails to designate a period certain, the benefit shall be paid in monthly installments over a period certain equal to 120 months. The amount to be distributed from the Trust each month shall be determined as follows:

(b) For the Plan Year in which benefits commence, the Participant's account(s) shall be valued in accordance with Section 7.5. The monthly benefit payable shall be an amount equal to the quotient obtained by dividing the amount determined under the preceding sentence by the number of months determined in Section 10.1(a). Such benefits shall continue to be paid until the Participant's account balances have been adjusted in accordance with Article V.

(c) As of each Allocation Date, the monthly benefit payable shall be adjusted by dividing the Participant's or Beneficiary's entire interest in the Trust by the number of months determined in Section 10.1(a) less the number of months for which benefits have been paid as of such Allocation Date. If the monthly benefits paid since such Allocation Date differ from the amount determined in the preceding sentence, the accumulated underpayment (or overpayment) since such Allocation Date shall be divided by the number of months for which benefits have yet to be paid before the next Allocation Date and the amount so determined shall be added to (or subtracted from) subsequent monthly benefit payments until a subsequent adjustment is made in accordance with this Subsection.

(d) Should the death of the last annuitant entitled to a benefit under this Section occur prior to the expiration of the period certain, any remaining balance in the Participant's Employer and Voluntary Contribution Accounts determined as of the Allocation Date immediately preceding death, reduced by any payments made since such Allocation Date, shall be paid in a lump sum to the Beneficiary in accordance with Section 9.2.

10.2 Lump Sum — The payment of a benefit occasioned by death or Disability shall be paid in a single lump sum. A Participant who is entitled to a benefit on account of separation from service who does not elect to defer the payment of such benefit in the manner prescribed in Section 9.3 shall receive a single lump-sum payment. In addition, a Participant who is entitled to a benefit on account of separation from service after his/her Normal Retirement Date, including benefits deferred under Section 9.3, may, not later than thirty (30) days after his/her separation from service, elect by written notice to the Plan Administrator to receive a single lump-sum payment.

ARTICLE XI — Plan Amendment and Termination

The Employer reserves the right to amend the Plan at any time and to terminate the Plan or discontinue contributions hereunder. However, in the event of such amendment, termination, or discontinuance of contributions, no part of the funds held in the Trust shall be used for or diverted to any purpose other than for the exclusive benefit of the Participants or their Beneficiaries, except as provided in this Article.

All amendments, including one to terminate the Plan, shall be adopted in writing by the Employer's board of directors. Any material modification of the Plan by amendment or termination shall be communicated to all interested parties and the Secretaries of Labor and the Treasury in the time and manner prescribed by law.

Upon Plan termination or discontinuance of Employer contributions under the Plan, all account balances shall be valued in accordance with Section 6.3. The Suspense Account shall be allocated and reallocated to the Employer Contribution Accounts of all Participants in the manner prescribed in Section 4.4(c) up to the limits of Section 4.5 determined without regard to compensation paid after the date of plan termination or discontinuance of Employer contributions. The Trustee shall then, as soon as administratively feasible, pay each Participant and Beneficiary his/her entire interest in the Trust in a lump sum and shall pay any remaining amount to the Employer. In case of any Participant whose whereabouts is unknown, the Plan Administrator shall notify such Participant at his/her last known address by certified mail with return receipt requested advising him/her of his/her right to a pending distribution. Except as provided in the following sentence, if the Participant cannot be located in this manner, the Trustee shall establish a custodial account for such Participant's benefit in a federally insured bank, savings and loan association, or credit union in which the Participant account balance(s) shall be deposited. However, if proof of death of the Participant satisfactory to the Plan Administrator is received by the Plan Administrator, he/she shall pay the balance to the Participant's Beneficiary.

ARTICLE XII — Administration

12.1 Named Fiduciary — The named fiduciaries shall be:

(a) the Plan Administrator, and

(b) any person designated by the Employer as a named fiduciary in the manner prescribed in Section 12.2(a).

12.2 Appointment of Plan Administrator, Other Designated Named Fiduciary, and Trustee —

(a) The Employer shall designate the Plan Administrator (if the Employer is not to be the Plan Administrator), the Trustee, and any person described in Section 12.1(b), in a written statement filed with the Employer's board of directors. No appointment of a Plan Administrator or a person described in Section 12.1(b) shall become effective until the party designated accepts those powers and duties bestowed upon him/her in accordance with the terms of the Plan in writing filed with the board. The appointment of the Trustee shall become effective at such time as the Trustee and the Employer execute a valid written trust which definitely and affirmatively precludes prohibited diversion. The details of any appointment described in this Subsection shall be recorded in the minutes of the board, and notice of any appointment shall be communicated at those locations customarily used by the Employer for notices to Employees with regard to labor-management matters at worksites of the Employer.

(b) The resignation of a Plan Administrator, a person described in Section 12.1(b), or a Trustee shall be made in writing, submitted to the Employer, and recorded in the minutes of the board. The discharge of any person described in the preceding sentence shall be effectuated in writing by the Employer and delivered to such person with the details thereof recorded in the minutes of the Employer's board of directors. Appointment of a successor shall be carried out in the manner prescribed in Subsection (a).

12.3 Administrative Expenses — Except for commissions on acquisition or disposition of securities, the Employer shall pay the administrative expenses of the Plan and Trust, including the reasonable compensation of the Trustee and Plan Administrator and reimbursement for their reasonable expenses.

12.4 Plan Administrator's Powers and Duties — The Plan Administrator shall have the following powers and duties:

(a) To construe and interpret the provisions of the Plan;

(b) To decide all questions of eligibility for Plan participation and for the payment of benefits;

(c) To provide appropriate parties, including government agencies, with such returns, reports, schedules, descriptions, and individual statements as are required by law within the times prescribed by law; and to furnish to the Employer, upon request, copies of any or all such materials, and further, to make copies of such instruments, reports, and descriptions as are required by law available for examination by Participants and such of their Beneficiaries who are or may be entitled to benefits under the Plan in such places and in such manner as required by law;

(d) To obtain from the Employer, the Employees, and the Trustee such information as shall be necessary for the proper administration of the Plan;

(e) To determine the amount, manner, and time of payment of benefits hereunder;

(f) Subject to the approval of the Employer only as to any additional expense, to appoint and retain such agents, counsel, and accountants for the purpose of properly administering the Plan and, when required to do so by law, to engage an independent Qualified Public Accountant to annually prepare the audited financial statement of the Plan's operations;

(g) To take all actions and to communicate to the Trustee in writing all necessary information to carry out the terms of the Plan and Trust Agreement;

(h) To notify the Trustee in writing of the termination of the Plan or the complete discontinuance of Employer contributions;

(i) To direct the Trustee to distribute assets of the Trust to each Participant and Beneficiary in accordance with Article X of the Plan; and

(j) To do such other acts reasonably required to administer the Plan in accordance with its provisions or as may be provided for or required by law.

12.5 Designated Named Fiduciary's Powers and Duties — A Designated named fiduciary described in Section 12.1(b) who is appointed pursuant to Section 12.2(a) may, subject to the approval of the Employer only as to additional expense, appoint and retain an investment manager to manage any assets of the Trust (including the power to acquire and dispose of such assets). The investment manager shall be the person designated by the designated named fiduciary in a writing filed with the Employer's board of directors, and details of the appointment shall be recorded in the minutes of the board. No appointment shall become effective until the investment manager enters into a signed agreement with the designated named fiduciary which sets out such enumerated powers and duties. In the event that an investment manager is appointed pursuant to this Section, it shall be his/her responsibility to establish and/or maintain a funding policy for the Plan in accordance with Section 12.6.

It shall be the responsibility of a designated named fiduciary to afford any Participant or Beneficiary whose claim for benefits has been denied by the Plan Administrator, a reasonable opportunity for a full and fair review of that decision.

If no designated named fiduciary is appointed pursuant to Section 12.2(a), the powers and duties described in this Section shall reside with the Plan Administrator.

12.6 Trustee's Powers and Duties — The powers and duties of the Trustee shall be to manage and control the funds of the Trust in accordance with the terms of the Trust Agreement forming a part hereof. Unless an investment manager has been appointed pursuant to Section 12.5, upon acceptance of the Trust, it shall be the duty of the Trustee, at a meeting duly called for such purpose, to establish a funding policy and method to carry out the objectives of the Plan. Thereafter, following the close of each Plan Year, the Trustee (or the investment manager, if one has been appointed) shall convene a similar meeting to review and, if necessary, revise such funding policy and method. If an investment manager has been appointed pursuant to Section 12.5, it shall be the duty of the named fiduciary who has chosen such investment manager, to establish a funding policy and method to carry out the objectives of the Plan and to thereafter review and, if necessary, revise such funding policy and method. All actions taken with respect to such funding policy and method and the reasons therefor shall be recorded in the minutes of the Trustee's (named fiduciary's) meetings and shall be communicated to the Employer. The general objective of the funding policy of this Plan shall be at all times to maintain a balance between safety in capital investment and investment return. All of the Trustee's other powers and duties shall be governed by the Trust Agreement forming a part thereof.

12.7 Allocation of Functions — Any person or group of persons may serve in more than one fiduciary capacity with respect to the Plan (including service both as Trustee and Plan Administrator). Where more than one person serves as Plan Administrator, such persons may agree in writing to allocate among themselves the various powers and duties prescribed in Section 12.4 provided all such persons sign such agreement. A copy of any such agreement shall be promptly relayed to the Employer.

ARTICLE XIII — Miscellaneous

13.1 Mergers, Consolidations, and Transfers of Assets — This Plan shall not be merged into or consolidated with any other plan, nor shall any of its assets or liabilities be transferred to any other plan.

13.2 Assignment and Alienation of Benefits — Benefits provided under this Plan shall not be subject to assignment or alienation.

13.3 Communication to Employees — The Plan Administrator shall furnish to each Participant and each Beneficiary receiving benefits under the Plan a copy of a summary plan description and a summary of any material modifications thereof at the time and in the manner prescribed by law.

13.4 Number — Whenever words are used in this document in the singular form, they shall, where appropriate, be construed to include the plural.

13.5 Construction — The terms of the Plan shall be construed under the laws of the State of the situs of the Trust except to the extent that such laws are preempted by Federal law.

_____   _____
(Date of Adoption)   (Employer)

                              By: _____
                                        (Officer)

Trust Agreement for Investing Contributions under a Variable Prototype Retirement Plan

(NAME OF YOUR CORPORATION)

UNDER THE TRUSTEESHIP OF THE TRUSTEE NAMED BELOW AND IN THE APPLICATION.

SECTION 1 — Introduction

The _____ (hereafter referred to as "Employer") has established a Retirement Plan (attached hereto as Exhibit A [this is Appendix C]) for the benefit of the participants therein (the "Participants") pursuant to the Internal Revenue Code of 1954 as amended. As part of the Plan, the "Trustee" shall establish a Trust Account for the investment of contributions under the Plan in regulated Investment Company Shares and any other investments considered prudent at the discretion of the Trustee, upon the terms and conditions set forth in this Agreement.

The Employer shall ascertain that the Participant has received a copy of the then-current Prospectus for the Investment Company Shares to be acquired whenever the same are to be so acquired, whether by reason of a contribution thereto (either by the Employer or by the Participant) or otherwise. By remitting such a contribution, or otherwise instructing the Trustee regarding the acquisition of such shares, the Employer shall be deemed to warrant to the Trustee that the Participant has received such a Prospectus.

SECTION 2 — Receipt of Contributions

The Trustee shall accept and hold in the Trust such contributions of money on behalf of the Employer and Participants as it may receive from time to time from the Employer other than those which it may be instructed to remit to the Insurance Company in payment of premiums in accordance with the Plan, if the insurance option is selected.

The Trustee may accept assets transferred to it from a trust serving any other qualified retirement plan which is maintained by the Employer, for the benefit of any of the Participants, provided that the Employer represents that said other plan satisfies the applicable requirements of Section 401 of the Internal Revenue Code of 1954, as amended, and provided that the Trustee has received a description of the assets and such other information as it may reasonably require. The Trustee will not accept assets which are not either in a medium properly designated by the Employer for investment hereunder or in cash, unless it is determined that their prompt liquidation is feasible. In that event, it will promptly effect liquidation of such other assets, and then shall make appropriate credits to the accounts of the Participants for whose benefits assets have been transferred, all in accordance with the instructions of the Employer. Amounts shall be credited as contributions previously made under the Plan of the Employer either by the Employer or by such Participants, as the case may be.

SECTION 3 — Investment of Receipts

3.1 Contributions shall be applied to the purchase of Investment Company Shares at the price and in the manner in which such shares are being publicly offered, or to any investments considered prudent, at the discretion of the Trustee.

3.2 If the insurance option is selected, the Employer may remit to the Trustee insurance premiums which constitute contributions under the Plan or, for purposes of administrative convenience, the Employer may forward premiums directly to the insurer. The Trustee shall accept and hold in the Trust Account or pay out as premiums on insurance, all contributions under the Plan which it may receive from the Employer. Each contribution shall be accompanied by written instructions of the Employer which direct how the contribution is to be held, allocated to Participants' Accounts, or paid out as premiums on insurance. The Trustee need not accept or need not invest a contribution which is not accompanied by adequate instructions. All contributions, except those allocated to payment of insurance premiums, shall be applied to the purchase of Investment Company Shares or to any investments considered prudent at the discretion of the Trustee, and shall be credited to each Participant's Account in such proportions as is designated by the Employer.

3.3 If the Trustee is instructed to allocate a part of a contribution for the payment of insurance premiums, its sole responsibility to the Employer or any Participant shall be to pay the premiums to the insurance company in accordance with the instructions, and its liability for a mistake or omission shall be limited to the amount of the premium involved. In all respects involving insurance premiums, the Trustee shall be deemed to be the agent of the Insurance Company. The Trustee shall have no liability with respect to money transferred to an insurance company pursuant to such instructions, and the Trustee shall not be responsible for remitting to the Insurance Company any premium or for taking any other action before the end of the seventh (7th) full business day following its receipt of the contribution, authorization, direction, or information which enables it to make such payment or take such action.

3.4 The Trustee shall not be obligated to receive a contribution, instruction, or request from a Participant unless the same is forwarded by the Employer, but it may do so in its discretion.

3.5 The Trustee shall have no responsibility to verify the accuracy of any information supplied by the Insurance Company, and the Trustee shall not incur any liability for its distribution of any inaccurate information supplied by the Insurance Company.

3.6 Whenever feasible, all dividends received on common stock shall be reinvested in such stock.

3.7 All dividends and capital-gain distributions received on Investment Company Shares shall be reinvested in such Shares.

3.8 Whenever feasible, if any distribution on such common stock may be received at the election of the shareholder in additional shares of stock or in cash or other property, the Trustee shall elect to receive it in additional shares.

3.9 If any distribution on such Investment Company Shares may be received at the election of the shareholder in additional Investment Company Shares or in cash or other property, the Trustee shall elect to receive it in additional Shares.

3.10 All investments acquired by the Trustee shall be registered in the name of the Trustee or of its nominee.

SECTION 4 — Distributions

Distributions from the Trust shall be made by the Trustee in accordance with written directions of the Employer or the Plan Manager who shall have the sole responsibility for determining that directions given conform to provisions of the Plan. Depending on the Employer's directions, the Trustee shall either (1) transfer the appropriate amount of cash and number of shares of stock, Investment Company Shares, and/or other Trust investments into the name of such Participant, his estate, or his designated beneficiary; or (2) redeem to appropriate number of shares of stock, Investment Company Shares, and/or other Trust investments and distribute them in accordance with the Payment of Benefits Provision of the Plan.

SECTION 5 — Voting and Other Action

The Trustee shall deliver to the Employer all notices, prospectuses, financial statements, proxies, and proxy-soliciting material relating to the shares of stock and Investment Company Shares held in the Trust. The Trustee shall not vote any of the shares of stock or Investment Company Shares except in accordance with the written instructions of the Employer.

SECTION 6 — Administration and Reports

6.1 The Trustee shall adopt rules for the conduct of its administration which it considers reasonable and which do not conflict with the substance of the Plan.

6.2 The Trustee may construe and interpret the Trust Agreement, correct defects, supply omissions, or reconcile inconsistencies to the extent necessary to carry out the purposes of the Plan.

6.3 The Trustee shall disburse from the Trust Account to such persons, in such manner, in such amounts, and for such purposes as the Plan provides.

6.4 The Trustee shall keep a record of all its proceedings and acts and shall keep such books of accounts, records, and other data as may be necessary for proper administration. The record shall include accurate and detailed accounts of investments, receipts, disbursements, and other transactions. Such records shall be open to inspection and audit by persons designated by the Employer, and Participants may examine records pertaining directly to them at a convenient time and place.

6.5 The Trustee may authorize any agent to act on its behalf and may employ actuarial, legal, investment advisory, clerical, accounting, or other services to carry out the Plan, the cost for which shall be borne by the Trust Fund.

6.6 Within ninety (90) days after each Plan Year or following its removal or resignation, the Trustee shall file with the Employer an account of its administration of the fund during such year or from the end of the preceding Plan Year to the date of removal or resignation. Neither the Employer nor any other persons shall be entitled to any further accounting by the Trustee.

SECTION 7 — Trustee's Fee and Expenses

Any income taxes or other taxes of any kind whatsoever that may be levied or assessed upon or in respect of the Trust Account shall be paid from the assets of the Account and shall, unless allocable to the Accounts of specific Participants, be charged proportionately to their respective Accounts. Any transfer taxes incurred in connection with the investment and reinvestment of the assets of the Trust Account, all other administrative expenses incurred by the Trustee in the performance of its duties including fees for legal services rendered to the Trustee, and such compensation to the Trustee as may be agreed upon in writing from time to time between the Trustee and the Employer shall be paid by the Employer, but until paid shall constitute a charge upon the assets of the Trust Account.

However, if the Employer so directs, such expenses may be charged in whole or in part against the Trust assets, and shall, unless allocable to the Accounts of specific Participants, be charged proportionately to their respective Accounts. The Trustee may designate an administrative agent who may be a corporation or individual(s) to perform any of the duties or functions of the Trustee. Fees charged by such agent or other expenses incurred by the Trustee shall be paid in whatever time and manner required by the Payee.

On termination of the Trust, transfer of the Trust, transfer of Trust assets under Section 4, or on resignation or removal of the Trustee, the Trustee may reserve in connection with any payment or distribution, an amount adequate to assure it of its fees and expenses, or other liabilities, properly incurred or to be incurred.

SECTION 8 — The Trustee

8.1 The Trustee shall carry out the instructions of the Plan Manager which are in accordance with the provisions of the Plan and Trust Agreement. The Trustee, acting in a uniform and nondiscriminatory manner, may adopt forms, including requests for selection of an investment medium or designations of beneficiary, or feasible to permit effective administration. The Trustee shall be entitled to rely upon written orders or instructions from the Plan Manager.

In case of the death of a Participant, the Trustee may require the submission of appropriate certificates, tax waivers, and other documents or evidence in perparation for distribution.

The Trustee must, within the area of its responsibilities, act with the same care that a prudent man familiar with such matters would exercise on acting in a like capacity in a similar enterprise having similar purposes. The Trustee shall, under the direction of the Plan Manager, make available to the Participants the opportunity to diversify investments within their Accounts in order to minimize the risk of large losses.

8.2 In addition to such powers as the Trustee has by law and under other provisions of the Plan and Trust Agreement, the Trustee will have the following powers, subject to the limitations set forth in Sections 2, 3, 4, and 12 hereof: (a) to deal with any part or all of the Trust Fund; (b) to retain uninvested such cash as it may deem necessary or advisable, for reasonable periods of time, without liability for interest thereon; (c) to enforce by suit or otherwise, or to waive, its rights on behalf of the Trust, and to defend claims asserted against the Trustee or the Trust, provided that the Trustee is indemnified to its satisfaction against liability and expenses; (d) to compromise, adjust, and settle any and all claims against or in favor of it or the Trust; (e) subject to the provisions of this Plan, to vote, or give proxies to vote, any stock or other security, and to waive notice of meetings; (f) to vote or otherwise oppose, or participate in and consent to the reorganization of any company, to pay assessments and expenses in connection therewith, and to deposit securities under deposit agreements; (g) to retain securities in unregistered form, or to register in the name of nominees; (h) to make, execute, and deliver any instruments necessary or appropriate to fulfill the powers described herein; (i) to exercise any other incidental powers necessary to apply the duties and authorities of an owner respecting all or any part of the Trust Fund.

8.3 The Employer and the personal representative or successors of the Employer shall have the sole authority to enforce this Agreement on behalf of any and all persons having or claiming any interest in the Trust by virtue of the Plan or Trust Agreement.

SECTION 9 — Amendment

This Trust Agreement may be amended at any time, in whole or in part, by either the Sponsor of the Investment Company Shares or by written agreement between the Employer and the Trustee. A copy of any amendment made by the Sponsor shall be mailed to the Employer and the Trustee, who shall be deemed to have consented to the Amendment unless within thirty (30) days after the date of its mailing, the Employer and the Trustee agree to continue under the original Trust Agreement, or take such other action negating such implied consent. However, the Employer cannot proceed under the procedures respecting prototype plans if the Trust Agreement is other than that offered by the Sponsor.

SECTION 10 — Resignation or Removal of Trustee

10.1(a) The Trustee may resign upon thirty (30) days' written notice to the Employer, and may be removed by the Employer upon thirty (30) days' written notice to the Trustee.

(b) If a group of Employers have adopted the Plan, the Trustee may resign upon written notice to the Sponsor, and it may be removed by the Sponsor upon written notice to the Trustee.

10.2 The Employer [if resignation or removal of the Trustee is made under Section 10.1(a)] or the Sponsor [if resignation or removal of the Trustee is made under Section 10.1(b)] shall appoint a qualified successor Trustee who shall notify the resigning or removed Trustee in writing of its acceptance of appointment.

10.3 As soon as reasonably convenient after receipt of notice under Section 10.2, the then Trustee shall transfer to the successor Trustee the assets of the Trust Account or Accounts affected by the appointment, and all records pertaining thereto.

10.4 If the Trustee resigns or is removed by the Sponsor as to the entire group of Employers under the foregoing Section 10.1(b), the Trustee (in case of resignation) or the Sponsor (in case of removal) shall notify each Employer of the fact of removal or resignation and of the fact of appointment of a successor Trustee, notification shall be given in writing to each Employer in accordance with the records of the Trustee, within ten (10) days after acceptance of appointment by the qualified successor Trustee. Failure to notify any Employer shall not affect the designation of the successor Trustee as to that Employer.

SECTION 11 — Distribution Upon Termination

The Trustee may elect to terminate the Trust Account if within thirty (30) days after its resignation or removal pursuant to Section 10, a qualified successor Trustee has not been appointed which has accepted such appointment. The Trustee shall terminate the Account upon termination of the Plan pursuant to its terms. The trustee shall terminate the Account if the Trustee terminates the Plan for reason of abandonment as provided in Article XI of the Plan. Termination of the Trust Account shall be effected by distributing the assets thereof as provided in Article XI of the Plan. Upon completion of such distribution, the Trustee shall be relieved from all liability with respect to all amounts so paid.

SECTION 12 — Prohibited Transactions

At no time shall it be possible for the Trustee to engage, directly or indirectly, in any of the following transactions with the Employer or any other party in interest, except for exemptions authorized by appropriate authorities, including Employees, advisors, consultants, or any person controlling or controlled by the Employer, or an Employee organization having members included as Participants of the Plan and its employees, officers and directors and affiliates, and relatives, partners, or joint venturers of any of the persons heretofore enumerated.

(a) Lend any part of the corpus or income of the Trust except for applying insurance or annuity values for premium payment.

(b) Pay any compensation for personal services rendered to the Trust. The Trustee may contract or make reasonable arrangements with a party in interest for office space, or legal, accounting, or other services necessary for the establishment or operation of the Plan, if no more than reasonable compensation is paid therefor.

(c) Make services available on a preferential basis.

(d) Acquire for the Trust any property from or sell any property to.

SECTION 13 — Miscellaneous

The assets of the Trust shall not be subject to alienation, assignment, garnishment, attachment, execution, or levy of any kind, and any attempt to cause such benefits to be so subjected shall not be recognized by the Trustee.

This Trust Agreement shall be construed and administered in accordance with the laws of the state of domicile of the Employer, unless the Employer and Trustee otherwise agree in writing.

In the event of any conflict of the provisions of the Plan and the Agreement, an interpretation that would best suit the continued qualification of the Plan and Trust shall prevail.

Any notice from the Trustee to the Employer pursuant to this Agreement shall be effective if sent by first-class mail to the Employer at his or its address on the Application or such other address as the Employer most recently has furnished to the Trustee, calling attention to it as a change of address.

Any distribution to a Participant, his estate, or his designated beneficiary, shall be considered to have been duly made if sent by the Trustee by first-class mail to the address specified by the Employer for the purpose; or, if none, either (i) in care of the Employer at the address of the Employer for purposes of notices hereunder, or (ii) the last address, if any, of the Participant on the Trustee's records, whichever the Trustee selects in its absolute discretion.

At no time shall it be possible for any part of the assets of the Trust to be used for or diverted to purposes other than for the exclusive benefit of Participants in the Plan and their beneficiaries.

SECTION 14 — The Trust Fund

Amounts received by the Trustee from the Employer shall be invested in the name of the Trustee or its nominee. The Trustee shall obtain a Tax Identification Number for the Trust Fund. Property contained in the Trust Fund may not be combined with any other property owned by any other person or entity, nor may any property in the name of the Trust Fund return, under any circumstances, to the Employer.

It is contemplated that the Trust Fund will be a single indivisible fund. However, the Trustee, at its discretion, may adopt such bookkeeping procedures as it considers necessary and desirable, depending upon the nature of the Retirement Plan and its reporting requirements.

Accordingly, where the contribution from the Employer is allocated to Participants on the basis of unit or dollar amounts, the Trustee shall keep such separate bookkeeping records as it deems desirable to show such separate portions. Any such treatment for bookkeeping purposes shall, of course, not affect the degree to which the rights of a Participant have been reduced through incomplete vesting.

Similarly, the Trustee may install bookkeeping procedures to control and identify contributions received from Employees. Any contributions received from Employees shall be maintained in a separate portion of the Trust Fund. In the event that Employees make both mandatory and voluntary contributions to the Trust, the Trustee may, within its discretion, establish separate procedures to distinguish the Mandatory Contribution portion from the Voluntary Contribution portion. Where Life Insurance contracts are purchased by the Trustee, it may adopt such bookkeeping procedures as it finds necessary to report the receipt of premiums, changes in reserve values, or other developments affecting such contracts.

Date:_____

Employer: _____

By:_____
      (Authorized Signature)

The named Trustee(s) acknowledges receipt of a copy of the Plan and Trust Agreement and hereby accepts its appointment as of this _____ day of _____, 19__.

Trustee(s):
_____
_____
_____

Appendix E

Adoption Agreement

1. INFORMATION ABOUT THE EMPLOYER

Name _____

Business Address _____

_____

Nature of Business _____

Tax Identification # _____

Employer's Fiscal Year _____

   Subchapter S Corporation ☐ Yes ☐ No

Date of Incorporation _____

2. THE TRUSTEE

The Employer appoints the following Trustee(s) in accordance with the Trust Agreement, effective on the date that the Employer and Trustee execute said Agreement.

Name(s) _____

_____

Business Address _____

_____

216

3. PLAN MANAGER

The Employer appoints the following Plan Manager to perform the duties provided in the Plan and Trust Agreement.

Name(s) _____

_____

Business Address _____

_____

4. PLAN YEAR

The Effective date of the Plan shall be _____

Plan Year shall mean the employer's fiscal year unless a different Plan year is selected as follows: _____ to _____

Anniversary date shall be the last day of the Plan Year unless a different date is selected as follows _____

5. PLAN COMPENSATION

Plan Compensation shall mean all income paid the participant.

☐ A. In the Plan Year

☐ B. In the Fiscal Year ending within the Plan Year

Unless the following item(s) would be excluded:

☐ C. Bonus

☐ D. Overtime

☐ E. Commission payments

☐ F. Other remuneration _____

If integrated formula is selected (under option 15 (c)) there shall be no exclusions.

No more than $100,000 of the earnings of a more than 5% shareholder in a Subchapter S corporation may be considered.

6. APPLICATION OF FORFEITURES

In accordance with Section 4 of Article VIII, forfeitures under the Plan shall be applied in the following manner:

☐ A. Be reallocated in the same proportion that the current year's contribution is allocated among participants.

☐ B. Be used to reduce subsequent contributions by the employer.

☐ C. Be reallocated among all participants except for those who have a greater than 5% stock interest in the corporation, in the proportion that the current year's contribution for such participant bears to the total contribution for all such participants.

7. YEARS OF SERVICE
In accordance with Section 5 of Article III, years of service shall include previous service with _____

---

8. NORMAL RETIREMENT AGE
Normal Retirement Age under the plan shall be the _____ birthday (no less than 60 nor more than 70). The Normal Retirement Age shall be 65 unless otherwise specified. If an integrated formula is selected, the Normal Retirement Age shall not be less than 65.

9. EARLY RETIREMENT
☐ A. There shall be no early retirement under the Plan.
☐ B. A Participant who has attained age _____ (no less than 50) with _____ years of participation shall be fully vested and shall be entitled to take an early retirement if he so desires.

10. ELIGIBILITY REQUIREMENTS
A. Employee Classification
☐ (i) All Employees
☐ (ii) Salaried Employees Only
☐ (iii) Hourly Employees Only
☐ (iv) All employees except for those who are subject to a Collective Bargaining Agreement unless such agreement provides for their inclusion hereunder
☐ (v) All employees except for commission salesmen
☐ (vi) All employees at_____

Specific site, department, or division

B. An employee is one who after commencing employment works 1,000 hours during the following twelve months.

C. Years of Service

Immediate Vesting Requirement

All present employees who have completed three years of service.

Employees hired after the effective date when they have completed three years of service.

Otherwise, all present and future employees after completing one year of service and reaching the minimum age.

D. Minimum Age

☐ (i) Present Employees: _____ years of age (maximum of 25)

☐ (ii) Future Employees: _____ years of age (maximum of 25)

All officers, shareholders, supervisors and highly compensated employees must be able to meet the eligibility requirements for future employees on the plan's effective date under options (C) and (D) above.

11. MANDATORY CONTRIBUTIONS

In accordance with Article IV of the plan, a participant must make contributions in accordance with the following formula:

☐ A. No mandatory contributions shall be required under the plan.

☐ B. For an otherwise eligible participant hereunder, he must contribute _____ % of his compensation (percentage selected by employer cannot exceed 6%).

☐ C. For an otherwise eligible participant to participate hereunder, he must contribute _____ % (not to exceed 6%) of his compensation in excess of his Social Security Wage Base (unless option A above is indicated, this formula must be used if the plan is to be integrated with Social Security on an excess basis only).

12. VOLUNTARY CONTRIBUTIONS BY EMPLOYEES

☐ A. An employee is permitted to contribute an amount not to exceed 10% of his Plan Compensation each year.

☐ B. _____% is to be read in place of 10% above.

☐ C. Participants shall not be permitted to make voluntary contributions hereunder.

13. VESTING

The employee's interest in employer contributions shall become nonforfeitable in accordance with the following schedule:

☐ A. 100% immediately upon becoming a participant

☐ B. Ten-Year Rule.

10% per year after the first full year of participation.

☐ C. Five- to Fifteen-Year Rule

Years of Service	Nonforfeitable Percentage
5	25
6	30
7	35
8	40
9	45
10	50
11	60
12	70
13	80
14	90
15 or more	100

☐ D. Other_____

_____

_____

(No slower than 50% vesting after five years of service if age and years of service total 45.)

14. CONTRIBUTIONS BY THE EMPLOYER

In accordance with Article VI of the Plan, the employer shall annually make contributions out of its Net Profits in accordance with the following:

☐ A. The employer shall contribute such amount as annually determined by its Board of Directors.

☐ B. The employer shall contribute such amount as annually determined by its Board of Directors; however, in the event that the Board of Directors does not act within its fiscal year, the company shall make a contribution in accordance with the following:

☐ (i) The company shall contribute _____% of the compensation of the participants.

☐ (ii) The company shall contribute _____% of its Net Profits for such year.

☐ C. The employer shall contribute _____% of the compensation of the participants.

☐ D. The employer shall make contributions in accordance with the level of its Net Profits as follows:

If the Annual Net Profit is:			The employer's contribution as a percentage of the participant's compensation shall be:
1. Less than $.....			...%
2. $.....	or more, but less than	$.....	...%
3. $.....	or more, but less than	$.....	...%
4. $.....	or more, but less than	$.....	...%
5. $.....	or more		...%

☐ E. The employer shall make a contribution of _____% (not more than 7%) of compensation in excess of the Social Security Wage Base (as defined hereunder). This option may be chosen by itself or in conjunction with any other contribution formula hereunder.

15. ALLOCATION OF THE EMPLOYER'S CONTRIBUTION

☐ A. In the proportion that each participant's individual compensation bears to the total compensation of all participants.

☐ B. In the proportion that each participant's points bears to the total points of all participants where each participant is credited with _____ point(s) (no more than 2) for each full year of continuous service and _____ point(s) (no more than 2) for each full $100 of compensation.

☐ C. Allocated on the basis of _____% (not more than 7%) of the participant's compensation in excess of Social Security Wage Base, the balance, if any, to be allocated in the proportion that each participant's individual compensation bears to the total compensation of all participants.

If contribution option 14(E) is chosen in conjunction with this allocation formula or if another contribution formula is chosen and contributions are made in a manner so that there are no participants other than those participating on an excess basis, then any forfeitures will be used to reduce the amount of employer contributions for such year. Any balance remaining shall be allocated in the proportion that each participant's compensation bears to the total compensation of all participants. For purposes of allocating such remaining balance, a participant shall include employees who are otherwise eligible except for the fact that their compensation is below the maximum amount of wages subject to Social Security taxes.

If this option is chosen and there are participants for whom an allocation is made other than on an excess basis only, then forfeiture will be allocated as follows:

☐ (i) To reduce employer contributions.

☐ (ii) In proportion that each participant's compensation bears to that total compensation of all participants.

16. SOCIAL SECURITY WAGE BASE

For purposes of this Plan, Social Security Wage Base shall mean:

☐ A. The Social Security Wage Base in effect for the year in which the Plan Year begins.

☐ B. A stated dollar amount of $_____ (may not be more than the Social Security Wage Base as in effect when the plan is adopted or amended).

The Employer (a) acknowledges receipt of the current prospectus of the named fund or security, and represents that each Participant has received such prospectus, (b) represents that each new Participant will receive the then current prospectus, (c) on behalf of himself and each Participant consents to the Plan and Trust Agreement, (d) represents that he will file such information with the Internal Revenue Service as the Service may require, and any other filings required by the State or Federal laws for any taxable year, (e) agrees to vote or instruct the voting of shares as requested by Participants concerning their mandatory and voluntary contributions, (f) realizes that neither the Sponsor nor Broker-Dealer can furnish legal advice, and (g) acknowledges and agrees to the Fee Schedule listed under the investment instructions, for the maintenance of Participant accounts, if applicable.

DATE:_____

EMPLOYER:_____

BY:_____
　　　　　(Authorized Signature)

The named Trustee(s) acknowledges receipt of a copy of the Plan and Trust Agreement and hereby accepts its appointment as of this _____ day of _____, 19_____.

TRUSTEE(S):

_____

_____

_____

Index